Peter
LOUGHEED

Peter
LOUGHEED

a biography by
Allan Hustak

McClelland and Stewart

Copyright © 1979 McClelland and Stewart Limited

All rights reserved

ISBN: 0-7710-4299-x

McClelland and Stewart Limited,
The Canadian Publishers,
25 Hollinger Road,
Toronto, Ontario.
M4B 3G2

Printed and bound in Canada

Canadian Cataloguing in Publication Data

Hustak, Allan, 1944-
Peter Lougheed

ISBN 0-7710-4299-X

1. Lougheed, Peter, 1928-   2. Politicians –
Alberta – Biography.

FC3675.1.L69H88   971.23'03'0924   C79-094137-6
F1078.L69H88

To my mother

PROLOGUE

A biography written at midpoint in a politician's career inevitably has its limitations; obviously, the longer the work can be delayed, the more definitive it can be. This is not an authorized biography. Although Peter Lougheed read it before publication, and objected to portions of it, the final interpretations of the man and his government are mine and mine alone.

The book could not have been put together if it had not been for the co-operation of Peter Lougheed, his warm and generous wife Jeanne, and his brother Don, who made themselves available for a series of interviews.

I am indebted to Ted Byfield of *Saint John's Edmonton Report* for taking time from an overcrowded schedule to read the manuscript. I have benefited immeasurably from the co-operation of Jim Seymour, Harold Millican, Ted Mills, Art Smith, Hayden Smith, John Francis, Peter Savaryn, Dave King, Jim Edwards, John Ballem, Marv McDill, Ken Moore, Eric Geddes, Peter Macdonnell, and David Wood.

There are others who submitted to interviews who are not mentioned here. If they are not identified, it is because they insisted that the price for their help be anonymity.

I express my thanks to the efficient librarians at the *Edmonton Journal*, Maureen Warren, Pat Garneau, and Adeline Northey; and from the Premier's office, Joe Hutton and Jane Simmons. I also stand in particular debt to Ray Beswick who helped to prepare and type the manuscript and to Jan Kureluk and Dilys Andersen who worked on the early drafts.

At McClelland and Stewart, Jack McClelland has been particularly patient and constructive; Anna Porter offered encouragement when the project was only an idea. I especially want to mention my editor, Ruth Fraser, whose fastidious and unerring eyes have been indispensable.

I also owe a debt of gratitude to Tom Gould and Don Cameron at CTV who gave me the opportunity to begin the work; Hugh Doherty, and Dolores MacFarlane at the CBC who allowed me the time to finish it; and to Allan Fotheringham and Isha Badong-Romanowski, Wayne Zimmer, and Deborah Peaker who helped in other ways.

In many quarters, Peter Lougheed is viewed as being larger than life. Theodore White once said a reporter cannot afford to have a hero. If I have succeeded, even to a degree, in presenting Peter Lougheed on a more human scale, revealing both his strengths and his weaknesses as I see them, then I have accomplished what I intended when I began writing this book.

A.M.D.G.

Allan Hustak
December 1978
Edmonton, Alberta

CHAPTER I

Late on the afternoon of August 23, 1938, a boy broke into a large sandstone mansion at 707 13th Avenue, SW in Calgary. The building that Calgarians simply knew as "the big house," was one of the finest and most beautiful homes in the city. Now a faded testament to affluence, it had been seized for tax arrears from a family of high degree, but diminished fortune. Its contents were to go on public auction the next day.

Even though he had just turned ten, that boy, Peter Lougheed, was confronted with part of his past and was made aware of its potential to shape his future.

He had spent some nights in the mansion when he was too young to remember; from time to time he had visited his grandmother there before her death and before the family's economic decline during the depression. He had never had the opportunity to appreciate the luxury it once represented. The house, formally known as "Beaulieu," was typical of the late Victorian opulence in the colonies – windows of leaded glass, architectural details of carved mahogany. There was a time when its appointments included rich oriental rugs, palms, ferns, and furnishings of brass and teak. Marble for its eight fireplaces had been imported from Italy.

As young Peter wandered through the twenty-six silent rooms, he was ignorant of the fact they had once been used to entertain men of wealth and power. For example, two

9

British princes who later became Kings, Edward VIII and George VI, had occupied its bedrooms. The Duchess of Connaught, who had visited "Beaulieu" with her husband the Governor-General, described the house in her diary as "very comfortable, a little garden 'round'." Set against the stately homes of England this was not understatement, but in the Canadian West, the place was a monument. Like the bluebloods they entertained the Lougheeds had considered themselves aristocrats: they remained aloof enjoying public esteem if not public affection.

As he witnessed the auction from a "secret" hiding place, Peter was made aware of the indignity of social decline. The highest price paid for a canvas from a collection of valuable oil paintings was $125.00; the entire library of several hundred volumes bound in leather sold for $22.00 – the original bid on the entire lot of books was ten cents.

After the first day of the two day sale, he was dismayed and came out from his hiding place. "Tomorrow people will be coming with money, not just five or ten dollars," he declared to a newspaper reporter. "I want to be around for that."

But the second day went no better than the first. He watched as the property was picked over and snapped up by 2,600 bargain hunters. Whether he sensed a need to preserve a modicum of dignity, or had a precocious sense of public service, the ten year old Peter suggested the house be converted into a hospital.[1]

A family acquaintance says that Peter Lougheed never forgot that auction: through it he discovered how much more galling it is to move down the social register than it is to be born poor and to have to climb.

As he grew older he took confidence from the knowledge of his distinguished background and pledged to assert himself against present family circumstances and the absurdity of economic depression.

The Lougheeds had risen with Calgary. Sir James Alexander Lougheed, the man who built "Beaulieu," was the grandson of one of four brothers, who for reasons lost in time, emigrated to Canada from Ireland in 1815.[2] The family ancestry can be traced to sixteenth century Scotland. The first Lougheeds were originally called "Boyd." That was the household name of the Earl of Kilmarnock who led his horse guards to be slaughtered at the Battle of Culloden in 1746 during the Jacobite Rebellion.[3]

The Earl was executed for his loyalty to Bonnie Prince Charlie and his relatives fled Scotland. They settled in County Sligo, Ireland, near Loc Head. Not being particularly anxious to be identified with Kilmarnock, they dropped the name "Boyd" and adopted the place name instead. The Lougheeds who came to Canada in 1815 settled in what is now southern Ontario, near Brampton. It was there on September 1, 1854, that "Jimmy" was born.

He was a serious youth. He studied the classics and graduated from Osgoode Hall. Admitted to the Ontario Bar in 1881, he articled with a Toronto law firm. He was ambitious and his ambitions were stirred by the "national policy" of Sir John A. Macdonald's Conservative government. The building of the transcontinental railroad captured his imagination as he recognized the prospect of a fortune to be made on the Western frontier.

With a letter of introduction to the chief engineer of the Canadian Pacific Railway, he made his way to Medicine Hat where he caught up with a trainload of railroad executives, including Sir William Van Horne, and persuaded them to give him a job as company solicitor in Calgary.

Calgary, when he arrived there on a hand car in the autumn of 1883, a collection of perhaps a hundred tents on the banks of the Bow and Elbow Rivers, was to be a future railroad divisional point. He rented out the back half of the only log cabin in town and hung out his shingle.

The railroad syndicate offered land for sale three months after his arrival in Calgary, and the CPR's Town Sites Sales book records that Lougheed initially purchased five lots at $300.00 apiece. Their location, more than a mile west of the townsite, seemed a curious choice. Conventional wisdom speculated that the town would expand to the *east*. Whether Lougheed in his position with the CPR had access to privileged information isn't known, but he continued to amass property, some thirty lots in all, to the *west*. The railroad, by the simple location of its station, could virtually dictate the direction a town would expand. Local opinion could be, and more often than not, was ignored. In Calgary, the CPR built its station just one block away from Lougheed's property. His fortune and his future were guaranteed. The land he bought on speculation bordered on 7th and 8th Avenues, the heart of the new town.

On September 16, 1884, Lougheed became a pedigreed Westerner through marriage. The *Calgary Herald*'s account of the wedding left no doubt as to its social significance.

> Last evening, the youth and beauty of our town might be seen wending their way to the Methodist Church, where a scene of no common interest was being enacted. Before the hour the building was packed, a number having to satisfy themselves with a peep through the windows. The principals were James Alexander Lougheed, Esq., Barrister, and Miss Isabella Hardisty.

"Belle" Christine Hardisty was born in 1858 at Fort Victoria, in the Northwest Territories. William Hardisty, her father, was an English Army officer; Mary Allen, her mother, was a Métis. Her father's family has been in the West for three generations in the service of the Hudson's Bay Company. One of her uncles was Lord Strathcona; another, Richard Hardisty, was the area's first Senator. Her only brother, also named Richard, was a Canadian Militia Officer who was killed at the Battle of Batoche during the Riel Rebellion.

Belle grew up in the east. She was educated at Wesleyan College in Hamilton and moved to Lachine, Quebec, when her father retired. After his death she returned to the West to be with her uncle, the Senator. It was while visiting him that she met her future husband. In the homogeneous nature of frontier society at the time, there was nothing unusual about the interracial marriage. But later, as James Lougheed's position grew, he had to face taunts of discrimination about his "Indian" wife. If it ever bothered them they never let it show. And Belle, as "first hostess of the West," contributed to her husband's career.

Their first home was a frame shack which had been abandoned by the tailor who built it. It was originally located on what is now 8th Avenue and 1st Street SW. Later, it was moved to 4th Avenue and 4th Street, (where the Three Greenhorns Restaurant stands today). It was rebuilt with a unique architectural feature for Calgary: a bay window.

In the summer of 1889, Senator Richard Hardisty was killed in a wagon accident during a trip to Saskatchewan. The local residents immediately petitioned Sir John A. Macdonald for another Senator. Red Deer's Methodist minister, Leo Gaetz, wrote Macdonald as follows:

> James Lougheed is a gentleman of culture, ability and position, with a thorough knowledge of, and faith in, Alberta. He is a Conservative of Conservatives, a good address, and will make a first class representative.

James Millward, President of the Calgary Liberal-Conservative Association had a more compelling reason for Lougheed's appointment: "The people here would be well pleased should you appoint a man from Calgary, for the late Senator was an Edmontonian. Now, a Calgary man would be fair play."

That sentiment was echoed in the *Calgary Tribune*:

> Calgary is the largest and most progressive centre in Alberta, or for that matter in the northwest, and surely she ought to have some claim on the government. Hitherto she has received fewer favours from the government than any other point in the northwest, and it is but fair that she should have some little favour granted.

The favour was granted. In November, in the last appointment the Prime Minister would make to the upper house, Macdonald named Lougheed a Senator. The *Tribune*, noting that the Senator was worth nearly $70,000.00 concluded:

> His prosperous career since coming to Calgary is a striking example of what may be accomplished by men of push and ability to make their homes in the west.

Senator Lougheed is probably the youngest man in the Senate.

At thirty-five, he was.

The story may not be true, but there are those who recall that the new Senator expected Calgary could eventually replace Ottawa as the Dominion capital. Apocryphal it may be, but it illustrates the confidence in the northwest that often prompted him to resort to boosterism during his career.

> We have there (in Alberta) incomparable agricultural capabilities, (he said in his maiden speech to the Senate.) Our mountains, our plains, our rivers teem with mineral wealth, our grazing land in the production of nutritious grasses unequalled in the continent, our climatic conditions are most favourable, and these with other natural advantages, when developed, I am satisfied will eventually make (Alberta) the dominant portion of the Dominion.

It was a trust sometimes naive, but never misplaced. As a Liberal-Conservative, Lougheed quickly earned a reputation of being more liberal then conservative in social matters, a position adopted by his grandson who ignores party labels.

Lougheed's contributions to the Senate were modest. His expanding law practice and a growing family were his main priority. In his book, *Calgary Cavalcade: From Fort to Fortune*, Grant MacEwen writes, "Lougheed knew all about the frontier's rough processses of law, especially as they applied to smuggling whiskey, stealing horses and rustling cattle." He was not, as some suggest Calgary's first lawyer, but he was from the beginning the city's most successful one. That success was due to his determination to "cover the territory."

As business grew, he began a nationwide search for a suitable law partner, and his choice would have historic significance: Richard Bedford Bennett of New Brunswick joined the firm in 1897.

His relationship with Bennett remained for the most part professional; they were never close friends. It is hard to see how they could have been. Bennett, vain, austere and reserved was, even at twenty-seven, obnoxiously aware of his own genius. Lougheed took Bennett to his first political meeting in the West, encouraged his political career, and played an important part in offering Bennett the Conservative nomination as territorial councillor, the first step in a career that would see him elected to the provincial legislature, the House of Commons, and eventually, the Prime Minister of Canada.

Bennett was a strict Methodist Sunday School teacher, a militant prohibitionist who disapproved of his senior partner's zest for some of the more unrefined aspects of frontier life. Nonetheless, Lougheed encouraged his partner's talents, making the firm of Lougheed and Bennett one of the largest and most respected in the West by the turn of the century.[4]

As the practice grew, so did Bennett's resentment over the way it was working. An associate remembered that Bennett was making $4,000.00 to $5,000.00 a year from his own clients. He had to share that with Lougheed, and did not like it altogether. The success of the firm allowed Lougheed to pursue his original interest in real estate. His buildings began to dominate the Calgary skyline. There were four of them: the Clarence Block, the Edgar Block, the Norman Block and the Douglas Block, named after his sons. (He also had two daughters, Marjorie and Dorothy.) Then came the Lyric Theatre and, in 1912, the handsome Lougheed Building. His shrewd investments in real estate and petroleum continued to grow. Through the company known as "The Canadian Western Natural Gas, Light, Heat and Power," he was one of the original promoters of the Turner Valley oilfield. As early as 1903 it had been producing artificial gas, but when the Dingman Well came in on May 14, 1914, shares jumped from $12.50 to $200.00 each. For several years after that, Lougheed was assessed half the taxes in the city of Calgary.

There is some suspicion that not all of his wealth was earned legitimately. In order to deal with unsettled claims of Alberta's Métis population the federal government issued scrip certificates for 160 acres of land. Many of the Métis recipients of the scrip were persuaded by unscrupulous entrepreneurs to surrender their certificates for as little as a bottle of whiskey. The illegal practice reached scandalous proportions and when a number of prominent Albertans faced prosecution for scrip fraud, Lougheed originated a bill in the Senate which imposed a three year statute of limitations on any such charges. In doing so he clearly protected a number of reputed millionaires, the foundation of whose wealth was built on fraud committed against the Métis.

In 1905 Alberta and Saskatchewan became provinces. Speaking that year in the Senate, Lougheed expanded the confidence he had expressed in his maiden speech. They were prophetic words:

> I may safely say that the time will come within the observation of many honourable gentlemen present when those provinces will occupy a more important position numerically, commercially and in many other respects than any of the other provinces of Canada. Their natural resources and the various possibilities which are to be found within their boundaries of those provinces are calculated to make them more important in the various respects which I have pointed out than any of the older provinces.

Lougheed, by virtue of his seniority and as a tribute to the new province, was elected as Sir Mackenzie Bowell's replacement as Conservative leader in the Senate in 1906. The irrepressible Bob Edwards, who rarely had anything good to say about politicians in his *Calgary Eye Opener*, endorsed the election.

> As a man of affairs he is regarded with the respect which success brings. Some say he is hard, but that is probably due to his disinclination to let the other fellow get the best of him in business deals.

As Conservative leader in the Senate, Lougheed was guided by two principles: his allegiance to the Canadian Pacific Railway and his loyalty to the party which had created that railroad and named him to the upper house. His blatant disregard for what some saw as a conflict of interest earned him a rebuke from Bob Edwards, who came to call the Senator "an offensive promoter of corporation interests to the detriment of the people." Edwards further suggested that Lougheed had "intrigued for the appointment to the Senate in order to be in line for cabinet office in the sweet bye and bye." This was nonsense, but other editorials agreed.

> The Golden Star is out with the statement that Senator Lougheed would make a better sheep herder than leader of the Opposition in the senate, (chided Edwards).
>
> Exception must be taken to this. We have known many excellent sheep herders, men who enjoy the respect of their fellows, whose characters were irreproachable. To compare them with Lougheed is a gratuitous insult to the sheep herding fraternity, and should be resented. The Conservative party is certainly out of luck; it now has no leader at all. Lougheed is merely a C.P.R. solicitor of no particular note. The only note he ever aspired to is one bearing interest at the rate of two per cent per month.

While that may have been the typical Edwards overstatement, it was not without justification. When the fledgling Canadian Northern Railway proposed expansion of its branch lines, the Senate rejected and sent back to the Commons the enabling government legislation. Lougheed defended the position by explaining that it was the Senate's duty to control the public purse; to act as a "bulwark against the clamour of the mob." Ignoring the financial scandals that surrounded the construction of the CPR, he bitterly attacked the CNR for attempting to embark on "an orgy of extravagance,a recklessness that is nothing short of being a national tragedy."

With Lougheed's support in committee, the books of the CNR were subjected to what the London Advertiser complained was a "miserable inquisition at the hands of the C.P.R."

The railroad was followed by the arrival of the automobile, and the Lougheeds, arbiters of taste and fashion in Calgary, bought a bright red Pope-Toledo in the summer of 1909. An accident involving the car eventually led to the admission of traffic into Canada's national parks. It happened this way.

Prior to 1912, motorized vehicle traffic was not allowed beyond park gates. The Senator had warned his family against driving to their rustic log cabin in Banff National Park, a warning Belle decided to ignore. Her first opportunity came when Lougheed returned to Ottawa for a fall session. Driving at the top speed of 20 k.p.h., her party set out for Banff. As soon as she attempted to drive beyond the park gates, the car was seized and a summons issued. The impounding incident remained in his memory. Later, when the Conservatives were returned to office in Ottawa, Lougheed approached the new Minister of the Interior, who agreed that the ban on automobiles in national parks was ridiculous. So, the law was changed.

In 1911, Lougheed attended the coronation of King George V in England and returned with perceptive criticism of England's attitude to a rapidly changing Canada. He made public his criticisms, not a particularly astute move because popular opinion was against questioning Canada's historic respect for Britain. (Later, his grandson, Peter, as Premier of Alberta, would show the same intransigence at constitutional reform in his efforts to strengthen Alberta's role in a changing Confederation.)

Following the federal election on September 21, the Conservatives under Borden defeated Laurier and the Liberals on the question of reciprocity. The Liberals had proposed the elimination of tariffs on raw Canadian products sold to the United States. Albertans agreed with the Liberals and, as usual, bucked the national trend. Six of the seven federal seats in Alberta went Liberal.

As a Conservative Senator Lougheed was named to the cabinet as Minister Without Portfolio. It was a mediocre cabinet, at best, and Lougheed emerged as a stabilizing influence during the divisions which soon faced the government following the introduction of Borden's Naval Bill in 1912. Lougheed was instructed to negotiate a compromise to get the bill through the upper house. He failed. Because of this failure and because he had been rebuked at home for his stand against reciprocity, he was expected to retire from the Senate. But with the outbreak of World War I in 1914, partisan politics was set aside and Lougheed was named Acting Minister of the Militia. His talent in executive administration served him well in the new role. The Governor-General, the Duke of Connaught, wrote to Princess Louise: "Lougheed has done admirably; he is an honourable gentleman, a businessman, and all the militia council are delighted to work under him."

For his efforts he was knighted by the King in June, 1916. Sir James Alexander Lougheed was the first and only Albertan to be so honoured. (Although Bennett later received a peerage he had to leave the country to accept it.) The Lougheed family's connections with royalty are even today the basis of gossip. One such tale told by older members of the Ranchmen's Club in Calgary relates how the Senator attempted to marry his daughter Dorothy to the Prince of Wales. (Another bit of common gossip told with equal relish but without any foundation intimates that Peter is in fact the illegitimate son of the Prince.)

With the end of the war, soldiers returned to civilian life with a growing list of grievances. Lougheed was appointed head of the Military Hospitals Commission, whose recommendations became the foundation of present day veterans hospitals, vocational training programs, pensions, and disability allowances.

In July, 1920, Arthur Meighen succeeded the ailing Borden as Prime Minister. Sir James became Minister of the Interior, a position which then signified Western leadership. He was also named Superintendent of Indian Affairs and Minister of Mines.

Still in the Senate, Lougheed was also chairman of the Natural Resources Commission. His determination to strengthen government control over a neglected resource policy laid the foundation for the policy that his grandson would one day pursue as Alberta Premier.

In 1921, acting upon "discretion of the minister," Lougheed rescinded federal oil regulations in the Mackenzie River valley. Imperial Oil had staked claims at Fort Norman in 1914; six years later they made their first find. In suspending their exploration and drilling rights, Lougheed explained he wanted to "head off wildcatting."

The *Edmonton Bulletin* complained that "presumably the decision is another outcrop of the fatuous notion that the way to make the country rich is to hold back its resources from use."

But Bob Edwards supported his old foe on this issue:

Sir James knows what he is doing. Doubtless, what he has in mind is his duty toward the Canadian people who own, or at least are supposed to be the rightful owners of the natural resources of this Dominion. If he were to sit passively in his swivel chair in Ottawa, and allow the Standard Oil Company, aptly enough referred to as 'the octopus' to stretch its tentacles over our oil bearing regions and squeeze out the riches for the benefit of the United States, then Sir James would not be protecting the interests of Canada. These interests are precisely what, as Minister of the Crown, he is delegated to protect.

In another attempt to consolidate federal resource control, his department reserved forty-nine sections of the tar sands along the Athabasca from "sale or other disposal, that is from exploration, experiment, and development."

His efforts in this direction were short lived. In the general election in the autumn of 1921, Meighen was defeated. The direction of government policy was altered. Lougheed was forced to turn his attentions to his old job in the Senate and his Calgary law practice.

In 1922, Lougheed's second son, Edgar, was graduated from Dalhousie Law School and was expected to establish his future with his father's firm. By this time, Bennett had reached a prominence of his own, and Lougheed moved to dissolve their twenty-five year old partnership. In doing so he activated an unfortunate and undignified legal affair that outraged Bennett and dragged through the courts for more than a decade. As far as Bennett was concerned, the firm of Lougheed and Bennett had been created by a single partnership agreement. In requesting dissolution, Lougheed's statement of claim listed three partnerships and asked that all three of them be dissolved. At the same time, he asked for the appointment of a receiver of the partnership assets. Bennett felt betrayed. In his view there were but two equal partners, he and Lougheed. But before Bennett was served with Lougheed's statement of claim, the Senator made a legal mistake. He obtained a court order, *ex parte*, appointing the Royal Trust Company as receiver of all assets. In spite of the court order, Lougheed's lawyers continued to use the offices and the supplies of the old law firm of Lougheed and Bennett. Acting vindictively, but within his legal rights, Bennett ordered the trust company to remove all of the assets. In three days, everything from the office furniture that he had shared to the brass nameplate from the door was under lock and key, and of no use to either partner. Lougheed made one futile attempt at reconciliation: the mess was never sorted out during his lifetime.

In the autumn of 1924, Lougheed contracted pneumonia; it was the first time in his life that he had been seriously ill. He was confined to his Rideau Street apartment in Ottawa for several months before returning to Calgary to recuperate.

An invitation from Conservative leader Meighen asking him to participate in the 1925 election seemed to revive him. He reluctantly returned to Ottawa where he grew weaker. A week before the vote, a slight bout of bronchitis was complicated by a second pneumonia attack. Once again he was confined to bed.

On the night of the election, Lougheed listened to the results on the radio at his bedside. In spite of his antagonism, the ailing Senator was relieved to learn that his estranged partner, Bennett, who had lost his seat in the previous election, was returned to the Commons. The Liberals appeared to have been defeated. Meighen carried 116 seats, the Liberals 99 seats, and the balance of power was held by the Progressives with 24 seats.

But Lougheed was not to know the eventual outcome: during the night of November 2, 1925, he suffered a relapse and died.[5] He bequeathed a legacy of public service that would be continued not in the lives of his children, but with his grandson.

Sir James left an estate worth just over one and a half million dollars. In terms of purchasing power today that was a substantial fortune. Most of it was in real estate. Under the provisions of his will, Lady Lougheed was given use of the family mansion until her death, and was to be provided with an annuity of $8,000.00. The remaining income was to be divided among the Senator's five remaining children.[6]

Named as executors were two of his sons, Clarence and Edgar. As well additional executors were Edmund Taylor, the man who, through the brokerage firm of Lougheed and Taylor, had managed the Senator's business since 1911, and the Royal Trust Company. Because of its position as receiver of assets in the yet unresolved dispute with Bennett, Royal Trust refused to act.

Edgar, the lawyer, was the only one of the Senator's sons with a university degree; he was expected to defer a career in law to manage his father's estate.

Edgar Donald Lougheed was an unprepossessing man with high cheekbones, black hair, and a toothbrush moustache. Born on December 19, 1893, he had been in his youth a high spirited individual, but came to be intimidated by his father's position. Temperament and circumstances beyond his control denied him the opportunity of coming out of the Senator's shadow and equalling his accomplishments. As a boy, he was educated at Western Canada College in Calgary and at McGill. With the outbreak of World War I, he enlisted in the Royal Canadian Army Service Corps. He spent much of his time overseas in Britain organizing shipments of food and supplies to the front, though for a brief period in 1916 he saw action in France. Accustomed to luxury and privilege, he engaged in lavish living to relieve him from the unremitting pressures of war, and while on leave generously entertained friends and acquaintances at the best hotels and clubs in London.

He returned to Canada with the rank of captain in June, 1919; that fall he enrolled at the arts faculty at the University of Alberta in Edmonton. When he graduated, the university newspaper remarked, "In order that the U of A may recuperate, Edgar Lougheed has decided not to take his master's degree, but to go on in the profession of law." He went to Nova Scotia to Dalhousie University for his LLB. It was there that he met the woman he would marry: Edna Alexandria Bauld. She was eight years his junior, the youngest of eight children, and the daughter of a prominent Halifax wholesale food merchant. The Baulds were wealthy, but not excessively so. Her father had made a fortune during the war, but the family's finances reversed in the early 1920s. Edna and Edgar were married June 2, 1924, at Christ Church in Dartmouth. The wedding, according to the society columns of the day, was "one of the smartest social events of the season."

Mary Dover, at present a social lioness of Calgary, remembers the wedding. She recalls Edna as a "petite, determined, vivacious woman with large eyes and an engaging smile." The newlyweds returned to Calgary in the summer of 1924, just before the visit to the Lougheed home of His Royal Highness the Prince of Wales. They took up residence in a small bungalow on a street directly behind "the big house": their dwelling was a wedding present from the Senator.

Their first son, who was to take his father's name, Donald, was born on April 13, 1925. After the death of the Senator in November of that year, Edgar assumed his responsibilities as executor. In order to pay the succession duties, the family who owned the bulk of the original Royalite Oil shares sold them. The shares had been acquired in the original financing of the Calgary Oil and Gas Company; their value had steadily increased and had they not been sold, the Lougheed family today would own Royalite. Edgar took out a mortgage on a larger house at 1731-9A Street to accommodate his growing family.

A second son was born on July 26, 1928, under the influence of Leo, the astrological sign that is said to lend itself to those of "incomparable judgement, of great courage who desire to rule and sway; humane, yet sufficiently spirited to be great leaders of men." The birth announcement took no notice of the auspicious stars; the Herald simply reported that "Edgar and Edna Lougheed are to be congratulated on the birth of a son." In the presence of 200 invited guests, the infant was christened Edgar, after his father, and also given the name Peter. Lady Lougheed, who already had four grandsons, and who had let it be known that she wanted a grand-daughter, reacted frivolously. "You've named the boy after my cat who is also called Peter," she teased. The parents were not amused.

At the time of Peter Lougheed's birth, Calgary was a booming city of eighty thousand people. The Robin Hood Flour Mill dominated its skyline, a symbol of the city's stolid agrarian tradition. Calgary was founded in 1874 by North West Mounted Police Colonel James Macleod and named after his ancestral home in Scotland. Its economic livelihood depended on the railroad, cattle ranching, and related industries: meat packing, saddlery, and leather goods. But there was reason for new optimism. Gas flares from "Hell's Half Acre" – the Turner Valley wells 50 kilometers to the southwest – illuminated the clouds at night and cast a rose-coloured glow over the sleeping city. The promise of a fortune to be made in petroleum had, by 1928, inspired speculators, hucksters, and men of vision. It may have been "Cowtown" but it had class with a capital "K." The price of a seat on the Calgary Stock Exchange, located in the basement of the Lougheed Building, was $4,000.00. On the evening that Peter was born, his father handed out cigars to clients assembled in the company's boardroom to follow the Gene Tunney-Tom Heeney championship bout direct from New York city.

Calgary had already achieved national recognition. Its most distinguished resident R. B. Bennett had been leader of the Conservative opposition for less than a year, and was certain to be the next Prime Minister of Canada. Provincially, voters had asserted their independence from the traditional domination of eastern political parties and in 1925 had installed in Edmonton as Premier, another Calgary lawyer, John E. Brownlee, as head of their own United Farmer's government.

The night spots were alive; down at the Grand Theatre,

Clara Bow was starring in her first "dramatic motion picture," "Ladies of the Mob." In the cabarets, young men and women danced to the latest hit – Nat Shilkrit and the RCA Victor Orchestra's version of "Get Out and Get Under the Moon." But as another writer, put it, "People at the end of the twenties were dancing the charleston on the edge of a volcano."

The euphoria ended in October, 1929, but the effects of the depression on the Lougheed estate were, at first, imperceptible; the decline in rental revenue was gradual as lessees quietly closed their offices or moved out. Edmund Taylor, the manager of the Lougheed holdings and one of the executors of the estate, died in 1930. Although it was discovered that the brokerage firm of Lougheed and Taylor was losing money at the time of Taylor's death, Edgar, determined to preserve his father's good name, insisted that shareholders be paid the full value of their investments. Taylor's death was followed by a number of tragedies that were to plague the Lougheed family through the depression. Edgar's younger brother, Douglas, an avid sportsman and championship golfer, took his own life early in 1931; he was only thirty. Two years later, Clarence died in his sleep, leaving Edgar alone to face the task of managing the Senator's estate. Although he had a talent for organization, he was not suited for commerce, and his job was not made any easier by the fact that a number of relatives were dependent on his economic success in management.

As the depression deepened, distant members of the family who had been provided for in the Senator's will had to be abandoned. The Senator's brother, Samuel, who had been left $1,000.00 a year from "surplus" income, learned with dismay that there was no "surplus." In order for him to qualify, the next income of the estate had to exceed $40,000.00; as shown in the income tax returns for 1933, the net income did not exceed the sum of $18,000.00 total. Samuel was advised by his nephew to "apply to the city for assistance until the depression is over."

In order to economize, Edgar's remaining brother, Norman, and his family moved into the big house with Lady

Lougheed. It was not a satisfactory arrangement and Edgar soon found himself the scapegoat for the family's economic anxiety. He began to drink.

By 1935 the full effect of the depression had completely swamped the real estate market; Edgar was forced to lower rental fees for many of his tenants.

Lady Lougheed died on March 13, 1936, a month short of her seventy-seventh birthday. The matriarch whose influence had stiffened Edgar's faltering hold on the family fortune was gone. A court case saw the family mansion seized for non-payment of taxes. Edgar lost his own home on 9A Avenue; the family was forced to move to modest accommodations on the top floor of the Moxam apartment block, which ironically stands right next door to Beaulieu. The Metropolitan Life Insurance Company which held most of the mortgages on the Lougheed properties agreed not to call them provided a deal could be worked out with Edgar. Invoking a clause in his father's will which requested that "the Royal Trust Company shall make periodic supervision for the purpose of proper management," Edgar accepted the role as Estate Manager.

In allowing the Royal Trust Company to act as a judicial trustee, he accepted a salary far below his previous annual income. He had little choice; that was better than no income at all. It was a humiliating experience, and years later, Edgar was heard to complain about how his family was "brought to its heels by the callous money lenders from the east." He became a quiet, brooding figure who sought solace in alcohol. To relieve the daily pressures Edgar would often walk through the front door of the Lougheed Building, pass directly through a back door into the alley, straight through to the beer parlour of a neighbouring hotel. In spite of his serious drinking problem, he remained friendly and human with people and that left a lasting impression on his children. "He had a great humility which perhaps I didn't appreciate at the time," Peter confides. "He was very relaxed with people who were from a low income; he was very much at home with people from all walks of life, from the banker to the bus driver to the fireman."

Edna too suffered as the depression grew progressively

worse. As a result of years of continuing failure, she suffered a brief nervous breakdown and underwent psychiatric treatment. Peter didn't find out about the nature of her illness until years later. "As far as I was concerned, there was a time when she was ill, and then she came back." These domestic disruptions could not help but have an effect on the young Lougheed. Yet given the advantage of hindsight, he claims he was too young to recognize the gravity of the situation. It is unreasonable to assume that he would not be marked or have some visible memory of such misfortunes that so greatly affected his formative years. His silence about his childhood is a good indication of his ability to blot out unpleasant memories and compartmentalize his life.

Depression was followed by war, and in 1939, Edgar found a house to rent for $50.00 a month at 1218 Sifton Boulevard, then on the outskirts of the city. Through the windows of a cupola which occasionally served as Peter's bedroom, there was a commanding view of the Elbow River, and of the Currie Military Barracks beyond. The house had a rehabilitating effect. There was room for a large garden, "a victory garden," as they were called during the Second World War.

"It became a real project," says Don. "We grew enough potatoes to last from the middle of August clear through to next February. I remember Mother canning fifty pints of peas in one week."

As gas rationing came into effect, Edna was one of the first of her social set to be seen on a bicycle. To conceal whatever nervous energy might remain, she started smoking two packages of cigarettes a day. And she took up bridge, determined to become a master bridge player.

"Master bridge players have to be aggressive," says Mary Dover, and "Edna was certainly that."

On February 26, 1940, she was admitted to hospital to give birth to her third child, but the infant, Edna Bliss, was delivered still-born. Determined not to leave the hospital without a daughter, the Lougheeds adopted a baby two days later, and called her Barbara.

From their house on Sifton Boulevard, the family man-

27

aged to emerge from the setbacks and fears of the depression. Peter remembers those formative years with nostalgia. True, his father's drinking continued to cause "sporadic difficulties," but they were happy years. "We were in the depression when everyone else was in it; we went through the war, and everyone else was in it. The pressures of a youngster growing up then were nothing like they are today. I was a very lucky guy. In spite of the crisis time they were to me days that I remember as happy, easy going and fun."

In 1944, to his mother's disappointment, Donald left home to enrol in engineering at the University of Alberta. Edna had expected him to go into law. "Mother thought an engineer was someone who drove a train," he explains. After his departure, there was no doubt that Peter was destined to be the lawyer.

With the end of the war, rent controls which had been a barrier to the Lougheeds improving their financial situation, were lifted, and soon Edgar had almost clear title to what remained of the Lougheed properties. The family moved again, this time into a large house at an address which appropriately reflected their growing financial stability: 2215 Hope Street.

In the spring of 1951, Edgar went on a business trip to see his brother Norman in Victoria. He decided to return through Washington state, where the family had friends. As he sat down to dinner in the Marine Dining Room of the Olympic Hotel in Seattle on the evening of March 30, he suddenly collapsed and died. The King County Coroner's record shows his death due to coronary occlusion. He was fifty-seven.

Notes

1 During the Second World War the house was used as a residence for the Women's Arms Corps. It was later turned over to the Red Cross, and today is headquarters for that organization in Calgary: the Lougheed monogram may still be seen in the frosted glass on the front door. Two other doors have been removed and are now the property of Peter Lougheed.

2 Another descendant of one of the four brothers moved to

California around the turn of the century, changed the name to its phonetic spelling, LOCKHEED, and established the multi-national aircraft corporation of that name.

3 The Lougheed and Boyd family arms are almost identical: both display a hand with two fingers extended to the sun at the zenith.

4 John E. Brownlee, Alberta Premier from 1925 to 1934, articled with the firm.

5 King refused to resign, deciding to meet Parliament instead. In doing so he precipitated a constitutional crisis and challenged the authority of the Governor-General. It was resolved in a general election which saw King and the Liberals returned to office with a resounding majority.

6 A daughter, Marjorie, died in 1917 when she was only twelve.

CHAPTER II

Peter Lougheed's position in Alberta's social hierarchy was secure from birth. The family's appreciation of the patrician prerogatives of money and power became part of his assumptions about himself and the world. The proverbial silver spoon in his mouth may have been a little tarnished by the depression but he was resilient and would learn to apply his own polish quickly. His mother helped; Edgar's drinking had strained their relationship so she devoted her position, affection, and attention on her children. There was never any question in her mind that her boys would not succeed. "She challenged us daily to meet her expectations," Don remembers. "It wasn't a case of whether we would win, but what she could do to help."

Peter agrees: "She taught us to enjoy competition, to compete against ourselves. I guess because of her, I enjoy competition most."

To Edna Lougheed it wasn't enough just to compete. It wasn't even enough to win. One had to win well. She may have been charming, but underneath her gracious manner was a steely determination. She was authoritative, with an immense courage that refused to compromise the family's dignity even through the most discouraging circumstances. She was charitable and prepared to tolerate those less socially fortunate as long as the socially deprived remained content and in place. "She was living in a dream world long after the real world had collapsed," explains a former neighbour.

The Lougheeds almost always had a maid; their house was always immaculate.

Dinner was usually formal, served on fine china, crystal, and linen; Edna rang a silver bell for service. One of their domestics, from an eastern European country, objected to the patrician attitude. She abruptly quit. After that she was referred to as the "communist maid."

There is a myth – and it is a myth – that at the age of twelve, Peter Lougheed declared his intention to be Prime Minister of Canada one day. If he did, he cannot remember the occasion, but confesses that at a young age he did indicate a desire to be involved in public life. "But I don't think I ever defined the target," he says. "Naturally, I suppose people presume that when you say that, you want to go ultimately as far as you can get. Yes, it is a myth." No doubt his first unconscious influence was his grandfather. The general attitude in the family was to idolize Sir James. But unconscious is the operative word; without a number of other motivating factors, his grandfather's reputation alone would not have been enough to influence his subsequent career. Peter is not simply the sum of all of the elements in his background. His most important qualities would be developed and acquired on his own.

His educational progress through grade school was predictable. He was enrolled for the first grade at Strathcona School for Boys, a private institution. He hated it, although he recalls it was the only time he stood at the head of his class.

"There were only two of us in grade one, and the other fellow was sick for six months."

Lack of family finances prevented him from continuing at Strathcona, and he was sent to Earl Grey Public School where he was to early display his indefinable qualities of leadership. "Peter had three things going for him as a kid," his brother volunteers with a touch of admiration in his voice. "He had self-confidence, an attribute people that age don't generally have; he was better looking than average and that attracts attention; and, third, and perhaps most important, he was much better than an average athlete, and that won him the recognition of his peers." Whatever his success at sports, it nourished him.

One of his teachers, J. Winston Churchill, remembers that he tried harder than the rest. "He had the ability to lift a team back into the fight when they seemed to be out of it."

It was at Earl Grey and later at Rideau Park Public Schools that he met and made the friends who would be at the nucleus of his adult life: Jim Seymour, Harold Millican, Bud Milner, Bruce Redmond, Harry Irving, Ted Allison, John Hantho, Fred Wilmot, and later an older friend of his brother's, Harry Hobbs. All would later play a part in the subsequent Lougheed career. Together they engaged in all the team sports. Peter couldn't skate well, but he managed to make the Elbow Park Pirates hockey team; he wasn't all that good at basketball, but he faked it. "He simply stepped in and filled whatever vacuum exists in any gang of young boys," explains Seymour. "He was the guy who called us up to organize the parties, the athletics and our daily recreation. He was a natural organizer."

But football was his game. He remembers playing touch football and other sports several hours a day, 365 days a year. His efforts soon won him the nickname "the Demander." He methodically continued to plot the activities of his growing circle of followers. "All of the games, whether cowboys and Indians, table tennis, or football were set up as win or lose situations," says Millican. "He'd divide us up as the Winnipeg Blue Bombers, the Calgary Broncs, and the Regina Roughriders; it was all organized, and together we'd run through an entire league schedule which Peter drew up. More often than not, he'd be the winner."

In 1944 the group found itself at perhaps the most class conscious of Calgary's four high schools: Central High had its own system of fraternities, the most influential bore the vaguely pretentious name "Kappa Kappa Tau." The atmosphere quickly allowed the group to exercise its influence.

Ivan Head, former foreign policy advisor to Prime Minister Trudeau and now President of the International Development Research Centre, was a student there at the time and remembers, "Peter was loyal to his intimate circle of close friends, and they to him. The fact is a good number of these people were not his equals in intellect, or competence, nor in drive. Many followed him around because they admired him, not because they were his equals. He was like a king with his courtiers."

A girl he dated found it disturbing. "It evoked some envy you understand. Nothing malicious, but looking back I guess you'd have to say there was a certain insecurity there, and his circle of friends certainly fed his ego, which even then was enormous."

Lougheed denies any suggestion that he was the dominant person of the group, but when pressed admits he may have been the "catalyst," or a "bit of a leader." Those who succeed as leaders are rarely academics; Lougheed may not have been an intellect at high school, but he was an achiever. He was good at English, Geography, and Social Studies, average in mathematics and the sciences. His weak point, perhaps significantly, was French.

"I was an extrovert, always doing things, just so busy in sports that any serious reading was limited," he admits.

The world was at war as he grew into his teens, and he joined the Sea Cadets faced with the prospect of going overseas to fight after he graduated. He was not mechanically inclined, and perhaps because the family usually had a domestic around, even through the depression, he was clumsy at such simple tasks as putting up outdoor screens or mowing a lawn. "He literally didn't know how to separate cream from the milk in those old fashioned milk bottles we used to get," recalls Seymour. He lost interest in his bicycle, acquired a driver's licence and got the use of his father's car, a black Hudson Terraplane, which his gang promptly dubbed "the Black Maria." He had a teenage crush on a pretty girl named Twila Robbins, and by the eleventh grade he was considered sufficiently infatuated with her to be "going steady."

Through high school he worked at odd jobs: carrying blankets around the Bay, working at Purity Flour Mills, and in the summer of 1945, he went to Banff with "ten dollars and came back with eleven and had a great time." He and a classmate, Peter Turner, caddied by day at the Banff Springs Hotel, just across the street from the family summer cottage, and they regularly played touch football. He returned to school at the end of the summer to play offensive halfback with the West End Tornados. On November 1, 1945, the team came from behind 6-0 at half time to defeat the Winnipeg Fort Rouge Rods 18-6, and to win recognition as Junior Football Champions in Western Canada. The *Herald's* account of the game singles out "little Pete Lougheed," as deserving special mention.

> Lougheed was a thorn in the side of the Winnipeg Fort Rouge Rods all afternoon, and was the individual ball carrying star of the game.

He gained almost twice the yardage along the ground as the entire Winnipeg backfield. He made the most brilliant run of the game, galloping fifty-seven yards, putting the Tornados back in the contest. The team victory was especially sweet because on the same day the professional Calgary Stampeders dropped a game in Winnipeg. The coach of the Fort Rouge Rods, Fritz Hanson, admitted the Tornados teamwork was "as good as any I've seen in a junior football club."

That year, the "Calgary Mafia," as Peter's group was called, engaged in the predictable shenanigans of high-spirited adolescents. Though not legally old enough to drink, they would collectively go through their parents' liquor cabinets, mix together whatever they pilfered, and consume the resulting concoction. To keep the "Black Maria" on the road, they occasionally siphoned gas from other cars. (Gas was rationed during the war.) Most of the gang smoked, but determined to remain physically fit, Peter didn't. "I didn't even touch coffee until I was twenty-three."

Few students in their final year at high school know what they will do when they graduate, but one event gave Peter a definite sense of purpose. The 1946-47 yearbook reveals that Peter proposed the first students union at Central. The idea was accepted by 95.6 per cent of the student body who elected him high school president. According to the yearbook his "live wire executive worked hard to produce a lot of concrete benefits including inception of a students union, booster club and boys athletic association."

The sense of purpose shown by these accomplishments was reinforced by a vocational interest test. The test prepared by California's Stanford University was administered on May 15, 1947; it revealed that Lougheed had a low aptitude for mechanical, scientific, or artistic endeavours, but the assessment of one natural talent was extraordinary. He was called before the examiner to be told that in all of the tests conducted, no one in North America had scored so high under the heading of persuasiveness. As a vocational choice, the examiner suggested that Peter would be excellent in advertising or as an author-journalist. A handwritten addition to the list of prospective careers added another professional alternative: mortician.

The assessment left no doubt in Peter's mind that he would use his natural persuasive talents to pursue a career in law and in politics.

So gifted a person at so young an age might be expected to be insufferable. Peter was not. In addition to his mother's driving ambition he had also inherited his father's placability. Because of sports, preoccupation with wealth and status in the conventional sense was eliminated.

"Friendships were very strong, and it was all done with a tremendous amount of dedication. It was natural to play touch football five or six hours at a time," he remembers. A psychologist might say his involvement in sports was rooted in insecurity, that he used athletics to escape an adolescence shadowed by sorrow. If he had any short-coming an acquaintance volunteers it was that "he was very serious. I don't think he ever managed to develop a sense of humour. If he did, he rarely revealed it."

In the autumn of 1947, he and most of the Calgary clique arrived at the campus of the University of Alberta in Edmonton. "Half a football team moved up with him," remembers Dr. Maury Van Vliet, Athletic Director on campus at the time. "Peter was a stumpy little character," but Van Vliet, who played college ball when he only weighed 145 pounds, recognized that Peter wasn't the weakest player. He, along with Calgary cronies Harold Millican and Harry Hobbs, back from service in the navy, were accepted as members of the Golden Bears Intercollegiate Football Club. To the press, Peter was the "swivel hipped half." His reputation as the star of the Tornados championship victory had followed him.

"He was aggressive, feisty, eager to learn, anxious to win, extremely coachable, and extremely co-operative," Van Vliet still recalls with delight.

He played two seasons with the Golden Bears, and edited the sports page of the campus newspaper, *The Gateway*. He offered himself as a candidate for chairman of the university athletic board and waged one the few unsuccessful campaigns in his life. "Peter felt he was well known as an athlete and could win with no effort," explains his roommate Ken Moore, "But when he lost it taught him never to take anything for granted – and after that he didn't." His team, the Golden Bears, was at the top of the league. It had no competition, so had run up a deficit of about $900.00. The students' council voted to abolish football from the campus.

The year was 1948. The Edmonton Eskimos were starting up and the club bought the Golden Bears' green and yellow uniforms, and picked up Peter Lougheed, Hobbs, and Ken Moore in the deal as well.

"That first year the Eskimos were a crazy bunch of people," admits Hobbs. "The team was made up of a bunch of American imports that I'd swear the scouts picked up in some of the bars . . . fellows who hadn't played ball for two or three years, and who saw the opportunity to make a few bucks and get a holiday in Canada at the same time." By comparison, Peter was reasonably attractive material. He was, however, the lightest player in the league (160 pounds) and as a pro he hardly forfeited his amateur status. The Eskimos paid him $200.00 a season. Nor was his performance on the field particularly distinguished. Canadian Football League records make no mention of Lougheed during his first two years with the club. Even by 1950 his contribution is listed as two runs for a total of eight yards. He is one of the first to recognize his limitations: "I was fast," he says, "I don't know about how good."

One contemporary, present *Globe and Mail* columnist

Dick Beddoes, more accurately reported, "Lougheed was hired to run back kicks. The old punt runner always gathered a crowd, but as an Eskimo he got to play a lot of left end of the bench."

Still, Coach Annis Stukus was impressed by Peter's grim determination to play the game. "He had the guts of a burglar, he was no bigger than a minute, no one could stop him, he never seemed to get hurt," says Stukus. After awhile you forgot just what a runt he was. He was one hell of a team man, but every now and then I'd have to plead with him: 'for God's sake, you're supposed to BACK the other players."

Normie Kwong, one of the all time great fullbacks of the team agrees: "He was a trier, maybe a little small, but he took his punishment and never whimpered."

The team trainer, Tiger Goldstick, remembers Lougheed as a "loud, mouthy young bugger. He had so many big words for his age, you could never win an argument with him."

In the summer of 1948 Peter became infatuated with a young woman he had met on campus. As a football player, he cut a wide swath with the ladies, but he was impressed with Jeanne Estelle Rogers from the moment he saw her in the campus cafeteria.

Jeanne, the vivacious daughter of a Camrose doctor, was studying voice and piano in her freshman year; a review of one of her recitals commented on the "brilliant quality and fine range of her voice." She was also studying Latin, German, and Psychology. She would be the first to admit that she was spoiled. "Peter and I were both gregarious individuals," she says. "I suppose it was inevitable that we'd get together."

One classmate suggests that "Jeanne displayed a certain style, I guess you'd have to call it finesse, that in spite of his achievement, Peter didn't have. I think that was part of his attraction to her."

Peter asked a mutual friend to arrange a blind date. Jeanne refused. He persisted, and finally she accepted an invitation to go out with him to a football game. After that first date, they began to see a lot of each other.

"Naturally, she got quite a number of phone calls, but I

was usually ten days ahead – I had her all booked up," offers Peter. The incident that brought them together occurred during a winter holiday break when Jeanne attempted to exert her independence. Peter had returned to Calgary, and in his absence, Jeanne accepted a date to go on a sleighride.

When Peter found out about it he was jealous and demanded that she break the date. Jeanne resisted.

"But I want you to be my girl," Peter confessed.

Jeanne broke the date. The degree of Jeanne's influence was obvious on Peter's behaviour in the final year of his legal studies. "Peter could be as pugnacious as a bantam rooster, but I think because of Jeanne he became more studious. She was a moderating influence on his behaviour and you could detect him becoming more mature in his dealing with others around him," says one of Jeanne's sorority sisters.

After Calgary won the Grey Cup in 1948, the Eskimos were preoccupied with selling football back to Edmonton. Peter was committed to that, and to selling it back to the university.

After one particularly bad showing during a Western Football Conference Thanksgiving tour, Stukus pulled him from the bench and sent him home. Although he was upset, some say he came to accept that what was important was not so much to play the game, but to have the image of being a professional football player. Lougheed is hurt by the suggestion. "Being a football player with Eskimos was dubious advantage as far as my aspirations on campus were concerned," he says.

Beddoes was probably the first writer to recognize a public future for Peter. "It was obvious he was doing all of the right things at University. He always made the most of what he had; I knew he would be somebody of some account." A classmate, Dolores McFarlane, sums it up when she says, "He was the golden boy."

A Beddoes' column in the *Edmonton Bulletin* in October, 1950, records that

> Pete Lougheed, who hasn't seen much action in the Eskimo backfield this season is busier at the University than a mother of triplets on washday. He is among

other things: secretary of the Student's Union, a big wheel in a fraternity, and an assistant coach of the varsity High School football team.

The fraternity mentioned was Delta Upsilon, a jock group of well-connected members, many of them from Calgary: their frat house was once the home of Alberta's first Premier, A. C. Rutherford. Lougheed predictably was elected fraternity president, and used the position to create his own establishment on campus. In a telling anecdote, Walter Stewart, writing in *Maclean's*, reports:

One of his chores was to announce Fraternity members and their dates at the annual dance – to name perhaps 200 people correctly as they sat at long tables in the ballroom. It's a kind of game to see how many mistakes the fraternity president makes; every proper introduction is saluted with a cheer, every small slip with laughter and groans. Nobody ever gets a perfect score, of course. Until Lougheed. He poured over the invitation lists, and on the big night, named every person in the hall correctly, and without hesitation.

Jeanne first recognized Peter would be a politician when Peter often deserted her at university functions. She would find herself standing alone while Peter "gladhanded" everybody in sight. Harold Millican relates a story he believes indicates at least an awakening of Peter's political involvement. "It was in the summer of 1949, in the St. George's Hotel in High River. Over several beers, Peter got to talking about putting his family name back into public life. He was ignorant of the simple mechanics of politics, and expressed curiosity about things like constituency associations and poll captains."

Millican, the son of a prominent Liberal lawyer (the provincial constituency of Calgary-Millican is named after his father) invited Peter to attend a Liberal rally, and Peter agreed to go, but at the last minute, didn't. Had he gone, he might have become a Liberal. "It could have gone either way," he admits.

His college roommate, Ken Moore, confirms Peter's early interest in politics: "Following our studies we often sat and talked into the late hours. He had sought acceptance by doing things for his high school and university. It was obvious he wanted to go on to serve his province and his country. There were only 6,000 students on campus and his potential as a leader of a political party was obvious."

In the spring of 1950, Beddoes remembers the "muscular mafia" were sitting around deciding who should run in the election for campus president. "Lougheed wants to run," someone said. "That little squirt," someone else scoffed. "Tell him to wait his turn. We're backing somebody else this year."

He waited.

On January 12, 1951, the campus newspaper blazoned the headline FOOTBALL RETURNS, and reported:

> Peter Lougheed, Secretary of the Students Council brought in a brief in which he embodied figures to show that reinstatement of football on the campus would be a sound financial move, even after the purchase of an entire new set of uniforms and equipment for the team.

Two months later, just after his father's death in Seattle, Lougheed sought the nomination for president of the university's student council. His opponents in the contest included William "Rip" Klufas, a war veteran enrolled in agriculture, and Ivan Head.

The election was a contest of personalities and an intense campaign, the like of which had never before been mounted on the campus. Klufas was the established candidate. A Wing Commander with the Royal Air Force, he had been decorated with the Distinguished Flying Cross. He was a superb speaker, immensely likable, and a farm boy who exemplified the best of rural values. He opposed the influence of fraternities as "fancy little clubs of unearned privilege that serve no useful purpose." Peter immediately invited him to his own. (Today, Lougheed's view of fraternities has changed to that of his former opponent: "What they do is physically isolate you from meeting people you would otherwise meet. But I didn't have enough maturity to see that at the time".)

Klufas, now principal of Edmonton's Bonnie Doon High

School remembers his youthful opponent with respect. "I was thirty-three years old at the time, yet I couldn't treat Peter as a youngster. He was advanced beyond his years, a gentleman and a man. I had to treat him as an equal."

During the campaign, Klufas objected to the fact that the university had sold the Golden Bears' uniforms and equipment to the Eskimos – university property which it was now necessary to replace. Lougheed shied away from the football issue, confident that his reputation in that area was well established.

After two weeks of spirited debate, the results of the first ballot were not decisive. Lougheed was ahead of Klufas by only a handful of votes. Head, who was considered too sophisticated and too much of an intellectual to have popular appeal, was eliminated. On the run off, Klufas gained just one vote.

Lougheed won.

Ivan Head suggests that one of the consequences of that election is that "it pretty well decided that he wanted to devote part, if not all of this adult life, to the public sector. It was obvious that he had the ability to gather the confidence of an electorate." At least he recognized that if he could not excite crowds, he was on his way to winning them.

Violet Henry, who had been elected vice-president of the student council by acclamation says that to Peter's credit, "he was sensitive enough to recognize that he wasn't the preferred candidate for president, that people didn't come on automatically to him." Henry observed Peter developed a "polite style of leadership," that took his deficiencies into account. Now executive organizer for the United States National YMCA Development Group in New York city, she admits that she favoured Ivan Head for the student presidency. That, as well as the fact she won by acclamation could have made Peter resent her presence on council, but as it turned out, she wasn't "considered a token female," and was made to feel "very much a part of the student administration."

"There wasn't anything particularly outstanding about our executive, or about Peter as president," she recalls. "We all were *practising* leadership, and we certainly didn't accomplish anything memorable." Another member of the student executive agrees, but adds, "Peter was an athletic extrovert, and on the surface he seemed to be accommodating, but we discovered that underneath he was determined to have us do things his way."

Garth Fryett, secretary of the student's council, felt that Peter was "very quick at bringing viewpoints together, to arrive at a consensus, and to determine the necessary course of action."

If any of his former classmates offer any criticism of Peter it is that he "was perhaps quick to take offence, perhaps a little oversensitive to personal criticism."

Peter deliberately avoided identifying himself with any of the political parties on campus; he wanted to leave his options open. There is a photograph of him in his capacity as student's union president, looking uncomfortable in the presence of Conservative opposition Leader, George Drew. His impression of Drew was less than favourable.

At the time, Peter particularly admired C. D. Howe's brutal ability to get things done. Howe, dubbed "the minister of everything" in the St. Laurent Liberal cabinet, was the type of personality Peter respected for individual strength, regardless of political affiliation.

"Although we knew he came from a conservative background, Peter never indicated his political leaning," says former classmate Merv Leitch, "he was interested in broad political questions and social reform, but not in partisan politics."

"Knowing his style," adds Harry Hobbs, "he wasn't going to commit himself until he assessed all of the parties, all of the options, and decided where his philosophies fit." He certainly couldn't be expected to identify with the grey leadership of the ageing St. Laurent, nor could he be inspired by the austere preacher, E. C. Manning, who was the Premier of Alberta at the time.

Ken Moore remembers the young Lougheed as "a person who knew where he was going. It was easy to live with a person who was serious about the future." They studied well together, and if Peter was not an outstanding student in his law class, he was a good one. One of his teachers recalls "he was not an intellectual student but he was knowledgeable." "Quiet, competent, efficient and methodical," is the way Fryett remembers him in class. "He was never one of those guys who monopolized the class because they felt they know everything."

"If he wasn't all that imaginative, he had a solid grasp of the essentials," says one of his former professors, and the Dean of the Law Faculty, Wilbur Fee Bowker, and recalls that "in spite of his many extracurricular activities, he was responsive in class."

"Except," cautions Ken Moore with tongue-in-cheek, "he would never have made it in the military, he would have never made in it the army."

During his summers at university, Lougheed and Moore served with the Canadian Officers Training Corps, and they gained their commissions. Moore suggested that Peter was not comfortable with the discipline of military life: "I remember one summer evening at Currie Barracks walking past the general who was commanding the Western Canadian military establishment, a war hero. Peter passed him without saluting. The general glared, Lougheed glared right back and continued on his way without saluting."

Another anecdote deals with a route march. "The sergeant showed us a map and told us to walk from point A to point B. Lougheed felt he knew the area and didn't need a map. We were the first group out – after wandering around for three hours we hadn't arrived at our destination but Peter wouldn't admit he was lost. Right to this day he claims he was following me," says Moore.

At the end of March 1952, Peter was one of twelve students to receive "Executive A" gold rings at the university's annual colour night. The ring, which he wears to this day, was presented in recognition of his "outstanding service to life on campus." He was also the recipient of a special award,the Joseph Dolson Oliver Mothersill memorial scholarship, worth $150.00, given for "good citizenship and active support of student government." One award that he expected to get, but didn't, was the university's "Block A," presented to students who excelled in athletics. He was disappointed.

"I felt I deserved the Block A. I don't know the politics involved as to why I didn't get it." "Perhaps," he rationalizes, "it was because I only played the one sport, football."

Jeanne, who had graduated a year earlier, had continued her singing lessons and planned to "set the world on fire." But she succumbed to Peter's charm and allowed him to persuade her to take a business course.

"Peter was the first man who ever treated me like a woman," she told *Chatelaine* in 1971. "I'd always been treated as just a fragile young girl. But Peter made me feel like a woman, and I think that was part of his fascination. When a man gives you confidence in your judgement, I think your facilities just naturally mature. I don't think I knew I was a woman before I met Peter." "Doughy" was the campus vernacular for couple that was thought to be serious or in love. It was obvious that Peter and Jeanne were "doughy."

Peter and Jeanne were married on June 21, 1952, in a candlelight ceremony at the Metropolitan United Church in Edmonton.

They left for a honeymoon at Harrison Hot Springs in British Columbia, and spent the rest of the summer with their in-laws. Peter worked at a Calgary law firm. Both were relieved, when at the end of August, they set out for Boston in Peter's first car, a blue Ford which was a wedding present from his mother.

The drive took longer than planned, and the only accommodation the newlyweds could find before Peter registered for classes was a small apartment in a rundown building adjacent to an elevated rapid transit line. Their neighbours in the house were as Jeanne put it, "characters out of a Tennessee Williams' play." They still remember the place as their own "Streetcar Named Desire."

Then, as now, the Harvard Business School had a reputation as a place of privilege; only one out of every three applicants was accepted. But in the early 1950's, the university was in a phase of transition. The former Dean of the Faculty, McGeorge Bundy, recalls that "undergraduates were given the prize of admission for their promise, not for their performance." The standards of scholarship, while

44

high, were not terribly demanding, and the school was being opened to talented young men who demonstrated a capacity for public service. Nelson Aldrich, writing of the time in *Harper's*, noted that the atmosphere had changed so that "sons of the lower middle class were admitted to mix with the careless sons of obnoxious wealth, the ambition of the one bound with the style of the other, creating a new Republican class of leader."

For the first six weeks, Peter was intimidated; it was a vast and unpredictable experience. He was homesick. Each class had a division of one hundred; only fifty would pass. "It was terribly competitive, nothing like the University of Alberta; the pressure was constant," remembers Peter. There was little time spent on speculative theory; instruction was by the case method. Each class was a hypothetical corporate suite in which students were required to make and to defend their immediate decisions. The quality of performance depended not on individual brilliance, but on teamwork and on organizational competence." More than a month went by before Peter overcame his shyness and participated in class. When he did, he was drawn into a discussion by Edward Brown, his professor of marketing. Brown, who is credited with creating the concept for the first shopping centre in North America, changed his instruction tactics and instead of class participation, zeroed in on one student to discuss the particular subject he had selected. The student was Lougheed.

Fortunately, Peter had prepared for the lesson and after that session, he overcame his self-consciousness; "in fact, for the rest of the year, you couldn't shut me up."

Athletics was not a priority on the Ivy League campus although Lougheed would have been a welcome addition to Harvard's football team. There was no time, though, for him to participate in his favourite sport. He witnessed the low point in Harvard football on November 22, 1952 when Yale University sent in its student manager to catch the pass for the last point in a 41-14 conquest.

Among his teachers at Harvard, he discovered a distant relative of his mother's, Charles Bliss. Bliss was a professor in his control section of accounting and the surprise

45

discovery that he was related to Peter, added a human dimension to the impersonal atmosphere on campus. Another of his teachers was Keynes's disciple, Paul A. Samuelson, who later won the Nobel Prize in economics. Samuelson was the pre-eminent corporatist of his time. Although Lougheed admits he was "impressed" by the Keynesian theory, he was "too much of a pragmatist to adhere to it, to put absolute faith in it." Simplified, John Maynard Keynes advocated that government intervene in the market cycle in times of recession, by spending when private investment falls off and by restraining the public spending when private investment, in the course of the cycle, begins to expand. Lougheed was skeptical of the theory, explaining that while he agreed "government intervention is a major factor in the economy, I didn't think government fiscal policy could ever be that decisive."

At the end of the first term, Peter took a summer job in a training program sponsored by Gulf Oil. The discovery of oil at Leduc in 1947 had created a boom at home in Alberta, and "keeping his options open," he recognized that if he didn't like law, or if he decided to abandon the idea of a political career, there was a natural opportunity to become active in the oil industry. The training program took him and Jeanne to Tulsa, Oklahoma, and the experience left him with a lasting impression. In Tulsa he witnessed first hand the frustration of a community going through withdrawal pains after an oil boom had passed. "I was concerned, watching oil companies shrink and go elsewhere in the world as exploration in Oklahoma started to fade." He could relate to Tulsa. "It was like Calgary and Oklahoma city was like Edmonton," and the thought that Alberta might become an economic backwater once its natural resources were depleted disturbed him.

He returned to Boston in the fall for his second year, and enrolled in an option at the Harvard Law School, a class in International Finance. Jeanne took a job as a pool secretary in the communication department and at night helped Peter with his essays and his thesis.

Following his graduation from Harvard in the spring of 1954, Peter was prepared to return to Calgary, but Jeanne noted that "Boston was halfway to Europe." So they headed east. For fourteen weeks they toured the continent in a rented Simca, relying on an AAA guide to get them through eight countries. They considered the vacation a delayed honeymoon and spent their third wedding anniversary in Edinburgh, Scotland, in a hotel suite that Peter could barely afford. It was an idyllic time, the only time in his life that he was free of all obligations: "no mortgages, no responsibilities, no family, and no job."

The prospect of a job didn't really concern him. Harvard men have always believed, and quite rightly, that they are chosen to lead. Several large eastern corporations tried to recruit him. The Bank of Commerce in Toronto had been particularly aggressive. But he was determined to return to Alberta. In the autumn he went to article with the Calgary law firm of Fenerty, Fenerty, McGillivray, Prowse and Brennan. One of the firm's partners, W. A. "Bill" McGillivray, was the son of Alexander A. McGillivray, leader of the Alberta Conservative Party from 1925-29. Now Provincial Chief Justice, Bill McGillivray was a family friend who had acted for the estate of Senator James A. Lougheed and who handled Edna's legal affairs.

McGillivray had known Peter as a child and advised and encouraged him. "He didn't do a great deal of criminal law, but he was particularly competent at civil litigation. He did a lot of litigation for injured people and insurance companies." The firm also had a substantial oil and gas practice. In McGillivray's assessment, Peter quickly demonstrated that he was a "decent and competent articling lawyer."

Lougheed had deliberately decided against starting a family while he was still in University, and in June, 1955, nine months after he and Jeanne returned from Europe, their first son, Stephen Rogers, was born. "Another example of Peter's perfect planning," smiles Jeanne.

On October 10, 1955, Peter Lougheed became the first third-generation lawyer in Calgary when, under McGillivray's sponsorship, he was admitted to the Alberta bar. Although his salary with McGillivray was only $125.00 a week, the Lougheed's bought an older two-storey home in

47

Calgary's fashionable Mount Royal district at 2910 Montcalm Crescent. Jeanne designed and supervised construction of an addition. The architect, who didn't always see things her way, complimented her on the finished product, and admitted she had a natural flair for decoration.

Peter's degree in business administration gave him an advantage that other lawyers in Calgary didn't have. Aware that his Harvard credentials might be resented, he "tried to act as if I had never been, to forget about it." His apprenticeship with the law firm required that he work long hours, and he soon learned to adapt to the fifteen and sixteen hour days. Less then six months after his admission to the bar, he was approached by Everett Costello, general manager of one of the Fenerty's largest clients, the Calgary based Mannix Construction Company. At the time, Mannix was embarking on the establishment of a holding company and in the reorganization, a vacancy for secretary existed within the company's construction division. Costello offered Lougheed the position, but Peter was reluctant to accept because he felt he was too young and too inexperienced. McGillivray cautioned him against leaving private practice because "in the profession, a house lawyer doesn't have the prestige of a man in private practice." But several months later, he was approached again, and this time agreed to accept the job. McGillivray was disappointed. "Perhaps Peter was bored, or didn't like court, or he felt he'd be happier acting for one client as an advisor for corporate matters." Peter denies that he was unhappy with the Fenerty firm. "It was just that the options with Mannix could not be ignored." So on June 1, 1956, he went to work for the man whom he credits with having a profound influence on his life: Frederick Charles Mannix.

CHAPTER III

Even to those who are acquainted with him, Fred Mannix is something of a mystery, an enigmatic individual obscured in the protective shadow of corporate wealth and its power. He is a self-made man, whose energy and forceful personality have spawned an internationally respected construction company. Although his companies do business around the world, he has an unsparing Western Canadian outlook. He is an original backer of the "Canada West Foundation," a coterie of influential Westerners who joined forces in the late 1940s to strengthen the West's identity.

Peter Lougheed's family may have helped to build the city of Calgary, but the Mannix family helped to lay the foundations for the industrial development of Alberta. The company had its genesis in Stonewall, Manitoba, in 1898. Its nineteen year old founder, Fred Stephen Mannix, followed the railroad construction into Alberta with a horse team in 1903. According to a one account, as the city expanded, young Stephen "lent muscle to the feverish construction challenges and expansion of the day."

In the late 1920s the founder branched out into irrigation ditches and highway construction. With the expertise he acquired in earth moving, he pioneered coal stripping in Saskatchewan during the depression. In 1940, Mannix began major expansion in heavy construction on a national basis: airports, harbour facilities, and dredging. Yet for all of that activity, Fred Stephen ran the operation out of his hip pocket. He is known to have lost at least two fortunes during his lifetime. When, because of failing health, he was confined to a wheelchair in the early 1940s, he retired and sold majority interest in his company to one of the largest construction firms in the United States, Morrison-Knudson. One of the conditions of that sale was that his thirty-four year old son, Frederick Charles, become president.

Shortly afterward, the company was dealt a severe blow. An assistant manager, a project superintendent, and a field superintendent were killed when their plane crashed into a tree as it was attempting a landing at Coleman, Alberta, on St. Valentine's Day, 1947. The loss of several of his top executives galvanized Fred C. into action as he determined to regain majority control of his family's interests from Morrison-Knudson. He was well qualified to do it. As a mercurial young man, he had learned his father's business from the ground up, working in the field. Because of that experience, he developed a fierce loyalty to those he worked with. When he finally assumed control of his father's operations, he was able to motivate people and command an unusual loyalty.

"Although you work your ass off, and keep your mouth shut," says a former executive, "the experience is not without its reward."

Mannix has a paternalistic, almost feudal, attitude toward his employees because, as he sees it, "that's the way I was raised in the camps and that's the way I've always lived." By 1950, Fred Charles Mannix had repurchased the Morrison-Knudson interest and had regained majority control of the company.

"His genius is that he held all of the equity, hired brilliant management personnel, and had some good luck in ruthlessly achieving his will," volunteers another intimate. Mannix's own explanation is not so revealing. He modestly explains that "we went into many joint ventures with foreign companies which had more sophisticated systems and abilities. But we kept our eyes and our ears open, and with a little humility and understanding, tried to learn from them."

Through associates or subsidiaries of the management

company, Loram Company Limited, this group is now involved in construction (Loram International Ltd.), ranching (Manalta Holding Ltd.), coal mining (Manalta Coal Ltd.), the oil and gas business (Western Decalta and Pembina Pipe Line), equipment sales and service (Manark Industrial Sales), engineering and consulting (Techman Ltd.) and railway maintenance (Loram Maintenance of Way Inc.). Any estimate of the Mannix fortune is, at best, a guess; it is impossible to determine the extent of its wealth, for he discloses neither assets nor revenues. All of the Mannix group of companies, with the exception of Pembina Pipe Line Ltd., are private.

Fred Charles Mannix eschews publicity. A forceful man with a penetrating gaze and a serene voice, his attitude to wealth and its uses is rooted in free enterprise at its best. To Mannix, a man is not handed opportunity, he creates it. Yet he is known to be benevolent. He has made many substantial anonymous contributions to charitable works, universities, and to individuals.

He's been described as "a fifteenth or sixteenth century pirate, a privateer turned prelate," a description to which Mannix responds by acknowledging that "if you've travelled very far, I guess you always pick up friends or enemies." His enemies use the word "cunning" to describe him; his friends prefer the word "ingenious." But Mannix explains the philosophy that made him a giant in the world construction industry this way: "Our family and corporate heritage is based on three tenets: First, do as least as well as anyone else, or better than anyone else as to quality, speed and integrity. Second, don't get overextended. Our outfit endeavours to continue to judge its own capacity; in other words, it's like being a weight lifter – you have to know what you can lift. Third, do the job as is the intent rather than the detail. If we tried to do a detailed job the way they called for in some contracts, you'd never get it done. If a person wants a highway or dam built of a certain quality, you have to see that it gets done as intended. Don't fight through loopholes in a contract to try and get out of it."

They were precepts that Lougheed could respect and modify. Peter had only been with the company for a few

51

weeks when he was summoned to a board meeting called to determine whether Mannix Company was entitled to a two million dollar claim against Westcoast Transmission. Change orders in the construction of a pipeline near Chilliwack, B.C. were costing the company hundreds of thousands of dollars and Mannix was seeking a claim that included all of his costs, overhead, and profit.

Mannix demanded an opinion: did he, or did he not, have a two million dollar claim? All of the sycophants around the table agreed that he did, with one exception. When Mannix asked the young lawyer he had just hired for his opinion, Peter felt there were some non-supportable items in the claim, and replied, "I don't think you've got a very good case at all.' There was silence in the room. The company's administrative manager, Chip Collins, remarked under his breath: "Either this guy Lougheed is going to become one of the most significant people in the Mannix organization, or he's going to be gone the next day." But Mannix appreciated Lougheed's straightforward approach. Within a year, Peter earned his first promotion. In July, 1957, with the reorganization of the various companies, he became secretary and general counsel of Mannix Company Ltd.

"Lougheed was discerning enough to know what difficult contracts mean. Although it might be thick, he could boil it down so that an ordinary guy – and most of our people are ordinary – could understand it," Mannix explains. "In the contruction outfit, you need a lawyer who has administrative ability and Lougheed had it – he had good business acumen." One source suggests a father-son relationship developed between the two men, that "Fred was the father Peter never really had." But Lougheed dismisses the suggestion. "The way we operated, I assure you could not be a father and son."

Lougheed's arrival at the Mannix corporation coincided with the national debate over the proposed construction of the TransCanada Pipeline. The federal Liberal government had offered to finance a pipeline to carry excess natural gas from northern Alberta east to Ontario. During his years at Harvard, Canadian politics were of peripheral interest to Lougheed; but even to a casual observer, the pipeline debate was a dramatic period in Canadian political history. Because the Mannix company would be involved in the construction of any pipeline to be built, Lougheed had followed the political ramifications with "detached interest."

When the St. Laurent government introduced closure to force the bill authorizing federal funds for the construction of the pipeline, the Tories emerged from the debate more popular with the electorate than they had been in two decades. But three months later their leader, George Drew, was forced to resign because of ill health. The choice of his successor would pique Lougheed's curiosity in partisan politics. For with the selection of John George Diefenbaker as Conservative opposition leader, the party was in the hands of a Western Canadian for the first time since R. B. Bennett. And Lougheed, who was easily impressed by dynamic men of action, was mesmerized on election night, June 10, 1957, when Canadians unexpectedly denied the Liberals the right to govern and elected a Diefenbaker minority government. Watching the results of that election on television with friends, Lougheed for the first time admitted his Conservative affiliation.

Shortly after the election he asked a family acquaintance, Art Smith, who had just been elected MP for Calgary South how he might get started on a political career. Smith, a Calgary oilman who had risen from an alderman on city council through the legislature as an MLA to the Commons, felt that Lougheed was "just another bright boy to which I talk to at least one a week. I told him to get some experience by running for the school board or for city council. He needed a profile in the community if he wished to make the jump into senior levels of government. He didn't have one and the routine demanded that he go through countless service organizations."

Although Fred C. Mannix was aware of Lougheed's intention to become involved in politics when he hired him, Peter understood that the corporate policy was not to use the Mannix company as a tool for political purposes. He was not to become actively involved as long as he was on the Mannix payroll. But to Peter's general interest in politics, Fred Charles had no other objections, and in fact encouraged him to contribute his time and talent to community endeavours.

But Lougheed was not prepared to work with traditional service clubs; he was interested in supporting causes that might eventually support him. He had been involved with the Calgary Stampeders' Booster club, where one of his tasks was to arrange half-time entertainment. His efforts with the club attracted the attention of another member of the Calgary establishment, H. Gordon Love. Love, a pioneer broadcaster, owned CFCN radio and television, and was credited with establishing Canada's first news gathering bureau in 1928. He was a member of the Calgary Exhibition and Stampede board, one of the most visible community projects in the city, and he invited Peter to join. Lougheed accepted and his association with Love would afford him a premature insight into the effectiveness of television as a weapon. Peter objected to the preponderance of talent from the United States at the grandstand show, and was instrumental in promoting the participation of young local entertainers. A group of singers and dancers called "The Young Canadians" was eventually formed and remain, even today, a permanent attraction of the annual Stampede.

He then took another step up the corporate ladder. In July, 1958, he was named vice-president administration and was also appointed a director of Mannix Company Limited. David Wood, who had long since left his advertising agency in Edmonton to become director of public relations for the Mannix corporation, found himself reporting directly to Lougheed, and was impressed with his management technique. "He had learned to delegate authority. You knew exactly what to expect from him, and he gave you the authority to go with your responsibilities."

Lougheed confirmed his badge of social certification by being admitted to the Ranchmen's Club, a sanctuary for members of the Calgary establishment, and to the newer Petroleum Club. There was an addition to his family with the birth of his first daughter, Andrea Gaye in September. Peter was soon recognized about town as the ideal, young organization man. As secretary and general counsel at Mannix he was able to concentrate on the narrow jurisdiction of corporate law, and to hone his talent for negotiation. He built on the experience of those around him and Mannix became his greatest teacher.

"He wasn't afraid to take on large corporations, large organizations," notes Lougheed. "I saw him so many times, eyeball to eyeball against the big eastern corporations – and they blinked."

Lougheed's contracts with the corporate world expanded. He was exposed to the Bechtels, to United States Fidelity and Guarantee Trust, TransCanada Pipeline, Transmountain Pipeline, the St. Lawrence Seaway, and to the workings of provincial and federal governments. "Since I was involved with multinationals at an early age, I am not awed by them," says Lougheed. "In dealing with them I learned you can't rest on your accomplishments, you've always to keep moving ahead of the opposition."

A sample of some of the working files between 1959-1960 illustrate the scale of the projects in which Lougheed was involved. They include the South Saskatchewan River Dam, the Toronto Subway, development of the Great Canadian Oil Sands, Dewline Construction, a Bomarc Missile Site, the Northern Alberta Resources Railroad, railroads in Australia and Mexico, and a traffic tube in California.

"It was an invaluable experience," Lougheed admits. "If a man interested in politics said to himself, 'what would be a good thing for a future Premier to do?' I'd have to say: lay the foundation by spending five years with Mannix."

When Lougheed joined the Mannix corporation, it was agreed that he would only stay five years before returning to private law practice. By 1961, that self-imposed time limit was drawing close, and he was preparing to resign when he quite unexpectedly was asked to leave for London on twenty-four hours notice.

Mannix was one contractor of a consortium that was bidding on a contract to construct the Mangla Dam in Pakistan. The $462 million dam was a World Bank project and at the time the largest engineering feat in the world. Lougheed was a member of this team and through the summer of 1961 he moved between London, New York, and San Francisco, negotiating with the various French, Italian, British, and

American engineering interests involved. The work was so time consuming that he was unable to be at home for the birth of his second daughter, Pamela.

Mannix had decided that if he should get the contract, Lougheed would have to shuttle between Calgary and Pakistan or even set up a base there for the estimated six years that it would take to build the dam. Peter, who almost certainly would have refused ("it would have meant that I would have been too old to get into politics when I got back") never had to face the decision. In the final bid, Mannix failed to obtain the contract.

In December, 1961, Peter Lougheed resigned from the Mannix corporation. For his former boss, he had a high regard: "Fred Mannix places a high value on personal initiative, and respects and encourages those who display that. He has a strong feeling that the most significant thing that can happen in this country is for the individual to create and to control his own economic destiny. Literally hundreds of people using the experience they gained working for him have moved on to set up a whole range of independent companies.[2] The alumni of the Mannix company is really something. He's created an impact on the whole nation."

Peter was out to create an impact when he left the Mannix corporation to set up his own law firm. He had hoped to go into partnership with his college roommate, but Ken Moore had professional loyalties of his own which at the time prevented the two men from working together. Lougheed then approached Harvard graduate John Ballem, a social acquaintance who was a house lawyer with Pacific Petroleum. Ballem, who physically resembles Peter, had acquired a solid reputation in the oil and gas business. He had arrived in Calgary from Nova Scotia, a graduate of Dalhousie University. Ballem had political ambitions of his own, and the two men agreed that at some point in the future, perhaps five or ten years down the line, they might become involved in federal politics, but in their commonality of purpose they agreed they would set up "a law firm first and foremost." Lougheed felt a third partner, proficient in general practice was required, so they recruited Marvin

McDill, a native of Winnipeg who was with the Calgary law firm of Blanchard and Iredale.

On February 6, 1962, the firm of Lougheed, Ballem and McDill opened at the most exclusive address in Calgary at the time: 1600 Elveden House. As a new firm in town, their energies were devoted to building the practice. Lougheed had been retained by Mannix as a director and legal advisor and Ballem and McDill were able to bring over some of the clients they had in their previous contacts. Right from the start, they were involved in litigation. Peter rarely had big cases, the kind that represented substantial economic fees, but the clients he had were solid and the firm registered steadily increasing profits. He was rarely comfortable with criminal cases and as a prominent Calgary lawyer remembers, "Peter didn't really have that high a profile in the profession." There was automobile litigation; another lengthy case involving Marine Pipe and several large construction claims sought by the Mannix corporation, some of which reached the litigation stage. There were few criminal cases. "As a lawyer he was all show," recalls one colleague. "He could impress a client with his organizational flowcharts but he was often slow to get off his ass and build a case."

He acquired the beginnings of a small library, the mark of a successful lawyer. It contained volumes of Western Canadian history, political biographies, and a copy of one book that he read and reread with fascination: Theodore White's *Making of the President, 1960.* The Kennedy appeal was almost universal and White's account of John F. Kennedy's victory would, in the early stages of his own political career, serve as his bible.

There was an opportunity to become involved in municipal politics, but he rejected it. A Calgary alderman Bill Dickie was about to resign his seat on council to run for the Liberals in the 1963 provincial election. He tried to persuade Peter to run for city council.

Meanwhile, Conservative party fortunes on both the federal and provincial scenes were deteriorating. On June 18, 1962, Prime Minister Diefenbaker lost 92 of the 208 seats he had won in the 1958 election, reducing the Conservatives to a minority position. Although the West remained loyal to the Chief, Diefenbaker had been transformed in eastern Canada into a political liability. On April 8, 1963, he was turned out of office as the Liberals, led by Lester Pearson, won 129 Commons seats, enough to form a minority government.

One month later, Premier Manning called a general election in Alberta for June 17. The Conservative leader, Milton Harradance promised to field a slate of fifty-five candidates, but he could only recruit thirty-three. A Calgary criminal lawyer, Harradance was a native of Blaine Lake, Saskatchewan, and had learned his flamboyant courtroom manner as a young man, watching John Diefenbaker in action. His abrasive style of leadership earned him the nickname "Milton Arrogance." During the campaign, he flew around the province in his own P51 Mustang Fighter, complaining about the way the Social Credit government had usurped the rights of the individual. Social Crediters called for "63 seats in '63," and the results of the vote were not far off the mark. Manning was returned with sixty seats; the Conservatives with less than 13 per cent of the popular vote didn't elect a single member. Two Liberals and a coalition candidate comprised the opposition.

In January, 1964, Peter became a member of the Calgary Olympic Development Association, a committee that had worked for several years to promote Banff as the site of the 1968 winter Olympics. The committee felt its prospects were excellent; Canada, a ranking winter sports country, had never hosted the games. Lougheed was an enthusiastic booster of the concept because he believed if Banff was awarded the winter games "it would bring better skiing and recreational facilities to the park and to the foothills." In February, the delegation, its members sporting identical white Hudson's Bay coats, flew to Innsbruck, Austria, confident that the International Olympic Committee would award the games to Banff. However, Canada lost to France as the IOC voted 27-24 in favour of Grenoble. Although the loss was disappointing, the Calgary group was convinced it was now the front runner next time around and Lougheed agreed to serve as vice-president of a new committee established to secure the 1972 games. His involvement with the Olympic movement would be both an asset and a liability to his eventual political career. Initially, it provided him with a popular non-partisan platform from which he would get public recognition, but later it would be regarded as a losing cause.

Shortly after Lougheed returned from Austria, Milton Harradance resigned as leader of the provincial Progressive Conservative party. During the 1964 Easter weekend, Lougheed encountered Harradance in the dining room of the Mount Royal Hotel in Banff. Harradance, convinced that a man of independent means was needed to build the party, suggested that Peter "consider running for the leadership."

Lougheed was skeptical. There was no attraction in a moribund party that didn't have a single seat in the legislature. In the entire political history of Alberta, the Conservatives had never formed a government. In fact, the only period in which the party had managed to win respectable representation was for a brief eight years between 1913-21, during which eighteen members had been elected to opposition. With the victory of the United Farmer's government in 1921, Albertans made it clear they wanted no part of either traditional "eastern oriented" old line parties. The psychological separation from the Liberals and Conservatives became a divorce in 1935 with the election of William Aberhart and Social Credit. After 1940, the provincial Conservative party became extinct. D. M. Duggan, who had toiled at the leadership from 1929 to 1940, decided on the day he was re-elected in 1940 that he could best serve the province by joining a coalition to oppose Social Credit. Duggan resigned as Conservative leader and sat out one term as an independent. It took two decades before a successor was found.

Attempts to use John Diefenbaker's 1958 national victory to revive interest in a provincial Conservative party failed miserably. In the six years between 1958 and 1964 there had been three leaders: W. J. "Cam" Kirby, Ernest Watkins, and Milton Harradance. Peter had no reason to believe that he might succeed where others had failed. Still, there were more members of the party and old friends who had more confidence in his prospects than he had himself.

An Edmonton stockbroker, Arthur Gregg, the Senior vice-president of McLeod, Young, Weir and Company, was one of a number of party members who badgered the party president, Gerard Amerongen, to call a leadership convention. Amerongen, an Edmonton lawyer who managed the party from his law office in the Tegler Building, had a sensible reason for refusing. "I had no intention of making a laughing stock out of the Conservative party by calling a convention without some assurance that there would be acceptable leadership candidates." Gregg had in his employ Peter Turner, a young man who had attended Central High School with Lougheed, and who had caddied with him one summer in Banff. Listening to Gregg lament about the party's failure to attract suitable leadership material, Turner casually suggested that he might consider "Senator Lougheed's grandson." Gregg was aware of the Senator's reputation and although he didn't even know Peter, he was intrigued at the idea that James A. Lougheed's grandson might lead the party. "What did we have to lose? It was a chance worth investigating," he admits, "since we were desperate for members and desperate for leadership." Gregg went to Amerongen and insisted he seek out Peter Lougheed. "I didn't know Peter from Adam," Amerongen recalls, "but in order to get something going, I phoned him in Calgary and asked to meet him." They got together at the Petroleum Club in Calgary, and over coffee, Amerongen spoke at length about the "impecunious state of the party." Lougheed remembers the conversation as being "painfully frank," ending with Amerongen asking him point blank whether he might consider being a candidate for the leadership of the party.

If Amerongen expected to discern a coherent pattern in Lougheed's intentions, he was disappointed. "He gave me no assurance of anything," states Amerongen. "The most I could hope for was that he would give it some thought." Word of Amerongen's approach made its way to a select group of Conservative businessmen in both Calgary and Edmonton, people who considered Peter an ideal representative of their class with extraordinary credentials and administrative ability. The party had found its man; all it had to do was convince him.

A second pitch was made to him that summer. Hayden Smith, a sales executive with New York Life Insurance in Calgary, and two lawyers, Henry Beaumont and Garry Johnson, all of them intransigent Tories active with the Young Progressive Conservative Association, invited Peter to attend the annual YPC barbecue at Happy Valley. The three men were concerned that the Liberals had managed to win a toehold in the legislature. The Liberal leader, Mike Maccagno, a Lac La Biche theatre owner, and Calgary Alderman Bill Dickie had both been elected. The NDP leader, Neil Reimer, was waging a strident opposition from outside the legislature, an opposition in which Reimer functioned as "a lightning rod in order to get Manning out of the heavens and down into the street." Although Reimer's approach was antagonistic, he was scoring political points.

Smith, who had campaigned for Diefenbaker's Defence Minister, Doug Harkness, remembers that "all of us in the YPC recognized the need to make some kind of move that would neutralize the opposition's success." Smith sensed that unless the provincial party came up with a strong leader, the Liberals were in an excellent position to present themselves as the "Conservative" alternative once Manning decided to retire. Smith, Beaumont, and Johnson were favourably disposed toward Peter and pledged their support to him.

"We recognized that Peter was anxious to step into the limelight, but that he expected others to build the stage for him," offers Smith. "He just wanted to wait until events fit into his program because he's a highly programmed guy. I honestly think that *at that time* he felt it was beneath him to think in terms of doing some of the mundane things you have to do in the political arena – things like knocking on doors – he felt that he had arrived beyond that, and that *in terms of personal achievement*, he'd already proven himself," and in fact he had.

Rumours spread fast in politics and a reporter with CKUA in Edmonton, Jim Edwards, "heard stories – I didn't know whether they were cultivated or not – that Lougheed was planning to take on Manning. It was an act of faith with him. It was recognized that someday he was going to throw down the gauntlet and tackle Manning, and according to the rumours, that day was going to be the beginning of the end of Social Credit." But the rumours could not be confirmed for the simple reason that in the summer of 1964, there was no truth to them. Lougheed accepted the invitation to attend the YPC annual barbecue and although he could not be aware of it at the time, because he agreed to show up at all, he set in motion his political career. Still Lougheed was wary of the motive behind some of those encouraging him; he was not prepared to be the tool of any special interest group.

On the second last week-end in September, Peter Lougheed and Harold Millican and their wives drove to Jasper to visit an old University colleague, Clare "Swede" Liden. Although Millican and Liden were Peter's friends, they were both Liberals, and in their presence Lougheed could evaluate his political chances with objective feedback. The three men spent an evening around the fireplace discussing the situation. There had been other discussions, but this one was conducted with a rare intensity. Peter still harboured national ambitions, but Liden felt that "the opportunity for Peter to take over the Conservative party was clean and fresh. He could take it over and build it up as his own."

Nevertheless, Peter appeared reluctant. He felt he needed more time to devote to his law practice before he could commit himself to the uncertainty of politics. Millican sensed that the minority position of the Pearson government and the awakening "quiet revolution" in Quebec would lead to greater power for the provinces. "Provincial rights," he insisted, "will be the wave of the future." In words that anticipated one of Lougheed's later lines, he voiced the opinion that "the action is going to be in the provinces – in Alberta." But Lougheed wanted to be convinced. He didn't think there "was anything for me in Alberta." Liden was quick to dampen his interest in federal politics. "Why play second fiddle to someone in Ottawa when you can be the boss in Alberta? You know you only like to be the boss!" Liden proposed that Peter consider making informal visits to rural centres, "to overcome suspicions that you're a slick city lawyer." "You might even learn something about the people," he added. It was a pivotal conversation and although Peter was still not convinced, he was intrigued by the challenge. "Still, the odds weren't very promising," he concluded. The three talked until dawn when their wives, who had been kept awake all night, called them to bed.

The unresolved debate at Jasper was followed by an unexpected report in the *Edmonton Journal* on September 21, 1964, that Gerald Baldwin, the popular Conservative MP for Peace River was "willing to accept the nomination for the leadership of the Alberta Conservative party." Baldwin had been parliamentary secretary to Prime Minister Diefenbaker, and with the defeat of the government the previous year, he was free to entertain the suggestion. In the absence of any other candidate, he was the best prospect for the job. Baldwin was flattered by the prospect of assuming the leadership of the provincial party and toyed with the idea. The newspaper report was substantiated on October 6, when Baldwin was quoted as saying that if he won the leadership, his approach would be "to tell the people what I would do as Premier, not spending my time telling them what's wrong with the present government."

Gerald Baldwin, or "Ged" as he is commonly known, was in his late fifties. Not exactly an old man, but he seemed old. He had first run for political office as a Conservative in the 1935 provincial election. He was not the most compelling personality for the job, and Liden telephoned Lougheed in another attempt to persuade him of the urgency of allowing his name to stand for the nomination. "You've got one chance," Liden told him, "and it's now."

The prospect of Baldwin in the race altered Lougheed's perception of the situation, although he still felt the "timing was wrong." He sought the advice of his law partners, asking them whether it would be "a wise thing" for him to do. Ballem, who had always understood that Lougheed's ultimate ambitions were federal did not think much of the idea; McDill had the opposite view and thought "the provincial scene was the way to go." But both of his partners agreed that perhaps it was too early in the life of their law firm for Peter to plunge into a political career.

On October 26, 1964 for the first time in his life, Peter attended a political meeting. He had arrived in Red Deer with Hayden Smith, Garry Johnson, and Henry Beaumont to attend the annual meeting of the Alberta Progressive Conservative party, ostensibly to hear federal opposition leader John Diefenbaker address the two hundred delegates. Lougheed was not impressed. Diefenbaker's vintage remarks attacking Prime Minister Pearson for building "Berlin Walls between the provinces" were all that Lougheed had to applaud at the convention. The following day, more than half of the delegates abandoned the meeting to follow Diefenbaker to Edmonton. And once the policy sessions convened it became apparent that this was a week-end that might better be spent elsewhere.

Lougheed was invited to sit in as an "observer" at the party's executive meeting and became impatient as the group spent its time discussing federal political strategy. One figure, however, caught his attention. A tall Lincolnesque Edmonton lawyer kept steering the discussions to long-term planning and organization on a provincial basis. He was Lou Hyndman, (the grandson of Prince Edward Island's Premier from 1876-1879, Sir Lewis Davis), the chairman of the policy sessions that week-end. Hyndman had returned from Ottawa where he had spent nearly a year as the executive assistant to Richard Bell, Diefenbaker's Minister of Citizenship and Immigration.

Before his work in Ottawa, Hyndman had been an aide-de-camp to Alberta's Lieutenant-Governor, J. Percy Page. Lougheed recognized that Hyndman was one man in the party who would be an asset in the development of a provincial party. Although Peter had intended to keep a "low profile" at the convention, his presence was noted by the press and in summary of the week-end session, reporters speculated that "two names have been suggested as leadership contenders: G. W. Baldwin, MP for Peace River, and E. P. Lougheed, a Calgary lawyer."

With the leadership convention set for the spring of 1965, Peter recognized he would soon have to make up his mind and arrive at a decision. He conferred with his wife and Jeanne outlined her views and political philosophy. He was relieved to discover she was Conservative.

Both of them agreed he was taking a chance, that the time for him to embark on a political career might not be right. Early in November, Lougheed and Jim Seymour secluded themselves at Lougheed's family retreat in Banff where Peter drew up a list of the advantages and disadvantages of seeking the job. The disadvantages were obvious. Harradance had left the party with "absolutely nothing." "Absolutely nothing," Lougheed emphasizes, "nothing in terms of finances, nothing in terms of organization – and the party had nothing in terms of history."

Lougheed decided that if he won the nomination, he would have to fight at least three elections before he might be assured of any measure of success. He also had to consider that if he struck out completely, "the door would be closed forever to any ambition in federal politics." He reasoned that Albertans, in supporting Social Credit, were supporting a conservative philosophy. Because the federal Tories had held power so infrequently, the conservative label did not evoke hostility; in fact the Diefenbaker interlude had enhanced their reputation in the West: "It was a matter of selling the same free enterprise philosophy in a new package once Manning was gone." The idea that he could "build a party from scratch without owing anything to anybody" was the strongest attraction. He had an instinct that a "strong case could be made for provincial rights." His experience in Oklahoma convinced him that Social Credit was not legislating resource policy to the province's best advantage; he sensed that if Alberta was not to become an economic backwater once the resources were depleted, an industrial strategy that took advantage of the province's resource potential must be developed. A further consideration appeared on his list: a career in provincial politics would allow him to remain close to his family.

So he made up his mind to run. Although he had endlessly measured and assessed his chances, there can be no doubt that his decision was, in the ultimate event, a gamble. "The prize was not all that great." He leaves the impression that his decision was based more on a sense of competition than conviction. Still, it was the roll of the dice he could not afford to pass up, and with the prospect of a younger man in the race, Ged Baldwin "deferred to youth."

If Peter was enthusiastic about the gamble, his friends were not. His mother's protective instincts made her caution him about the pain of defeat; his father-in-law, Dr. Rogers, bluntly told him he was "crazy." Fred Mannix, a very important influence, reacted in grey flannel understatement as Lougheed resigned his directorship with the company: "That's really quite an undertaking," he said. It was a discouraging task to convince anyone that he was serious. As he returned from a Stampede board meeting in Chicago with Gordon Love, Peter told the broadcast executive of his intentions. Love didn't disguise his sympathies for Social Credit as he exploded: "It's a dumb move. You'll never beat Manning, he's a household word. You won't get off the ground and you won't beat Social Credit." Then he smiled. "But if you really insist on doing this foolish thing, I'll help you."

Peter's mind was on other things, however, at the end of November as he went to Lethbridge to formally announce plans for a membership drive that would "get the whole country" behind Banff's bid for the 1972 Olympics. There had been criticism that Calgary could not accommodate the crowds that would pour into the city for the games, but Lougheed suggested if the city could handle the Stampede crowds it should be able to handle the winter games without extensive expansion.

The first organizational meeting for Peter's leadership campaign took place at the Mount Rundle suite at the Palliser Hotel in Calgary on December 10, a full four months before the convention. Ideologists were absent from the Lougheed operation. All of the people gathered together were practical business executives.

"I don't think any of us really knew what we were getting into," says Brock Hammond, a public relations executive with British American Oil (later Gulf). "There," as Chip Collins recalls, "Peter unfolded his mind before us like a chart as he informed us of his decision." Lougheed insisted that it was imperative that he win 80 per cent of the delegates on the first ballot. To those who suggested the goal was unrealistic, Peter was patient but adamant.

"We have to win overwhelmingly," he argued. "The party is in such difficulty that we have to have whatever strength there is ALL behind the leader. We can't afford to emerge from a convention with a significant number of dissidents. I have to win in an overwhelming way!"

Politics consists of getting to know people, and he set out to learn who the key people in the Conservative party were, people like Edmonton lawyer Peter Savaryn, and Roy Watson, both important backroom federal party organizers. The task was relatively simple; there were only nine constituency organizations and seven of them were in Calgary and Edmonton. While on a trip to Edmonton, he was introduced to the president of the National Conservative Student Federation. Although now only twenty-three, Joe Clark, at seventeen, had already been private secretary to the former provincial Conservative leader, Cam Kirby. Earlier, Clark had achieved leadership of the University of Alberta's model parliament opposition Conservatives. Although some of Lougheed's friends found Clark's consuming interest in politics "kind of spooky for someone so young," Lougheed accepted his offer to help.

By February, Lougheed's activities caused the *Edmonton Journal* to report that, "It had been learned that Mr. Lougheed will let his name stand." Lougheed didn't deny the report, but promised he would have something to say in a very few days.

Asked to confirm that Lougheed would be a candidate, Milton Harradance said he wouldn't interfere, but he did just that, endorsing Lougheed as a "splendid man for the job." One week later, on February 9, Lougheed called a news conference to announce that he would be a candidate for the leadership. He concluded that "there is a real need for a political force to be developed in this province with responsible ideas. Such a political force can develop best within the framework and traditions of an established party. It should enlist the energies and aspirations of young Albertans, supported and guided by the many experienced persons who had had little opportunity to participate in the political affairs of the province."

"If elected leader, I will begin immediately to organize the energies and the ideas of Albertans who will join with us to meet the challenging future problems of this province."

Having thrown his hat in the ring, he decided it might be a good idea to see a legislative session in action; he had never seen one before, so he turned up in the visitor's gallery one day early in March, 1965, to watch Premier Manning preside over a particularly dull afternoon session. Manning spotted him and pencilled a note:

Mr. Lougheed.

I hope your visit to the assembly doesn't dim your enthusiasm to enter actively into provincial public life.

The first twenty-five years are the worst.

It's good to see you here.

E. Manning

The alliance between the Progressive Conservative party of Alberta and its new leader, Peter Lougheed, had been sealed before the first of the four hundred delegates arrived in Edmonton on Thursday, March 18, 1965, to register for the leadership convention. There were two other candidates in the running. Dunc McKillop, a bespectacled twenty-nine year old Calgary lawyer with R. B. Bennett's old law firm, admits he was a contender simply "to make a name for myself." He had been a candidate in the 1963 provincial election, and had polled 1,500 votes in Calgary's Queen's Park; one of the few Tories to place second in that election. McKillop, who was John Diefenbaker's godson, did not expect to win. He calculated that Lougheed would be no more successful than his predecessors as long as Manning was around and that, after a few years as leader, would "blow it." He was, he said, running for next time, building a reputation that would see him a serious contender for the convention that would be called to replace Lougheed.

The other candidate was John Scott, an Edson town councillor and party organizer. The Edson riding was vacant as a result of the death of the Minister of Lands and Forests,

Norman Willmore. A by-election was called for March 29. Scott was the Conservative candidate in the by-election and many felt he had only entered the leadership race to generate publicity for that effort. But Scott believed that if he was lucky, he could win both the leadership and enter the legislature nine days later. Scott was a pleasant enough man, getting on in years, who had no obvious or hidden qualities that would qualify him for the job.

But Scott withdrew at the eleventh hour, on the day the convention opened in the suitably sedate CNR hostelry, the Macdonald Hotel. He died in 1975, but his widow, Frances, alleges that he was "pushed around by monied people, people who can buy anything." Party officials deny the claim, and Gerry Amerongen says, "if he was bought off, it must have been at a pretty low price. There wasn't any money around at that time to do that sort of thing."

Peter and Jeanne arrived exuding confidence. His efficient organization had at least forty people greeting delegates for him in sharp contrast to the subdued campaign waged by Dunc McKillop. Lougheed's supporters wore discreet gold and green buttons smaller than a quarter proclaiming, "I'm for Peter." The buttons were everywhere. McKillop estimates he spent only $500.00 on his campaign and agrees that he was outhustled by Lougheed. In fact he almost didn't get nominated. When nominations were called from the floor, neither McKillop nor his seconder were present. It was discovered the program was ahead of schedule, and the meeting recessed while the candidate was rounded up.

Lou Hyndman nominated Peter. Joe Clark had persuaded his father, Charles Arthur, the respected editor of the *High River Times*, to provide rural balance by seconding the nomination. Jabbing the air with gestures reminiscent of John F. Kennedy, Lougheed appealed to the delegates to end their lethargy and called on his supporters to get candidates of "distinction, decency and ability." The world over, politicians rely on slogans to emphasize their ability to do the impossible, and Lougheed took his slogan seriously. He pledged that under his leadership, the Conservatives would provide "not an opposition, but an alternative."

He allowed room for skepticism about his efforts. "I will make mistakes, but they will be mistakes of commission, not omission." He declined to talk about issues, saying he wanted "to do his homework," before he offered solutions. "Let us consider," he concluded, "that the campaign starts right now and never stops." It was more than rhetoric; he meant it.

One delegate suggests that "McKillop drunk, was more articulate than Lougheed sober." McKillop wasn't drunk, but he did nurse a monumental hangover during most of Saturday's policy sessions. Nevertheless, most observers agree that McKillop delivered the better speech. But Lougheed was better organized; he had the convention in his pocket. The balloting proved anti-climactic. The chairman, George Lynch-Staunton, declared Lougheed the winner; he didn't even bother to read the result of the vote as the floor erupted in enthusiastic, sustained applause. Their excitement was uncomplicated; no one doubted that Lougheed had won. His margin of victory was never made public, but there can be no doubt it was overwhelming. He won because he was the best man for the job. But, as the *Albertan* commented, "Whether he is to be congratulated on his election . . . is, in the light of the party's past history and future prospects, a debatable point." The conservative *Edmonton Journal* on the other hand was ecstatic and gushed in an editorial that it was entirely possible for "Premier Peter Lougheed," to form Alberta's first Conservative government. "Mr. Lougheed himself presents an impressive blend of forward looking confidence with a family name appealing to old timers, and an outlook appealing to the post war wave."

The first task of the new leader was to appear on the hustings in the Edson by-election; he attended a public meeting where he spoke in support of John Scott. When the polls closed on March 29, the Liberal candidate, William Switzer, squeaked past Neil Reimer of the NDP to win the seat from Social Credit. Scott trailed a distant fourth with less than 500 votes.

The by-election gave the Liberals three seats in the legislature securing for them beyond all question the position of official opposition. The prospect of reversing the trend was disconcerting, but Lougheed could not harbour timidity in the course he had set for himself. As he had acknowledged at the leadership convention, it would be a "a long tough road."

Notes

1 The case was eventually settled out of court, at a meeting in the Waldorf Astoria Hotel in New York city. Mannix collected $1,000,000.00 from Frank McMahon, the Calgary oil and gas entrepreneur. "It was the first cheque for that amount I ever saw," relates Lougheed.

2 One example is Harold Milavsky, who was administrative vice-president of the Mannix Corporation, and who is now President of TRIZEC.

CHAPTER IV

Peter Lougheed may have been, as the *Medicine Hat News* described him, "Everybody's perfect candidate," but in the spring of 1965 his challenge was to conjure a following out of a void. He would have to overcome obstacles that might discourage a lesser man. The task as he saw it was to build personal support that cut across party lines. Initially, that meant emphasis on organization and image rather than ideology.

Robert Lorne Stanfield, the Premier of Nova Scotia, was prepared to help. According to Geoffrey Steven's biography, Stanfield, as president of the party in 1947, had faced the same situation that Lougheed now encountered in 1965. Without representation in the legislature Stanfield "revived dormant constituency associations, and organized meetings at which local Tories elected new officers."[1]

"It was exhausting, often discouraging, work but it paid dividends."[2] Gradually, Stanfield developed a network of contacts across the province, people, who if they believed the party could be revived, would go to work for it, and perhaps stand as candidates. When he returned to a constituency a second or third time he found that people knew him, and were coming to respect his dedication, determination, and skill as a political organizer.

In May, 1965, Lougheed went to Halifax for three days to sit down in Province House with Stanfield and seek his advice. He returned convinced that "there is some real essence to be learned from Stanfield's experience in Nova Scotia." The meeting with Stanfield left him satisfied that he couldn't delegate the job of organizing. "Stanfield taught me that the leader of the party has to be the principal organizer and has to work harder than anyone else. When everybody is a volunteer, the leader has to go to every meeting, no matter how small. He has to generate the enthusiasm himself – the contributions of the volunteers will be in direct proportion to the enthusiasm generated by the leader." There was something else. Impressed by Stanfield's attempts to attract industry through a Crown corporation, Industrial Estates Limited,[3] Lougheed gave serious thought to promoting a similar economic council in Alberta to induce secondary industrial development, convinced that a "major and energetic" selling job was required in the West. Albertans are traditionally committed to free enterprise and suspicious of government assistance to industry, so reaction to Lougheed's opening gambit was lukewarm. Nevertheless the *Medicine Hat News* supported the idea provided "the proposed agency did not offer any improper inducements."

On the heels of his meeting in Halifax, he accepted an invitation from Manitoba's Premier Duff Roblin and travelled to Winnipeg to discuss organization. Roblin advised him to look for candidates not on the basis of whether "they were the best Conservatives" but rather to "look for the best man regardless of his political affiliation." "The trick," said Roblin, "is to identify the candidate who can win." Lougheed became convinced that "the more non-political, the more apolitical a person is, the better chance he has of winning."

It was this appreciation of talent on a non-partisan basis that prompted Lougheed to consider arranging a speaking tour in Alberta for a French-Canadian law professor from l'Université de Montréal, Pierre Elliott Trudeau. Lougheed first met Trudeau at the end of June at Mont Tremblant during a conference organized by Power Corporation, a brainstorming session with upwardly mobile young Canadians: Lougheed was impressed by Trudeau's cool and cerebral approach to the "quiet revolution" then emerging in

Quebec. Trudeau dared to challenge the spirit of the new nationalism in terms which, at the time, made sense to Lougheed. For his part, Trudeau recalls that Lougheed "did not leave a particularly memorable impression." The Trudeau tour of Alberta never materialized. Three months after the meeting in the Laurentians, Prime Minister Lester Pearson called a federal election for November 8, and Pierre Trudeau joined the Liberals as a candidate in Montreal's Mount Royal constituency.

Through the summer of 1965, Lougheed continued to plan his own election strategy. He recruited a Calgary businessman, Ted Mills, as a constituency organizer; Rod McDaniel was put in charge of finance; and, Merv Leitch was given the responsibility of determining policy. Lougheed went to Ottawa to meet John Diefenbaker as well as the Progressive Conservative MPs from Alberta who promised assistance in building a provincial organization. Five ground rules were employed:

1. No radical statements such as "Premier tomorrow."
2. Fresh, new approach with emphasis on planning and participation by new people.
3. Personal dedication and confidence.
4. Team approach versus one man administration.
5. Emphasis on business experience.

By the end of July he had, as his priority, established a communications committee, responsible for organizing a preliminary election program for media exposure including slogans and advertising material. Appointed committee coordinator was John Francis, a Calgary public relations consultant, who had been a freshman on the University of Alberta campus when Lougheed was president. The committee also included Joe Clark's father, Charles; Jim Edwards, an Edmonton broadcast executive; Charles Cook, a Calgary radio personality; Horst Schmid, a German language broadcaster in Edmonton (who had been the campaign manager for federal Conservative MP Bill Skoreyko); David Wood and Brock Hammond, two Calgary businessmen; Ron Helmer and Doug White; Dale Smith, a public relations director in Edmonton; and, Carol Wilmot, a Calgary housewife (who was responsible for gauging feminine reaction to the candidate's performance). They gathered at the Palliser Hotel on August 21 in an attempt to respond to the growing change in attitudes in Alberta, but the degree of change was difficult to chart. The committee was to create an appealing image for Lougheed; he must not appear harnessed to personal ambition, but dedicated to the more practical ideal of a sense of mission, a sense of purpose.

In the rural areas, the Bible dominated political thinking; Aberhart and Manning were successful because they preached old virtues; Social Credit's economic theories had become an extension of Christian morals. Nominally, Lougheed is an Anglican. He believes in God, but also believes his faith is a personal matter; he does not subscribe to organized religion. His religious image was of great concern to the committee, for as Charles Cook explained, Manning, a preacher, has the image of "an honest man" while lawyers are perceived to be "crooks." Brock Hammond emphasized the point, but suggested that it would be naturally assumed "that as a Christian, Lougheed would carry his principles into office."

Other weaknesses in the candidate's image that concerned the group included the fact that Peter might be seen as being "too intensive and calculating" and that his "Ivy League" appearance was not attractive to rural groups." The degree to which the candidate's age might alienate voters was considered and it was decided that the word "young" would not appear in campaign literature; but it would be "implied in photographs and statements carefully selected to give the impressions of maturity," while subtly conveying his youthfulness. They examined whether Lougheed's connections to "an old Alberta family" might be resented and Jim Edwards concluded that it could be used to his advantage if Peter were promoted as the first "Alberta born Premier."

Lougheed had made his first television appearance on CFRN's "Face the Newsmen" shortly after winning the leadership and his performance was less than satisfactory: he tended to gesticulate too much, and cupped his hands close to his chest in a position best described as precious.

75

He had a minor speech impediment, a slight lisp. Saskatoon MP Dr. Lewis Brand recalls thinking that as a speaker Peter was a "lightweight." But in spite of Peter's handicaps he had, for a novice, displayed an uncanny ability to relate to the cameras. The committee agreed that "work should commence immediately regarding grooming Peter for subsequent appearance." A television sub-committee was struck to consider "formal, dramatic impact, imaginative production, use of film, etc." Gordon Love put his studios and cameras at CFCN at Peter's disposal after midnight for rehearsal purposes. His television training was easy. He had an intuitive grasp of technique – it was the mechanics he had to learn – how to relax in a studio with technicians around, how to shift naturally from camera to camera, how to modulate his voice for the right measure of sincerity, and how to pace his comments to the clock. He counted on Jeanne's flair for the dramatic. His wife attended the taping sessions and during the videotape playbacks proved to be his most valuable critic.

He had an opportunity to practise his television technique during the federal election campaign of 1965. Lougheed plunged into the federal campaign "to help elect seventeen Progressive Conservative MPs from Alberta." But he also adopted a strategical position regarding the federal party that he maintains to this day. On September 9, a press release was issued:

As provincial leader, Mr. Lougheed does not intend to comment on federal matters except insofar as they affect the provincial administration.

In taking this stand he guaranteed that his own efforts to build a party in Alberta would not be threatened by the internal quarrels which had already begun to divide the federal party. It also allowed him the convenience of influencing federal matters by being able to come down on both sides of an issue at the same time. This is an ideal situation for a provincial politician because it allows him to pursue his policies independently of the federal spectrum.

Opposition leader John Diefenbaker was fighting for his

political life; he had defused a challenge to his leadership earlier in the year, and many of those who pledged their support to him during the campaign were anxious to see him fail so they could rid themselves once and for all of the Western warrior should he prove to be unsuccessful. He wasn't, but then neither was Lester Pearson. On the night of the election Diefenbaker, who had campaigned vigorously and effectively, denied the Liberals a majority government and picked up two seats to give the Conservatives ninety-seven members in the Commons. The country may have rejected Diefenbaker but Alberta did not: fifteen of seventeen seats were Conservative; the other two, Social Credit.

The federal election over, Lougheed returned to two areas of personal endeavour: the drive to organize the first Conservative party convention since winning the leadership and the campaign to secure the 1972 Winter Olympics for Banff. Banff's position was suddenly jeopardized in mid-November when Montreal Mayor Jean Drapeau, in a surprise move, declared that he was going to bid for the 1972 Summer Olympics. It seemed unlikely that the International Olympic Committee would sanction both the summer and winter games in Canada in the same year. Because of his work on the committee, Lougheed's political reputation appeared to be tied to the success of his efforts to secure the winter games for Banff. He had flown to Olympic conferences in Madrid and Rome where the IOC assured the Calgary group that its selection of a site would not depend on the federal election results: both the Liberals and Conservatives supported Banff's application. Now eastern Canadian ambitions threatened Alberta's hopes. Lougheed appealed to Drapeau to bid for the 1976 summer games instead and challenged his action as not being "in the best interests of Canada or the Olympic movement." But the Mayor of Montreal was determined and replied that he would seek the endorsement of the Canadian Olympic Association for his application, at a meeting in Toronto at the end of November.

But there could be no doubt that Lougheed was getting mileage out of his Olympic involvement; it was a perfect vehicle for him to establish his credentials as he spoke to service clubs throughout the province, without pushing politics.

Except for the growing objections of environmental groups, public expectations about the winter Olympics had been magnified. Expectations about Lougheed's political image were also being raised. A column by the *Edmonton Journal*'s John Barr on October 25, 1965, was particularly significant. Barr had zeroed in on an article by a political science professor of the University of Alberta, George Bowering, who had described Alberta as a "cultural desert, a province inhabited mainly by ungrammatical, pro-Socred letter writers, stupid newspaper editors, fiery eyed fundamentalists, and right wing politics." Responding to that image, Barr chided Alberta's political academics for painting crude caricatures of the province and, in the same article, noted that

> a new breed of Alberta politician is appearing, represented in one instance by the attractive young leader of the Progressive Conservative Party, Mr. Peter Lougheed. Taking a page from John F. Kennedy's book, Mr. Lougheed is determined to enlist some academics in his cause, the better to inject some needed tonic into the flaccid veins of his party.

The article was copied and circulated to the growing number of Lougheed's strategists who were invited to the initial meeting of the party's campaign organizing committee. The expanded group met in the Maligne Room of the Macdonald Hotel in Edmonton on November 14, to co-ordinate all aspects of policy, publicity, communications, organization, and finance. At the meeting both short- and long-term organizational charts were fixed. Finance, under McDaniel, was expanded to include Edmonton lawyer, Peter Macdonnell and chartered accountant, Eric Geddes. Geddes, a Price Waterhouse executive, had been a federal party fund raiser in the 1957-58 election campaigns, but had become disenchanted with Diefenbaker's leadership. Merv Leitch had built the policy co-ordinating group to include an economist, Gordon Pearce, as well as the former party leader, Ernest

Watkins. It also included Dave Jenkins, who worked in the party's national headquarters during the election, and Robert Dinkel. Lou Hyndman, Neil Crawford, a former executive assistant to Diefenbaker, and Gerry Amerongen were all on the general organizing committee. Calgary lawyer Henry Beaumont was put in charge of planning the annual convention that would be held in January. Chip Collins was responsible for office administration.

It was the first phase of Lougheed's campaign and appropriately was designated as "image building." The committee would, according to the minutes, "make superior use of the media to the other parties. As much as possible the three TV and several radio stations in the province should tie together into an overall statement of party position." Lougheed prefers to call it the "identification process." "We took the view," he says, "that unless we got credibility with some seats in the legislature no one was going to pay any attention to policy. With the horrendous record of the Conservative party, without representation in the house, we could have had all the policy in the world and no one would pay any attention to it." But image building was a slow process; recognition of Peter in the public mind was not that easy to cultivate, as Charles Cook demonstrated in a letter to Lougheed:

During the course of a week in hospital Cook wrote "I heard your name pronounced:
LOW'-heed
LOUF'-head
LU'heed
and strangely enough, properly, once. Until you are better known you better hit the broadcasters over the head, continually, with the correct pronunciation of that beautiful, wonderful name." [The name is pronounced LAW-heed.]

Joe Clark expressed similar concern in a memo to Peter and included a number of recommendations. The following excerpts:

1. We can't always remember to inform you of picnics, annual meetings, Christmas parties, etc., at which

79

you might profitably appear. We can't rely on remembering. Some sort of system must be set up which would involve some 'little old lady,' of which the party has a few, receiving and reviewing newsletters of a variety of groups, and scanning the weeklies, and social columns of the dailies.

2. Statements you make in response to government announcements must be more widely circulated. Certain weekly newspapers should receive a copy. An 'I thought you might be interested letter' should accompany the first release to the weeklies.

3. However crowded your timetable, you would benefit from frequent speeches before friendly PC groups. On such occasions you should encourage questions to develop your proficiency at response.

I'd even go to the lengths of having a couple of hostile questions planted because a Tory group is likely to be too polite to give their Leader the grilling he needs.

4. Have more lunches with editorial writers, feature columnists; start going through the news people.

It was advice he pondered as he flew to Toronto on Monday, November 15, 1965 to oppose Montreal's application for the 1972 Summer Olympics, at a meeting of the Canadian Olympic Association. Technically, the COA demanded federal approval before it would consider a bid such as Montreal's. But Drapeau had the "unanimous approval" of the Quebec government and the COA waived the rule. Lougheed was concerned and said so. "After many years of hard work in the Calgary-Banff area by volunteer workers dedicated to the Olympic Movement, the position of the City of Montreal is most disappointing." It could conceivably result in losing both bids for Canada instead of being reasonably assured of the Winter Games in 1972.

Lougheed outlined his objections before the COA but he recognized that a complete rejection of Montreal's application wouldn't work. In numerical terms, Western Canada had only six representatives on the COA; thirteen of the thirty voting directors were from Quebec. When Lougheed finished, Drapeau made his pitch. He delivered a brilliant and passionate argument. In spite of Lougheed's efforts, the COA endorsed Montreal's bid, adding a clause that Banff's application would have priority at the meeting of the International Olympic Committee in Rome in April of 1966. It was a compromise that the Calgary group had to live with. They had assurance from Mayor Drapeau that "Canada is capable of handling both the winter and summer games," as he promised "to work with our friends in the West to prove to the world that Canada can support both." Lougheed didn't believe it for a moment and sheepishly had to say that "he was satisfied under the circumstances." But five months remained before the final IOC decision in Rome, and the Calgary committee redoubled its efforts to be successful.

Between his political organization, his speaking schedule, and his efforts on behalf of the Olympic Committee, the workload was prodigious. His family added to his concerns. Jeanne was pregnant with her fourth child. Then too, Peter was ignoring his law practice and his partners began to voice their concern. Ballem and McDill were prepared to accommodate his political ambition, but they were not prepared to finance it.

Their initial warnings went unheeded as Lougheed devoted more time to planning the party's annual convention. He spent sixteen hour days travelling from Camrose to Cardston, Jasper to Lethbridge, Vegreville to Vermilion. His refrain was consistent: Alberta was "neither a Liberal nor an NDP province. If there is going to be a swing away from Social Credit, it will be logically to the Conservatives." It was the rationale he used to express his conviction that "at the least, we will form the official opposition after the next provincial election."

Speaking to the Macdonald-Cartier Club at the King Edward Hotel in Edmonton on January 15, 1966, Lougheed outlined some of the details of the forthcoming convention, a convention that he said would demonstrate that his party was "a responsible alternative to Social Credit." Avoiding a personal attack on Premier Manning, he chided the government for creating "a myth of performance."

That declaration was conveniently accentuated within

the same week when Social Credit candidates for the model parliament elections at the University of Alberta amalgamated with the campus Conservatives after being refused campaign funds from the Alberta Young Social Credit League. Lougheed welcomed the coalition as an example of "the wide gulf between young Albertans and the Social Credit Party." The incident, trivial by itself, created a storehouse of political energy. Under Joe Clark's direction, Lougheed's alma mater would deliver volunteer manpower when it was needed.

On January 28, beneath a banner which proclaimed "the future belongs to us," fourteen of Alberta's fifteen federal Conservative MPs joined Lougheed on the platform of the Palliser Hotel ballroom for the party's annual convention.

They were astonished by the response; in spite of minus 40° temperatures outside, almost a thousand people showed up. Whether they came out of loyalty to their federal representatives or to hear Lougheed is debatable but not important. The Conservative MP for Calgary South, Ray Ballard, who had worked with Lougheed on the Calgary Stampede board admitted he attended with reservations: "Peter was not known as a Conservative person; we all recognized he came from a Conservative family, but there was some question in our minds as to what kind of policies he would come up with."

Lougheed, who found himself speaking to the largest Conservative convention in Alberta's history, dispelled any notion that he was not ideologically in tune with the Tories. He unveiled his party philosphy in "twelve guideposts."

1. He stated that "the public has a right to know. Public laws should be made in public," and he warned against "comfortable drift to government by cabinet or through order in council."
2. He declared his belief in local government and pledged that the proper role of provincial government is "guidance, advice and assistance to local government – not direction, control and restriction to their affairs."
3. He stressed the belief in the provincial government

which "gives strong support to the need in Canada for an effective central government."

4. He promised to "protect the individual citizen as much as improving the public good," and explained that "every single item of proposed legislation should be thoroughly examined by members of the legislature to determine its impact on individual Albertans."

5. He affirmed that the provincial government "should always have a long range plan for future development."

6. He promised "adequate warning should be given of proposed new legislation to encourage public participation in public affairs so that administration within a vacuum could be avoided."

7. He pledged "to establish a set of legislative priorities in relation to financial resources."

8. He saw as his greatest challenge the administration of welfare in relation to need without detracting from human dignity. In his view "proposed welfare programs should carefully weigh the dangers of compulsion and the unnecessary cost arising from compulsion."

9. He stressed the importance of "sound financial responsibility."

10. Significantly, he hoped to initiate the "full development of Alberta's natural resources."

11. He reaffirmed his support for "the free enterprise system."

12. He expressed the sentiment that "God's endowment of Alberta with such abundant natural resources complimented by the skills and talents of its own people, permits the development of a society second to none in North America."

The "guideposts" were hardly sensational new dogma; as one cynical observer remarked, "Peter overextended himself – Moses was content with ten."

But it was an impressive beginning, and as the *Albertan* noted, "The Liberal party could readily subscribe to most of Mr. Lougheed's guideposts; Social Credit is unlikely publicly to reject any of them and even the New Democrats would find some of them acceptable." But the speech was important because it demonstrated Lougheed's ability to distil the essence of a common denominator in Alberta society, and because it reflected an attitude and an approach to politics that would change after he came into office.

Notes
1 Geoffrey Stevens, *Stanfield*, (Toronto; McClelland and Stewart Ltd., 1973).
2 *Ibid.*
3 In 1965 Nova Scotia's IEL had fostered a Clairtone Electronics Plant, a Heavy Water Installation, and a Volvo Assembly Plant all of which later proved to be economic embarrassments to the government of Nova Scotia.

CHAPTER V

It is hard to imagine a low point in Peter Lougheed's career, but 1966 qualifies. For several months that year his political efforts and professional interests seemed to come apart. A bitter controversy erupted in his law office early in February when his partners requested that he remove his name from the firm. They claimed the practice was suffering because of Lougheed's political endeavours. To them it seemed that clients who preferred to be discreet in their political dealings were uncomfortable with the apparent partisan nature of the firm.

"We wanted Peter to adopt a low profile from a political point-of-view," explains Marv McDill. "We were a very youthful law firm, we were concerned that the public was not taking us seriously. To them it appeared that we were politicking all the time. And, in our view, the law practice was not to be used for political ends." John Ballem recommended a compromise, that Peter's name still appear on the firm's letterhead but in lower case letters and as a "counsel" to the law office. Ballem did not consider the idea as a denigration of Lougheed's position: "It would have been consistent with the fact that he was spending less time in legal affairs; everyone in the profession would have understood what had happened."

But Lougheed was affronted. The law firm was, after all, his idea; to tamper with the prestige of a name that represented three generations of Calgary lawyers was, in his mind, totally unacceptable. The dispute coincided with the premature birth on February 7 of his youngest son, Joseph. (Jeanne had endured a difficult pregnancy.) Lougheed was in no position to resign from the firm, even though he considered it. The practice represented an income which, at the time, he could not afford to relinquish. The party's fund raising efforts were still less than satisfactory. Although after a year under Lougheed's leadership party membership had grown from less than a thousand to four thousand paid members, there was only $27,800 in trust, not even enough to provide the leader with an honorarium. So, Lougheed endured the indignation and as a face saving concession proposed instead the reversal of the first two names. His partners accepted that: Ballem's name was given precedence and the firm was rechristened Ballem, Lougheed and McDill.

A week after being demoted in his law firm, Lougheed promised his candidacy in the riding of Calgary West; he announced he would seek to represent the area in the legislature. He had planned to run in his home constituency of Calgary-Glenmore, the seat held by Liberal Bill Dickie. He denied he was running away from a fight by not taking on Dickie, and explained "that in view of the limited opposition in the legislature, I should contest a seat held by Social Credit."

In order to improve the party's financial position the "Lougheed Club" was devised. An exclusive appeal was made to 150 people prepared to contribute $100.00 annually to build "a responsible alternative in politics." Members did not get much in return for their contribution, other than sporadic reports on party matters written on Peter Lougheed's personal stationery. Many of the initial members were already volunteers serving on various committees; the contribution was considered a test of the degree of their commitment to the cause.

"Those who put their own interests ahead of Peter's were ignored or demoted," claims a volunteer worker. "There was no second line of assistance: Peter expected total commitment from his friends, or nothing."

Eric Geddes explained it another way: "Peter rang the

86

bell for help, and his friends came out of the woodwork; they felt that if Peter was willing to make the sacrifice they were obligated to do all they could to support him."

Within three months, the Lougheed Club had filled its quota. The new source of revenue helped to defray, among other things, travel expenses. And, early in March of 1966, Peter travelled to Ontario again for meetings with Premier John Robarts and with Dalton Camp, the national president of the Progressive Conservative party. Camp, without being openly disloyal to Diefenbaker, was organizing a campaign to promote reform of the party constitution, reform that might allow the opposition to reassert itself. Camp had concluded that there are limits to the power of political leadership "and these should, from time to time, be appraised."

Camp recognized Lougheed as a prime resource of the party and tactfully suggested that the greatest contribution Alberta could make to the national party was to express its sentiment in favour of the principle of leadership accountability. Robarts opposed the idea, while Lougheed felt that if he was going to build a provincial party he could not get personally involved with the question of national leadership. He would not take sides.

As he had done with Roblin and Stanfield, Lougheed sought Robarts' counsel and took away from Queen's Park a strong recommendation from the Premier against "making commitments or promises on the long way up that you are not prepared to keep if you should ever get elected."

Lougheed returned to Edmonton in mid-March to preside over the opening of the party's first permanent headquarters, offices which had been scrounged on the fifth floor of the Imperial Bank Building on Jasper Avenue; a similar office was opened in Calgary a month later, in the Lougheed Building.

In the last week of April, Peter left for Rome where the final decision on the site of the 1972 Winter Olympics would be announced. Calgary's Mayor, Jack Leslie, was optimistic it "would be a Banff year." Although environmentalists and wild life conservationists had stepped up their attack against the use of national parks for the games, Lougheed was convinced that "Canada needs events such as Expo '67 and the Olympics to pull the nation together to achieve the national pride of holding a well run event."

The summer games were awarded first: Montreal lost to Munich, West Germany. Following that announcement, the Canadian delegation felt supremely confident that Banff would succeed in its third bid to host the winter games. But the Calgary group had failed to understand the psychology of manipulating the International Olympic Committee. Getting the nod from the hoary aristocrats of international sport was not so much a business proposition as a mating game, and Calgary had not followed the protocol of wooing the IOC members. Sapporo, Japan, not Banff was awarded the games. It was an astonishing decision in view of the fact that Japan had been the site of the summer games two years earlier. In explaining its choice, the IOC noted that Japan had been the successful applicant because it was never able to stage the games it had been awarded in 1940 because of the war.

"Who won the war anyway," Lougheed exploded, "the Allies or the Axis? It's hard getting slapped in the face and kicked below the belt at the same time." It was one of the few times he reacted without thinking.

He was concerned that Banff's failure to obtain the Olympics had damaged his political credibility. He declined to pose for a souvenir group photograph of the Calgary Olympic Committee. There was no point in being identified with a lost cause. The Olympic movement was past history. Lougheed was free to concentrate exclusively on laying the groundwork for an election. He continued to cultivate reporters, editors, and columnists he knew or needed to know. Studying the timetable, he continued to focus on fund raising, and began to attend a series of nominating conventions.

Early in June, 1966, Lou Hyndman was the first Conservative candidate to be nominated for the 1967 election. Hyndman defeated former party president Gerry Amerongen on the first ballot for the right to represent Lougheed in Edmonton West, the province's wealthiest constituency. The contest between Hyndman and Amerongen demonstrated a familiar pattern in future nominations: two or more equally competent and attractive candidates pitted against each other to give the nomination a competitive nature which in turn helped to stimulate public interest.

The nominating meeting in Okotoks-High River on June 22 was devised as a "media event" to give the Conservatives a rural profile. In a gathering reminiscent of the early Social Credit rallies, two hundred people gathered at a ranch near High River for a typical Western barbecue. Sixty year old Tom Hughes, a respected area rancher, edged out a local realtor, C. L. Rhyasen, by three votes. The winning candidate's reaction was typical: "I feel like a mosquito in a nudist colony," he said, "I know what to do, but I don't know where to start."

But the Hughes' nomination served to alienate Joe Clark from Peter Lougheed. Clark, eager to run himself, had his heart set on representing High River, his home town. Lougheed discouraged his aide's ambitions explaining that Clark was too young. It was the beginning of a cooling in relations between the two. "Peter was often aggravated by Joe's pedantic enthusiasm. In Peter's view Joe was very much a peripheral character in the party hierarchy. Peter had him pigeon-holed as a party worker and resented Joe's arguments on party policy which he felt were often unnecessary and immature," recalls an intimate of both.

The core of Lougheed's drive was to recruit candidates who, without being specific on details, could convince an electorate that Lougheed could be trusted. He believed that the political process should be an education not only for the voter but for the candidate as well.

In August, accompanied by Ged Baldwin, Lougheed toured the Peace River district in the northwest section of the province to find out first hand the nature of public grievances in the area. He "covered a great deal of territory" talking to homesteaders, inspecting rail and transportation facilities, visiting Indian reserves, and touring hospitals which were unable to admit patients because of a lack of permanent medical staff. At the conclusion of the tour he was convinced of "a definite need for accelerated growth in the north."

In September, Premier Manning called a by-election for

October 6 to fill the vacancy left by the death of Social Credit member William Kovach in the Pincher Creek-Crowsnest riding. It would be Lougheed's first test at the polls and, in theory, the climate seemed encouraging for the Conservatives. In the 1963 provincial election, the Conservative candidate, Frank Lynch-Staunton had been second in the riding, and in the 1965 federal election, Tory MP Lawrence Kindt had increased his majority in the corresponding federal constituency of Macleod. Optimists felt that Lougheed could sweep into the provincial legislature on Kindt's coat tails.

Apart from the tourists during the summer who explore the mountain reaches of southwestern Alberta, Pincher Creek is an insular area whose economy depends on coal mining and ranching. After an initial foray into the riding, party organizer Joe Clark reported that he "didn't like the looks of it." Key Conservatives in the riding suggested that Lougheed not waste time bothering to run a candidate.

But Peter was not willing to run himself; a more important test would be the provincial general election expected within eight months. There was no point in his risking personal defeat as a parachute candidate in a rural riding. Instead, Alex Wells, thirty-five year old chartered accountant from Blairmore, was nominated to carry the Tory colours into the fray. As campaign managers, Lougheed and Clark established headquarters in motel rooms at Frank and in Pincher Creek. The former Minister of Agriculture in Diefenbaker's cabinet, Alvin Hamilton, was brought in as the Conservative's keynote speaker at a fund-raising banquet. Wells had an identical twin brother, Stan, and between the two of them, they doubled their efforts, each of them campaigning in different locations as "Wells, the Conservative candidate." Even as a gimmick, the Tory twins were no match for the NDP's blitz tactics. NDP strategists had concluded that "the knack of political campaigning has disappeared from Alberta. You have to shake the tree." Their candidate, Garth Turcott, was not content only to shake the tree, but with help from T. C. Douglas and party organizers from Saskatchewan, Ontario, and British Colum-

90

bia, he uprooted it. Still, in the long run, it was Lougheed who collected all the apples.

The NDP campaigned to eliminate property tax and proposed free education at all levels. It soon became obvious that the Conservatives, whose only aim was to get a seat in the legislature, were not in contention. The contest was between Social Credit's Joseph Hanrahan and Turcott. Turcott's people were everywhere.

On the night of the by-election, following a see-saw battle, Turcott edged past Hanrahan by 136 votes to become the first NDP member to win a seat in the legislature in Alberta's history. Lougheed did not expect to win, but he did not expect to fail so completely. Wells captured fewer votes than the 1963 Tory candidate, and he dropped from second to third place, collecting less than a thousand votes.

The *Edmonton Journal* concluded that the by-election defeat discounted the idea that Lougheed was "a coming political force." "If this vote is any index of Mr. Lougheed's electoral potency," said the paper, "he looks headed for a pretty dismal future."

Although Lougheed felt the NDP victory was "terrifying" he conceded that the by-election was "a blessing in disguise for the Conservatives; a baptism of fire." Lougheed had been impressed by the NDP's door-to-door technique and learned from it; the experience also taught him "never again to take a vote for granted." "Our mistakes in Pincher Creek were due to inexperience," Lougheed admitted.

More political trouble was brewing for Lougheed as the federal Conservative party divided into pro- and anti-Diefenbaker factions which threatened to split the provincial organization. On October 22, the *Journal* touched a sensitive nerve by posing the question: "Where does Mr. Lougheed, as one of the bright new lights of the party, stand in the dispute between Dalton Camp (and many increasingly disaffected young Tories) and Dief the Chief?"

"Until he clarifies his position on the federal leadership of his own party," the paper reasoned, "his claim to speak for 'a new conservatism' will hardly be credible."

The following day, after an executive meeting of the

Alberta provincial party, Lougheed responded, and indirectly expressed his accord with what Camp was trying to do. He accepted an amendment to the provincial party's constitution that provided for a review of his own leadership. And his words spoke for themselves about his position:

The leadership is not a popularity contest. Neither is it a mandate of unlimited duration. If the majority do not find the continuation of my leadership acceptable, they are entitled to request a leadership convention.

A standing vote of confidence [which Diefenbaker favoured at the national level] is clearly unfair. The purpose of a secret ballot is to permit free expression of opinion without intimidation or unreasonable pressure.

In spite of the controversy at the national level, Lougheed appeared to have a solid grip on his own party when he was officially nominated as the Conservative candidate for Calgary West on November 2. 150 people were expected to attend the nominating convention in Richmond School, but twice as many arrived to endorse him unanimously as their candidate. In his acceptance speech, he appealed for a "responsible and effective opposition."

In a direct reference to his Social Credit opponent, Donald S. Fleming, he suggested "Calgary can no longer afford to have silent and obedient backbenchers represent it."

But a week later, during a special two day session of the legislature, called to make provincial tax laws conform to new agreements with the federal government, Lougheed was upstaged when the newly elected NDP member, Garth Turcott, used his maiden appearance in the house to hurl strident charges of a conflict of interest at a cabinet minister and a former provincial treasurer. Turcott demanded the resignation of Municipal Affairs Minister Alf Hooke, and also claimed that the former treasurer, E. W. Hinman, had been involved in a "tangled web of dealings" with two private companies.

Although the charges were dismissed by Premier Manning as nothing more than "malicious gossip" Turcott refused to let the matter lie; the result was widespread controversy which titillated the public through the winter and well into spring.

While Turcott was getting media attention on the provincial level, the furor surrounding Diefenbaker and the federal Conservative party continued to escalate. "It was one of the worst months I had as leader," remembers Lougheed. "Nobody was interested in provincial politics or the provincial Conservative party; people were talking about Camp and Diefenbaker and nothing else. We knew we were facing our first election within six months and no one even wanted to talk about it."

The Diefenbaker revolt came to its apparent conclusion at a national convention in Ottawa in mid-November. Lougheed was present in the Chateau Laurier's baroque ballroom as Diefenbaker was shouted down by the jeers of angry Tories, Joe Clark among them, who demanded that "responsibility and leadership be transferred to younger people."

Camp emerged victorious out of that turbulent convention and a resolution to hold a leadership convention before January 1, 1968 was subsequently passed. Through it all Lougheed remained silent. "He was appalled to see the way Diefenbaker was disgraced, but at the same time, I think he recognized what a liability Diefenbaker had become," suggests a confidant, "Peter just didn't want to make any waves that might submerge his own party in Alberta."

Many Diefenbaker sympathizers interpreted Lougheed's neutrality as indecisiveness; others felt his silence lent consent to Camp. A former Conservative cabinet minister suggested that "by refusing to come to the aid of the party [and many felt the party was Diefenbaker] Lougheed destroyed himself; he'll never be elected to anything." The federal MP for Edmonton East, Bill Skoreyko, was particularly vituperative: "I felt Peter owed it to Diefenbaker to declare his loyalty to him. There was no doubt that the Lougheed name was respected and recognized as a comer across the country; he could have had an impact in Eastern Canada where Diefenbaker was in desperate need of support." In Cardston, the Mayor, Dennis Burt, announced that he was "irritated" by Lougheed's neutrality, and abandoned the provincial Conservatives to run as an independent.

Diefenbaker himself was not at all perturbed by Lougheed's silence. "I was fond of Peter," he says. "Even then it was apparent he was going to be a powerful, able politician."

The Diefenbaker-Camp débâcle ended, but Lougheed's political trials did not. As a contribution to Canada's Centennial Year, Premier Manning was trying to formulate a "political realignment" which, if successful, would assimilate Alberta's Conservatives into a rejuvenated Social Credit party.

Early in 1967, rumours were rife that Manning would attempt to merge his Social Credit party with the faltering Conservatives, then seek the national leadership as Diefenbaker's successor. The distinguished Canadian journalist Blair Fraser lent credence to the rumours. Writing in *Maclean's*, he theorized that

> Manning and the western right would move into a position of authority and influence . . . instead of a so-called Conservative party, divided between eastern businessmen and western cowboys, they would restore a national party of genuine conservative opinion that would be supported for approximately the same reason in all parts of Canada.

Although both Lougheed and Manning deny it, there are those who claim that "proof positive" exists that early in 1967, Manning offered Lougheed the leadership of the Social Credit government. In view of what subsequently happened the theory makes sense.

Peter was determined that the party be established in its first election. "It would be better to be second in the legislature with five seats, than third with eight, behind the NDP or the Liberals." Financing a campaign was still a problem, and Lougheed privately indicated that while the party would be forced to field at least sixty-three candidates, as many as forty would be considered mere tokens.

Although he had pledged to produce "new faces," the Conservatives had nominated only eight candidates by the end of January, 1967. Lou Hyndman had begun his door-to-door campaign in Edmonton West. In Calgary-Bowness, chartered accountant Len Werry was unopposed for the nomination. Calgary Alderman Dave Russell, an architect, had announced his intention to run for the Conservatives in Victoria Park. Lougheed was also encouraged by the prospects of two former football players joining his political team: Don Getty in Edmonton West and Oskar Kruger in Edmonton-Strathcona South.

Invaluable assistance in laying the groundwork for an election came from Ted Mills, a young Calgary entrepreneur, whose main asset was a tireless gluttony for the punishment of organization. Mills was like a "country parson" who went from town to town to spread Lougheed's message.

In preparation for the election, the Conservatives held a party congress in Banff in mid-February where Lougheed proposed that a Premier be restricted to two terms in office. He also recommended live television coverage of the legislature to "upgrade public awareness of what goes on and to create an awareness of the farce in the Alberta legislature."

The legislature had resumed sitting in February, and Garth Turcott renewed the charges he had made against the government in November. He demanded a judicial inquiry into the allegations he had made against the two MLAs. Premier Manning, who was not used to having the integrity of his government questioned, was incensed. He moved what amounted to a vote of censure against the NDP member. The Premier's motion deplored "the impropriety of the honourable member from Pincher Creek in casting reflections on the character and reputation of other honourable members without presenting specific charges supported by evidence."

The House also directed Turcott to file with the Speaker "any and all specific charges relative to the insinuations he had made ... together with evidence justifying such charges."

The mood of the legislature was angry as both sides of the house severely rebuked Turcott by a vote of fifty-four to one in favour of the Premier's motion of censure. The strain on the youthful lawyer was evident; he appeared to have lost weight and seemed tired and haggard. On one occasion, after a stormy session in which he had been branded a "liar" by Highways Minister Gordon Taylor, Turcott had collapsed from exhaustion in the members' lounge. But he was back in the house two days later to file four specific charges and to table fifty-four supporting documents.

Turcott formally charged:

1. that the Honourable Alfred J. Hooke, the Minister of Municipal Affairs, used or attempted to use his high office for the personal gain of himself, his friends and his business associates in conflict with his public duty
2. that E. W. Hinman, the honourable member from Cardston (formerly Provincial Treasurer) used or attempted to use his high office while a member of the government for his personal gain in conflict with his public duty
3. that E. W. Hinman knowingly and deliberately misled this honourable assembly by falsely disclaiming any and all involvement in the affairs of the Edmonton Airport Hotel Co. Ltd. and Alberta Western Forest Products Corporation Limited
4. that the honourable premier has willfully and improperly questioned my integrity; that he has implied and insinuated wrongdoing on my part and that he has moved a motion (against me) without presenting specific charges supported by evidence.

The effect of Turcott's action had raised in the public consciousness the need for an opposition in Alberta. But the electorate was not impressed with the NDP Member's inexperienced behaviour and the strident, almost hysterical, approach to public business. In any event the charges precipitated an election. Just before the House adjourned, Premier Manning moved to defuse the issue by agreeing to have a judicial inquiry into Turcott's allegations against Hinman and Hooke.[1] One week later, during the evening of Friday, April 14, while Lougheed was on a flight between

Edmonton and Calgary, Premier Manning abruptly announced that the legislature had been dissolved, and that a general election would be held on May 23.

Lougheed, who represented a Conservative alternative to a government that was conservative in everything but name, was not anxious to fight an election on the NDP's charges. Within hours after his arrival in Calgary he took the initiative and invited Manning to participate in a public television debate. Manning refused. "A public debate would exaggerate our differences," the Premier replied, as he invited Conservatives to join his party in the fight against the NDP to "insure the preservation of political and economic stability in Alberta."

It was a shrewd move on Manning's part, for in retrospect, Lougheed has never been a more energetic or attractive campaigner than he was in 1967. In an election with no real issues, it was imperative that he establish his credentials, and Lougheed was incandescent.

His campaign received an unexpected boost on April 21 when Federal MP Dr. Hugh M. Horner announced he was quitting national politics to join Lougheed's team. At the time Horner was forty-two and was one of the candidates for the Conservative's national leadership convention which had been called for September. Horner had no hope of succeeding Diefenbaker and he knew it; he was having difficulty raising funds for his leadership campaign and the exchange of a career in federal politics for a chance at a seat in the provincial legislature was a convenient out. There were other factors: after nine years in the House of Commons, he had become disillusioned as an opposition backbencher; there was more money to be made in his home town of Barrhead as a pediatrician. Son of Saskatchewan Senator, Ralph Byron Horner, whose name is legend in Western Conservative circles, the doctor, like the rest of his family, has an intuitive grasp of rural populism. He is nothing, if not an individual, and his presence on the Lougheed team gave the urban based Conservatives their first element of credibility in rural Alberta. None of this concerned Premier Manning in the least. Confident of victory he abruptly left for Montreal and the opening on April 27 of Expo '67, an event which affected Canadians with greater enthusiasm than any election campaign.

The election campaign marked the beginning of the television era in Alberta politics. This was to be the first time a political party would use television to communicate its platform to the Alberta electorate. Peter Herndorf, a rising young television producer with CBC in Edmonton, arbitrarily decided to do an hour long special on Lougheed. Herndorf felt Social Credit was "dull" and visualized Lougheed as something of a political novelty; win or lose, Lougheed was worth a documentary. The concept was unique, which made the idea all the more attractive. While Lougheed may have been suspicious of Herndorf's intentions, he recognized television's growing presence as an unavoidable element in election drama. The inclusion of a five man production crew in his entourage – something Premier Manning didn't have – gave Lougheed the immediate trapping of success, which in turn contributed to an aura of even greater political authority.

In many respects, the 1967 campaign was a rehearsal for the 1971 election. Many were convinced that the campaign would be Manning's last, although there was no assurance of it. He had been Premier for twenty-four years and it was reasonable to expect his resignation after his twenty-fifth anniversary in office. Should Manning retire, it was imperative that Lougheed assess his probable opponent for some future contest. The succession was not defined. No doubt Gordon Taylor the Minister of Highways would be a contender; Raymond Reierson, the Minister of Telephones and a former Labour Minister, might also be in any leadership race. There was even a rumour that the Premier's son Preston was being groomed as Manning's successor, but that was unlikely since Preston was barely in his early twenties and lacked practical experience for the job.

It was Jim Edwards of CKUA who correctly advanced the name of Agriculture Minister Harry Strom. Edwards had covered the 1963 election as a reporter and was convinced that Strom was worth watching. He was an unknown quantity, but his credentials in the party were impeccable. He was genuine, sincere, and folksy. He had, in Edwards' opinion, "a dash that Manning didn't."

But was Strom interested in the job?

Edwards decided to sound him out. Following a conversation with Strom at Bow Island, Edwards was convinced that Strom "hungered for the leadership once Manning decided to retire." What was more important. Lougheed's communications experts were convinced that "the image makers could do a hell of a lot with the guy – he could be packaged as a tea totalling Lyndon Johnson."

Certainly the image makers did a good job in selling Lougheed. Even the *Toronto Globe and Mail* was convinced that the Conservatives in Alberta would elect a "corporal's guard" and "assert the kind of pressure in the legislature that might be turned into a government next time 'round."

Lougheed unveiled his party's campaign platform: a forty page inspirational, but suitably flexible, "Blueprint for the '70's." It suggested that the province's $600 million accumulated surplus could be used to provide more services without an increase in taxes.

Influenced by NDP tactics in the Pincher Creek by-election, Lougheed modified their technique and introduced a new brand of political campaign on a provincial scale. It was something of an athletic feat: he and most candidates literally *ran* for office. Accompanied by an advanced guard who rang door bells and set up introductions, he sprinted down more than 180 miles of streets up to more than 10,400 homes in Calgary West – not to talk politics – but "to touch the flesh." It was a brassy and irreverent approach to politics in the province and at least one Social Credit Member, Charlie Johnson, was seen to shake his head in disgust as he wondered aloud "Where has the dignity in politics gone?"

The Conservatives were having difficulty fielding a full slate of sixty-five candidates. At the last moment a number of sacrificial lambs were recruited: people like Larry Boddy, a university student in Edmonton (who considered distributing lawn signs which declared "THIS IS A BODDY

HOUSE") and Joe Clark who was dropped into Calgary South to run against the respected Speaker of the House Art Dixon.

At a major election rally in the Henry Wise Wood School auditorium in Calgary on May 15, Lougheed spoke about the mood of restlessness and anxiety he had encountered in the election:

"The time has come for Alberta to choose enthusiasm over complacency; expansion over drift . . . freedom over red tape . . . Conservative over Social Credit . . . Tomorrow over Yesterday."

He earned his spurs the following night in Edmonton at an all party candidates forum sponsored by the McDougall United Church; the occasion marked the first time that all four party leaders appeared on the same platform. Premier Manning was suffering from a bout of laryngitis. Lougheed was interrupted by applause ten times during his turn at the podium. The loudest applause from the crowd of 1,200 came when he was asked to describe the difference between his party and the others.

"The difference between Conservatives and Liberals," he said, "is that we believe that something that is needed to be done, needs to be done by the voluntary efforts of the citizens, not by the actions of a bureaucratic authority."

Between Conservatives and Social credit he explained "we believe that the first responsibility of the MLA is to the constituent not to the party."

And between Conservatives and NDP?

"I simply have not got enough time," he smiled.

Lougheed had not extinguished the fire of Manning's oratory, but he certainly had dampened it. The following day *Journal* reporter Eaton Howitt's prose gushed on about how "Peter Lougheed's star shone brightly over Edmonton." Party worker Dave King thought the evening was symbolic: "a marginal Anglican trouncing an evangelical Minister in a United Church."

Election day, May 23, 1967, was in Lougheed's memory a day "when the clock simply didn't move." But shortly after the polls closed, the suspense was over: to no one's surprise, Social Credit was returned for its seventh term. Manning had won again, but the real news once the votes had been counted was that the Conservatives, under the leadership of Peter Lougheed, would form the official opposition. Six Conservatives had been elected. Lougheed received the largest plurality – 4,452 to Mannings 3,202. Lou Hyndman had won in Edmonton and as an added bonus, so too had the only man with parliamentary experience, Dr. Hugh Horner in the rural riding of Lac Ste. Anne. The other three successful Tories were equally distinctive.

Don Getty, thirty-four, who unseated Education Minister Randolph McKinnon in Edmonton. Affable, handsome, and athletic (he was once described as being "Pat Boone" with macho). Getty, born in Westmount, Quebec, was the son of a steel pipe salesman. Raised in Ontario he came West in 1955 as a quarterback for the Edmonton Eskimos. After working in various capacities for Imperial Oil, he started his own exploration company in 1964. His entry into politics was motivated by the conviction that under a Lougheed government "the oil industry could be handled differently."

Dave Russell, thirty-five. Diffident, with a beet-red face and a sheepish smile, Russell obtained his degree in architecture from the University of Manitoba, and a Master's degree in landscape architecture from Cornell. Something of a cultural dilettante, he was a director of the Allied Arts Centre and the Calgary Philharmonic Orchestra who dabbled in oil painting for relaxation. Russell had been an alderman in Calgary for seven years and, frustrated by the lack of response to his suggestions on council, he decided to exchange a career in municipal politics for one in the provincial legislature.

Len Werry, forty-two, a gentle, soft-spoken man had a sad but rugged face, like a boxer on the skids. A reformed alcoholic, Werry had been a business tax assessor with the federal revenue department. In the early 1960s, he set up his own public accounting firm. Like Lougheed, his conversion to Conservative politics was inspired by Diefenbaker's election victory.

Although the Social Credit government was returned to office with fifty-five seats, Lougheed had polled an astonishing 26 per cent of the popular vote. The Conservatives had outdistanced the NDP which claimed "moral victory" with 16 per cent of the vote. But the moral victory didn't translate into any seats for them. Turcott was defeated, the NDP shut out of the legislature. The Liberals with only 11 per cent of the popular vote won three seats and an independent, Clarence Copithorne, was elected in Banff-Cochrane.

Had 1,500 more voters in six key ridings voted Conservative, the opposition would have doubled its representation. Tom Hughes came within 192 votes of capturing Okotoks-High River; Henry Beaumont almost won Calgary North; Paul Norris in Edmonton and Dallas Schmidt in Wetaskiwin were also near to the margin of victory, as was Basil Zailo in Redwater. But one of the most startling campaigns had been waged by Joe Clark in Calgary South. The rookie who had started late and had been dismissed because of his inexperience managed to come within 462 votes of displacing Art Dixon.

"We underestimated him," agrees Ted Mills. "We expected Clark to run, no one expected him to place." For many of Peter's loyalists, a Clark success was too hard to contemplate. Several of them agreed that in the election "Joe came too close for Peter's good. He wasn't of the calibre that Peter wanted for his team."

Note

1 A judicial inquiry conducted by Mr. Justice W. J. C. Kirby later found that both Hinman and Hooke had been "imprudent" in their business dealings, but the inquiry absolved both men of the charge of using public office for public gain and recommended that the government establish guidelines for the behaviour of cabinet ministers.

CHAPTER VI

With the exception of Dr. Hugh Horner the new opposition was as green as the threadbare carpet on the floor of the legislative chamber. The legislature, built on quicksand on a high hill overlooking the North Saskatchewan River, was a peculiar place in those days: a cathedral of dustbowl solidarity. And Ernest C. Manning was its bishop. Manning was concerned as much with the coming of the "antichrist" as he was with domestic affairs. Under his guidance Social Credit ignored conventional parliamentary rules and operated under its own system. The legislature was deemed to be above partisan politics; it was approached with a degree of reverence. Dealing with Manning Lougheed later observed was like "starting your coaching career against Casey Stengel."

When a photographer attempted to get a picture of the new opposition leader at his desk on the floor of the chamber he was denied permission. In defending the refusal Manning explained "the legislature's purpose is for the conduct of the house and it should be done in dignity. It is not for propaganda purposes."

The opposition had neither office space nor a research budget. Its business was conducted in the corridors or in the members' lounge. Lougheed, elected in May, would not assume office until the legislature opened the following February. (Under Social Credit, the legislature usually met for only one session a year.) But he immediately began negotiations with Premier Manning for what he considered to be "essential requirements." Armed with information from other provinces he argued he needed public funds to carry out his elected responsibility. "All we are asking," he insisted, "is to bring the provisions for the opposition into line with other provinces. Anything less is completely unsatisfactory and ignores the popular vote."

From the very beginning Lougheed behaved like a "Premier in waiting." Southam News reporter Don Sellar remembers flying with Lougheed to Calgary shortly after the election and was surprised to see that Peter was met by "an entourage." "He was always accompanied by one or two cohorts which gave him an impressive air of authority." Sellar observed that now that Lougheed was subject to public scrutiny he began to control his habits. He had started smoking cigarettes during his years with Mannix, but gave them up shortly afterwards. ("He never really inhaled," offers his wife Jeanne who goes through two packs a day herself, "it was easy for him. He just came home one day and quit.") Although he drinks sparingly – preferring gin and tonic or an occasional glass of wine – he no longer went into a liquor store to make his purchases. Aides bought it for him. (To this day he is cautious about being seen in public with a glass of alcohol in his hand. When a television film crew arrived in a room where he was meeting with Prime Minister Trudeau both men were sipping screwdrivers. As the cameras started to roll, Lougheed discreetly slipped his glass out of sight beneath his chair.)

The provincial election behind him Lougheed took his family to Montreal for Expo '67. As a centennial project he exchanged homes with a Montreal lawyer who had been on the staff of Quebec Premier Jean Lesage. The family enrolled in French lessons, but Peter soon discovered he wasn't a linguist and gave them up. The experience in Montreal exposed him to French Canada. Although it was a superficial introduction to Quebec nationalism, it left him with a respect if not an appreciation of Quebec's grievances. He recognized that Quebec and Alberta had many objectives in common which were being stifled by the federal government and financial interests in Toronto. The experience gave him "all sorts of ideas about how to improve our understanding of the Quebec situation." He pledged that if he were to head an Alberta government he would "consider taking senior cabinet ministers to Quebec city for informal discussions with the Quebec government. I'd like to have my number two minister in charge of intergovernmental affairs to work with Ottawa and the other provinces, and three or four red hot guys stationed in Ottawa as a nerve centre."

While Lougheed was relaxing in Montreal Premier Manning who was concerned with what he called "the advanced state of disintegration of federal politics in Canada" published his long awaited book which briefly threatened Lougheed's efforts as opposition leader. Manning's *Political Realignment: A Challenge to Thoughtful Canadians* advocated the polarization of Canada's political parties. On the left would be the NDP and left-wing Liberals; on the right, Conservatives, Social Crediters and right-wing Liberals united under a banner of social conservatism. As defined by Manning the new party would combine "humanitarian concerns of an awakened social conscience with a firm conviction in the value of freedom of economic activity and enlightened private enterprise."

Lougheed read the treatise without comment but was relieved when all of the major parties demonstrated a profound disinterest in being so realigned, particularly the Conservative party which that summer was preparing for a leadership convention in Toronto.

In recognition of Peter's "outstanding contributions to the party at the provincial level" he was invited to participate as one of two keynote convention speakers. "The invitation was a calculated and deliberate ploy by the party to make Peter a creature of the convention, not part of it," explains Dalton Camp. "The party believed in his future and that was a convenient way for us to protect him and to maintain his neutrality in what was shaping up to be a particularly hostile situation."

The convention, which opened in Toronto's Maple Leaf Gardens the day after Labour Day, was hot; Lougheed, cool. He refused to endorse any of the candidates. His speech was delivered under difficult circumstances. The crowd of six thousand was far more interested in hearing what John Diefenbaker was up to. Diefenbaker had no intention of gracefully surrendering the leadership. Accordingly Lougheed trimmed his remarks. His prepared text was a paste-up of previous speeches. He urged the delegates to look ahead, not back.

> The people of Canada are looking for a whole new political approach, one that is in tune with the changes going on in the rest of our contemporary society. The fundamental aspect of Canada today is change – rapid change from a rural to an urban society; rapid change from long hours to more leisure; rapid change, like it or not, from federally oriented legislation to provincially oriented legislation.

Diefenbaker refused to be put out of harm's way. At the last moment he entered the race in an attempt to succeed himself, a move that did neither him nor the party any good. He was eliminated on the third ballot. With a field of eleven candidates from which to choose the delegates preferred "to look ahead, not back," and on the fifth ballot they gave the leadership of the party to Nova Scotia's Premier, Robert Stanfield. So Peter Lougheed and Bob Stanfield assumed their duties as leaders of the opposition of their respective parties at about the same time.

Premier Manning eventually agreed that the government would provide the provincial opposition $10,000.00 and sparse office space on the second floor of the legislature. With the money Lougheed was able to hire Ted Mills as an executive assistant; Mills was a novice whose enthusiasm for the job was inspired by Allen Drury's political epic *Advise and Consent*. "All I knew about politics was what I read in that book," admits Mills. For his research assistant Lougheed selected an astute student of history and political science, David King, who was also president of the Alberta Progressive Conservative Student Federation. Lougheed engaged as his secretary Wylla Walker who had worked in a Red Deer law office, and shortly after recruited a secretary from his own law office, Linda Butler, to help her.

106

A meeting of the caucus and all unsuccessful party candidates was convened, and over buckets of fried chicken, the previous campaign was assessed. What Lougheed learned from that meeting was that "if the candidates had started earlier, if they only had more time, the election results would have been better."

The former Speaker of the House of Commons, MP Marcel Lambert, was called in to instruct the new MLAs on parliamentary procedure. Recognizing his own parliamentary inexperience Lougheed instituted a comprehensive opposition strategy independent of individual party concerns: he met with all ten opposition members in caucus once a week. He also began his efforts to get the independent member of the house, Clarence Copithorne, to join the Tories. Copithorne was amused by the idea. "I was leader of the third largest party in the legislature," he says, "and I felt the Conservatives had an obligation to join me if they really wanted me in their party."

Robert Stanfield whose national popularity was rising made his first political pilgrimage to Alberta in late November to appear with Lougheed as a guest speaker at a provincial party convention. Coincidentally, a provincial Liberal convention at the same time fell apart when four federal cabinet ministers cancelled their speaking engagements at the last moment.

Premier Manning had helped to solve the Conservative party's financial problems, but Lougheed's personal finances were in jeopardy. He was being made to feel more and more of an unwelcome partner in his Calgary law office. As John Ballem defines the situation: "Peter was drawing a salary as an MLA and a salary as leader of the official opposition. Our firm had carried him financially for three years during a time when his contributions were negligible." A new financial agreement between the partners was proposed by Ballem and McDill, a formula which they felt was "fair and extremely generous under the circumstances," but Lougheed thought otherwise and rejected it. "As a result, there was no alternative for Peter but to leave the partnership," says McDill. It was a painful episode. Not even Lougheed's friends knew how upsetting it was and even to this day he will not talk about it. But his wife Jeanne says, "Everything about it was kind of dirty. Peter carried those guys by taking a substantial salary cut early in the partnership."

So in December Lougheed joined his old college roommate, Ken Moore, as a partner with the firm of Macdonald, McIntyre, Cheeseman, and Moore. "I was glad to welcome him as a partner," admits Moore, "if for no other reason than to get my neckties back. During our university days Peter always came to me when he needed a tie, but he never returned any of them – why he's still wearing my neckties."

The association with the new firm was amicable. Peter's political activities were accommodated without question. "The thing about our relationship as partners," says Moore, who is himself a Liberal, "was that Peter could go out of the office for a week or two attending to political business, then come back and bury himself in a file and forget everything he had done outside the office. He has this remarkable ability to concentrate on the particular subject matter at hand and in several hours was right up-to-date and on top of any file that was handed to him."

Lougheed expected the same degree of concentration from his caucus. Each MLA was assigned to shadow two or three government ministers and Lougheed expected each of them to know as much about various government departments as the ministers themselves. "He was terribly demanding on all of us," says one of them. "In fact, we were ready to complain about the workload until we walked into his office and discovered that he was working harder than any of us."

The legislature opened on February 15, 1968, and Lougheed was sworn in as official Leader of Her Majesty's Opposition by Lieutenant-Governor Grant MacEwen. The government, anticipating a $100 million deficit, stuck fairly close to the homespun issues in its seventeen minute Throne Speech. The speech stressed "a concerted effort be made to restrain public expenditures and greater emphasis be placed on increased productivity." Shortly after the legislature opened Lougheed startled the house by moving an amendment to a routine motion establishing standing committees. He proposed that an opposition member chair the public accounts committee. The idea, which was later approved, originated with John Diefenbaker, who in 1958 first invited a member of the opposition to be chairman of the national public accounts committee.

Lougheed's maiden speech to the legislature on February 19 was lengthy, factual, and not very inspiring. Opening debate on the Throne Speech, he relied on statistics from the Economic Council of Canada to show that Alberta was at the bottom of the list in per capita income. "We've been hearing for a long time how great things are in Alberta, and we hear that this is due to the wisdom and judgement of the present administration." "The key question," he argued, "is how buoyant is the Alberta economy really?" He also observed the ritual of denouncing government bureaucracy, and promised the opposition would "take the lid off to find out what's really going on." To prove the point the opposition immediately filed twenty-four notices of motion, which usually lead to debate in the house. But opposition performance in that first session was lacklustre. *Edmonton Journal* editor, Andrew Snaddon's impression of Lougheed was that "he cowered behind a bowl of flowers that separated his desk from Manning's, hoping that Manning wouldn't pick on him." The opposition members were not alert enough to exploit government weakness. Lou Hyndman reveals a specific example. "We weren't even aware that we could introduce bills. I was reading the parliamentary rules and came across a passage which clearly stated ANY member could introduce a bill. We thought only government ministers could introduce legislation, at least that's what Manning led us to believe." But the opposition also discovered the effectiveness of "the question" and started to use it aggressively. For the first time the government was forced to explain in detail its actions and expenditures, something it had not been accustomed to doing.

In the same week that Peter made his maiden speech in the Alberta legislature Pierre Elliott Trudeau announced his candidacy to succeed Lester Pearson as leader of the federal Liberal party. Trudeau won the convention on April 6, 1968, and, in Gordon Donaldson's memorable phrase burst on the Canadian political scene "like a stone through a stained glass window." The new Prime Minister charmed his way into the national fabric, the personification of the Expo spirit which had overnight instilled Canadians with reckless abandon. Trudeaumania swept the land and with the federal election called for June 26, everyone was eager to jump on the bandwagon. Two Liberal MLA's, Mike Maccagno and Bill Dickie, announced they were leaving their legislative seats for a try at the House of Commons. Dickie's federal ambition was short-lived: he lost the federal nomination in Calgary South to Pat Mahoney. But he retained his seat in the legislature. Maccagno won the federal nomination in Athabasca and resigned. Lougheed did not actively campaign in the 1968 federal election but he did visit a number of ridings with individual candidates.

The excitement Trudeau engendered was rewarded on election day as the Liberals swept to a majority government. Four of Alberta's nineteen seats went Liberal, but Maccagno's wasn't one of them. After thirteen years in politics, the provincial Liberal leader decided he'd had enough and the by-election to fill his vacant legislative seat was called for August 20.

"We knew from the start that the Conservatives were in trouble in the Lac la Biche by-election when we couldn't find a candidate," admits David King who was sent into the riding to run the campaign. The provincial party had no organization in the riding, but it finally convinced Jack Bergeron, a twenty-seven year old Fort McMurray bush pilot, to run. The Conservatives had two objectives in that by-election: one was to place second and the other to at least retain their deposit.

Social Credit went all out to support their candidate, Dr. David Bouvier, a former Mayor of Lac la Biche. Bouvier won handily. Bergeron came second with 1,200 votes – not enough to keep him from losing his deposit. The unusual effort by Social Credit to give special attention to Lac la Biche was puzzling at the time. But, the government's motive was soon apparent. It wanted to present the seat to Ernest Manning before his retirement as a demonstration of party strength.

110

CHAPTER VII

A unique chapter in Canadian politics ended on September 27, 1968, when the dean of Canadian Premiers, Ernest C. Manning, resigned. He had been Premier for twenty-five years, six months and twelve days. Only one man had served longer as the Premier of a Canadian province. Nova Scotia's George H. Murray and his Liberal party were in office for almost twenty-seven years, from 1896 to 1923. As Premier, Manning had radically altered the proposed course of Social Credit; his political pragmatism and sound fiscal administration had made the movement respectable. With Manning's departure the party could no longer camouflage its sedentary failings and the stage was set for Peter Lougheed.

In a letter to members of the "Lougheed Club" early in November Peter paid tribute to Manning's "remarkable contributions" predicting that Harry Strom would be the next Premier. Lougheed wrote that a mere change in leadership was not enough, "particularly when we move from Mr. Manning to someone of lesser capabilities," adding he would strive for "a complete change in administration."

As Lougheed's strategists had anticipated, Harry Edwin Strom was chosen from among five candidates on December 6 at the first open Social Credit leadership convention ever held. Significantly Strom won with the support of those members of the party committed to reform. Six days later he was sworn in as the first Premier ever to have been born in Alberta. But nothing in his credentials indicated that he was exceptionally well qualified for the job.

The son of pioneer Swedish stock Strom was born the sixth of eleven children on July 7, 1914 on the family homestead at Burdett, near Medicine Hat. A gentle, strapping man (six foot three) Strom never lost his rough rural edges. He had cast his first vote for Social credit in 1935 (when Peter Lougheed was seven) but was never active in the party until his election in 1955 as a representative for the Cypress constituency. He was brought into the Manning cabinet in 1962 as Minister of Agriculture, a department he administered with uncommon zeal. His personality was tempered with a streak of stubborn evangelism. However, the moral catechism which sustained Manning was no longer enough for the Alberta of the 1970s: Strom was an anachronism in politics, the archetypical "nice guy" woefully out of touch with the mood of the electorate. And, he faced a panoply of problems. Declining oil revenues combined with record government spending imposed an immediate challenge with which the new Premier was forced to deal. He had to sort out fiscal priorities.

Lougheed called for an immediate election but the prevailing mood in the province was to give Strom a chance to prove himself. Expressing confidence that Strom would bring Social Credit "into greater contact with the 20th Century urban explosion," the *Calgary Herald* recognized "we can't expect him to have Manning's aura of appeal and authority," but it allowed that "he would make his own imprint in time." Edmonton and Calgary radio stations CHQT and CHQR ran a special documentary on the new Premier as an introduction to a comprehensive twelve hour series on the Social Credit movement. Lougheed was "somewhat disturbed" by the programming and the attention being focused on Strom. He suggested to his communications advisors that "in some diplomatic way we should make our views known to the management of the stations that there should be a more equitable distribution of time between the political parties."

Though Lougheed may have been momentarily eclipsed by

Strom's accession he received his own share of media attention at the end of January, 1969, at the party's annual convention in Calgary. Coverage of the convention was televised for the first time, although at the party's expense.
Lougheed mounted a challenge to the new government in a
thirty-four point recitation of the new directions a Conservative government would follow. He proposed a shift in tax
emphasis from property taxes to those who "had the ability
to pay." He set a goal of post secondary education for 50 per
cent of Alberta's young people. He promised increased funding for universities, day care centres, and mental health
treatment facilities. He expanded his original twelve guideposts and concluded with at least eight other promises that
were so meaningless that they fell into the "motherhood
category." The speech was well received but the apparent
contradiction between the massive government initiative in
education and welfare and the pledge of financial restraint
left many confused. The *Edmonton Journal* dismissed
Lougheed's ideas as sounding suspiciously like "what Social
Credit is doing in various fields." "The Conservatives have
not yet developed a credible policy platform in detail,"
griped the paper, "something the Conservatives must do if it
is to present that 'challenge' when the next provincial election arrives."

But policy was incidental to voters in the Edmonton riding
of Strathcona East involved in the February 10 by-election
called to fill the legislative seat vacated by Premier Manning. Manning had represented the riding since its creation
in 1948. In every contest he had consistently swept every
poll. And in every respect it was considered a "safe seat"
for the government. Manning publicly endorsed lawyer
William Johnson as his successor in the riding. It was felt
that Johnson, a disciple of Manning's "Social Conservatism," would one day lead the Social Credit party. The
by-election was considered a formality to assure him a
cabinet position. No one gave the Conservative nominee,
William Yurko, a chance. The party doubted his prospects. Party president Roy Watson insisted that Edmonton
Alderman Neil Crawford was the better man. Crawford had
served as an aide to Diefenbaker and Watson was so confi-

dent of his chances that he had several thousand dollars worth of campaign material printed with Crawford's name before the nominating convention was even held. But Yurko had the support of Edmonton's closely knit and powerful "Ukrainian community," about 15 per cent of the city's population, who organized on his behalf.

He won on the first ballot.

According to some observers, Lougheed was not overly optimistic about Yurko's chances.

A short introspective man with a broad Slavic face, Yurko was a chemical engineer. He had always harboured an ambition to be Canada's U.N. representative so in 1967 he had abandoned his $30,000.00 a year job managing a copper refinery in Arizona to return to his native Alberta to pursue a career in federal politics. His first attempt to win the Conservative nomination in Edmonton Centre for the federal election in 1965 left him disgruntled. He lost to Steve Paproski in a highly irregular and savage nominating meeting. "Ethnic discrimination was so thick at that convention you could cut the divisions with a knife," he remembers. Although Yurko is of Roumanian descent his family is related through marriage to several leading families of Edmonton's Ukrainian community. Consumed by an interest in human rights since childhood Yurko "hates discrimination on an ethnic basis with a passion." But his first brush with the political process taught him that "ethnicity in the echelons of political power is highly marketable." So in seeking the provincial nomination he enlisted the support of Edmonton lawyer Peter Savaryn and capitalized on his heritage.

Armed with little more than a stubborn determination to succeed he waged a strenuous campaign. Accusing the government of atrophy he canvassed more than 3,000 homes during the longest consecutive cold spell ever recorded in Edmonton. Near the end of the campaign the six Conservative MLA's joined him on the hustings. "The caucus was not particularly enthusiastic," Yurko recalls, "you could see it on their faces, they felt they were wasting their time." That was an understatement. Savaryn had to ask the caucus to give Yurko its support. The attitude of some party members was that Yurko had not played the game according to their rules so they weren't going to lift a hand to help him. "Dr. Hugh Horner felt I could win Strathcona East by 400 votes and said so," says Yurko. Horner underestimated Yurko's chances by forty-four votes. When the results were tabulated on the eve of Yurko's forty-third birthday he had scored a surprise upset taking the seat from Johnson by 444 votes.

"I added the ethnic touch," he admits.

For the Social Credit party the loss of Manning's seat was embarrassing. But to lose it three days before the legislature resumed its spring session was humiliating. When the session opened the government now faced a seven man Conservative opposition. The session, which lasted fifty-eight days, was an unusually long one. Premier Strom introduced a legislative program which was essentially Manning's but he added several innovations of his own. Revision of the Lord's Day Act made it possible for Albertans to go to the movies on Sunday and, at last, they could get an alcoholic beverage with their meals. A third of the 117 bills introduced came from the Municipal Affairs Department. There were amendments to the Human Rights Act which prohibited racial discrimination in housing or in apartments with three or more units. The province was carried into federal medicare. And, welfare laws were tightened. But perhaps of greatest importance to Lougheed, a permanent boundaries commission was set up to redraw the obsolete electoral map which would shift the emphasis from rural to urban representation.

On June 30, 1969, the personally popular Liberal MLA for Edson, William Switzer, died unexpectedly of a heart attack. A by-election in the large, economically diversified riding was set for October 28. In spite of the Liberal's competent candidate, Hinton lawyer Arthur Woods, the party had no hope of retaining the seat; Liberal credibility had been strained by real and imagined quarrelling among its leaders. As a result even good candidates were no longer to be taken seriously.

The government's chances of capturing the seat lay with the principal of the Edson Junior High School, Arthur Jorgenson, and the NDP had high hopes of winning the seat with their new leader, Grant Notley. Against Jorgenson and Notley the Conservatives put up an exuberant Jasper pharmacist "call me Bob" Dowling. (He had grown up in Camrose with Peter's wife Jeanne.) As president of the Rocky Mountain House federal constituency association, Dowling's interest in provincial politics was peripheral. He had "no intention of getting involved in Alberta politics." But the prospect of a resident in a federal park (over which the province had no jurisdiction) having a voice in Edmonton appealed to him. He knew he could count on a substantial support base in Jasper.

Only one major issue surfaced once the campaign got under way: the compulsory aspect of medicare. Jorgenson was hard pressed to explain why the contribution rates remained the same even though the federal government was now contributing to half the cost of the program. A series of well attended public meetings revealed that Jorgenson was not as strong in person as he was made out to be in the slick Social Credit campaign literature which papered the riding.

Dowling faced his opponents with confidence. He discounted Notley as being "nervous, unschooled and wet behind the ears." Dowling was perhaps more of a political novice than Notley but he had the strong organizational presence of Dr. Hugh Horner who had represented the region as a federal Member of Parliament. Horner was on familiar terrain as he stumped the riding to deliver his following to Dowling. While Lougheed and the other MLAs helped to campaign their presence was low key. "We didn't want city slickers attempting to impose their campaign style on the Edson constituency," explains Dowling. "It didn't work in Pincher Creek and would have been resented in Edson."

John Diefenbaker, who normally refrained from endorsing candidates in a provincial election, was persuaded to wire his support to Dowling "realizing you have much to offer your people in these difficult times." Diefenbaker's endorsement was potent.

The only uncomfortable episode in the campaign occurred when Doug Caston, publisher of the *Edson Leader* and the president of the Edson Conservative Association, declared he "was not interested in a Jasper man as an MLA" and threw his support to Grant Notley and the NDP.

Early returns on election day put Jorgenson and Notley ahead of Dowling. But when the last votes in Jasper came in to be counted Dowling carried 70 per cent of the polls from the mountain constituency to sweep to a 700 vote victory.

Lougheed's stature was reinforced by this second by-election victory in ten months. The urban based Conservatives now had rural credibility. They were communicating their freshness and it was becoming infectious.

The Edson victory left William Dickie as the only remaining Liberal in the legislature. Dark and handsome in the manner of a silent screen villain, Dickie was less than happy with the party's newest leader, Bob Russell. Russell, like his predecessors, was given the impossible task of leading the party from outside the legislature and he and Dickie disagreed on policy. Dickie, a self-confessed "right wing, free enterprise Liberal," was also becoming uncomfortable with what he considered to be the "left wing direction" of the federal party under the leadership of Pierre Trudeau. So, to no one's surprise, he enthusiastically accepted Lougheed's invitation to join the Conservative party. Dickie and Lougheed were old friends. Both were Calgary lawyers and as youngsters they had played hockey for opposing teams at the Mount Royal Skating Rink. It was Dickie who had tried to persuade Lougheed to run for the seat which he vacated on Calgary city council. On November 24, he became the ninth member of the Conservative opposition.

That left Clarence Copithorne the only independent in the legislature. While Copithorne was interested in being wooed by the Conservatives he continued to resist all approaches to join the party.

Early in 1970 Lougheed stepped up his efforts to build a coalition of special interest groups. Expecting to lead an opposition of at least thirty members after the impending election he began to pull out the stops in his campaign speeches. "Peter didn't expect to form the government in 1971 but it was realistic for him to believe he would command a strong opposition," says someone who is close to him. "Under the circumstances he occasionally said things he would never have even considered if he thought he would be Premier in 1971 – he was really aiming to win the government in the 1975 election.

During several public appearances early that spring he appealed to a tradition in Alberta of opposition to conventional party politics. He advocated the diminution of party discipline within the legislature. Lougheed claimed that MLAs should not be forced to vote along party lines, but according to the dictates of their consciences and their constituents. The concept was first advanced in 1903 by the Premier of the Northwest Territories, Frederick Haultain, who argued that it was nonsense to separate the province's best men into "hostile groups under names and for reasons which have nothing to do with the business entrusted to them." Haultain's theory was successfully employed in Alberta to elect both the United Farmer's government in 1921 and Social Credit in 1935. To revive the idea was blatant political opportunism on Lougheed's part, but he didn't believe in it for a moment. And, as Grant Davy, the chairman of the University of Alberta's political science department, pointed out, if Lougheed were serious "no one could really be held responsible for what is done or not done. You would not have responsible government in a sense of government being accountable to the people."

As the legislature resumed sitting at the end of January 1970 Lougheed tightened the reins on his nine man caucus in anticipation of an election. Claiming that Premier Strom had been overshadowed by Saskatchewan's Premier Ross Thatcher at a recent federal-provincial conference, Lougheed attacked Strom as being "timid, weak and cautious in his dealings with Ottawa" and promised a Conservative government would be "more aggressive." He challenged Strom to develop a non-partisan Alberta consensus for dealings with Ottawa and seized the initiative himself in proposing changes to a federal tax law which he felt hurt Alberta resource development. Lougheed was responding to proposals contained in a white paper on tax reform released by the federal Finance Minister, Edgar Benson. Lougheed predicted "a major economic and social upheaval of society if the reforms were established as policy." He articulated five major concerns with the Benson proposals:

1. The elimination of a low tax rate on small business would hurt the development of secondary industry.
2. Proposed higher tax rates for top income earners would result in an exodus of professionals from Canada.
3. Reduced incentives to foreign capital for investment in the province.
4. A proposed capital gains tax would mean a 100 per cent tax across the board.
5. An appreciation tax would encourage the take-over of Canadian owned companies by foreign interests.

In Alberta politics, as in any province, self-interest and special provincial objectives count most. In demanding that the Benson tax revisions "be withdrawn and not just tinkered with" he scored another psychological advance. In comparison the Social Credit response that it would "make representation to Ottawa on every single area which will have an adverse effect on Albertans" seemed puny.

As the session ended Lougheed once again set his sights on corralling the sole independent member of the legislature, Clarence Copithorne. Copithorne, "every inch a cowboy," cultivated the image with abandon, wearing Western boots, string ties, and a stetson in the House. He once tabled a hamburger during a supply debate as evidence of the poor fare offered in the legislative cafeteria, demanding "they fix the place up so you can at least get a good steak." Although he enjoyed his role as a maverick, Copithorne recognized that he could be more influential in bringing about the defeat of the government as a Conservative. So, on April 15, he announced that he was joining the Lougheed team. That gave the Conservatives all ten members of the opposition, and for the first time Lougheed felt that he was riding the crest. On the seating plan of the legislature he circled the names of government members that the felt would be defeated in the next election. His diagram had thirty-four circles – not enough to make the

Conservatives the next government. But Dr. Horner was more confident; he circled fifty-five.

Lougheed staged a whirlwind tour of the province that summer visiting every major city and many small towns. He made many speeches and at a picnic at Elk Island Provincial Park 6,000 people turned out to see him. He sat as an honoured guest at luncheon meetings, rode horseback in parades, and, at the end of it, believed he had shaken more than 200,000 hands. He also presided over nominating conventions. By September the Conservatives had nominated more than forty candidates. But in a province which had been one of the first to recognize women's suffrage, women were conspicuous by their absence from the Tory candidates' ranks.

An attractive and outspoken Calgary woman who was interested in running claimed she was discouraged by Lougheed from doing so because, she explains, "Peter was afraid I wouldn't fit into 'the team.' And, I wasn't prepared to shut up and be a sedate backbencher." The woman, who has since been successful in municipal politics, suggests "Peter is the dearest male chauvinist I know. He has always been one to appreciate obvious feminine qualities, but finds it hard to relate to women as political equals. In all his corporate and professional experience he's always dealt with women subservients and I think he feels emasculated by aggressive women."

Another woman, the wife of a prominent Edmontonian, who in her own right has had professional dealings with Lougheed complains: "although we have been introduced many times he fails to recognize me by name unless my husband is present. He knows who I am, but he can only identify me as an appendage of my husband."

The Conservatives did field two women candidates. The first to win a nomination was legal secretary, Catherine Chichak, who had earlier failed in her attempts to win a seat on Edmonton city council. The other, Helen Hunley, was the mayor of Rocky Mountain House, who during World War Two was in the Canadian army.

As the pace of nominating conventions quickened Conservatives assembled a respectable slate of candidates: Lougheed's friend from university days Merv Leitch, Edmonton alderman Neil Crawford, the editor of Calgary's *North Hill News* Roy Farran, Red Deer lawyer Jim Foster. An ethnic balance was also evident: Jewish lawyer Ron Ghitter, Ukrainians Julian Koziak and Dr. Ken Paproski, German Horst Schmid and former Edmonton Eskimo football star Normie Kwong. Lougheed had hopes for a black football star, Schenley award winner Johnny Bright, but Bright, confident that his high profile was sufficient to win the nomination overestimated his political popularity and lost to a little known economist, Les Young. Attempts were also made to recruit national television news reporter Peter Kent, a native Calgarian, but Kent didn't feel the Conservatives could win and declined to run.

In October, terrorists of the *Front de Libération du Québec* kidnapped James Cross, the British Trade Commissioner, and later kidnapped and murdered the Quebec Labour Minister, Pierre Laporte. Prime Minister Trudeau dealt forcefully with the crisis by introducing the War Measures Act. Impressed by Trudeau's display of leadership Lougheed was one of the first to endorse the federal government's use of the draconian legislation. Taking such a position, he differed from federal Conservative leader Robert Stanfield, who opposed the wholesale suspension of civil rights.

Convinced of growing support in northern Alberta Lougheed invested his effort in yet another swing through the Peace River country. During a stopover at Fort Chipewyan he met a sixty-five year old resident, Noel McKay, who complained about the downstream effects of the Bennett Dam in British Columbia on the Athabasca-Peace River Delta. McKay claimed that the dam had reduced water levels in Alberta and complained that trappers who could normally expect muskrats in the hundreds got only thirty-five that season. "If we lose our water," he told Lougheed, "we lose everything – fish, ducks, muskrats." Like any good politician Lougheed put the information away for a future broadside against the government for its ecological neglect. He returned from northern Alberta to meet his growing number of candidates and to review the platform for the next election.

The Conservative's organization was stronger than it was in the previous contest. The campaign was entrusted largely to Bob Dinkel. Co-ordinating his efforts were Jim Seymour and David Wood. Art Smith of Foster Advertising and his assistant Joe Hutton were engaged as consultants. Joe Clark, who had gone to work for the CBC after the 1967 election, offered his services but it was felt that Clark wasn't needed and his offer was rebuffed.

Over the Christmas holiday Lougheed received a letter from Peter Savaryn suggesting a campaign slogan. Savaryn kept a collage of various homespun philosophies under the desk blotter of his Edmonton law office. Among the clippings was a column with the words of an eighteenth century saint, Alphonsus Liguori:

Now is a word perpetually sounded by the clocks of time. Now is the slogan of a wiseman. Now is the flag of a serious man. Let us always remember this is a small word and whenever there is a job to be done, intellectual or physical, we should do it with all our capability, remembering that only now is the time for us, that now is ours, that tomorrow never comes.

The column was passed on to the communications committee, and at a policy meeting in Banff, the sentiment was written on a blackboard. Various phrases were considered: "Now is the time for us," "Now is ours," and "Now is the flag." Brock Hammond recognized the obvious. He walked to the blackboard and dramatically erased everything on the board except the single word "NOW."

"It was winner," observes David Wood. "There it was staring us in the face. It said everything that needed to be said."

A week later, beneath the party's chromatic orange and blue colours, more than 2,000 people gathered in Calgary's Palliser Hotel at a party convention described as "the largest political gathering in Alberta since 1935." It was a mammoth rally – one of those conventions orchestrated to promote peer approval and a feeling of joint accomplishment. Robert Stanfield, whose popularity had slipped, was conspicuous by his absence. One of the candidates, lawyer Ron Ghitter, captured the spirit of the occasion; "when history looks on this night, it will be remembered as the night the Alberta Conservative party turned the corner and grasped the momentum to win the 1971 election."

The legislature opened on February 11, 1971, for the last session before the election. Pre-election sparring was endemic as Lougheed sharpened his political teeth. He dispensed with his prerogative of studying the Speech From The Throne before giving his reply. Labelling himself as "leader of the alternative party in this house," he ignored the government's legislative proposals and delivered his own "Throne Speech" – a social action program to meet the needs created by unemployment (which had risen to almost 6 per cent), poverty and unjustice. The basis for his remarks was a detailed government report, *Social Futures: 1970 – 2005*, which painted a bleak outlook for Alberta's future. Lougheed blamed thirty-six years of Social Credit government for "contributing to the trend." Referring to the government as "the opposition on the other side," he proposed new opportunities for native people, new emphasis on education and health care, and he demanded an Alberta Bill of Rights to "take precedence over any other statute" to offset any decline in individual liberties.

Premier Strom refused to be baited. He gave a good natured account of his stewardship. "Social Credit," he chided Lougheed, "came to office because of its concern for social problems."

Meanwhile, outside the house, Lougheed put the finishing touches to the most important weapon in his campaign arsenal: television commercials. Social Credit had still not come to terms with the medium; Strom was awkward and uncomfortable before the cameras.

Initially, Lougheed had invited Peter Herndorf to manage the television campaign. But Herndorf, not willing to jeopardize his growing influence at the CBC, declined and recommended instead Perry Rosemond. Rosemond, a Canadian expatriate living in Los Angeles, had little experience with political advertising. But as he was later to demonstrate as the creator of "King of Kensington" and as a public affairs producer with the CBC's "The Way It Is," he had a solid grasp of television.

"What we did was kind of unique at the time," boasts Rosemond. "I flew up to Edmonton and talked to Peter for about four hours on audio tape. The promotional announcements were based on transcriptions of our conversations. It wasn't a contrived Madison Avenue approach. The commercials were based on Peter's own ideas, his own words. We shot the appropriate film, and distilled the essential Peter Lougheed." No scripts were written for the spots, the completed commercials had a documentary look.

Strom was content to campaign on his record, and to be fair, his legislative progress was considerable. A new age of majority was established, extending voting, drinking, and other adult privileges to eighteen year olds. An environment package was passed establishing the first provincial Department of the Environment in Canada. There was a wilderness areas bill and it was this legislation that the opposition zeroed in on as being "inadequate." To bolster its argument, Lougheed cited the ecological damage being done to the Athabasca Delta by the construction in British Columbia of the Bennett Dam.

Lougheed introduced a petition on behalf of trapper Noel McKay asking the government for an agreement with British Columbia so that "they will never again do anything to the rivers that will hurt the delta and have a bad effect on the living of the trappers and their families."

Implicit in the petition was the suggestion that McKay had been deprived of his livelihood as a trapper because of the downstream effects of the BC dam in Alberta.

In the government's response two days later, Health Minister James Henderson accused Lougheed of "deliberately attempting to mislead the house." Henderson claimed that McKay had not trapped for a living since the Bennett Dam had been completed in 1967, and therefore could not have been affected in any way by its construction.

To prove the point, Henderson made public confidential welfare documents which revealed that since 1963 McKay had declared no income from his traplines. The documents further indicated that McKay had been confined to a TB sanatorium for two years, and since leaving the hospital, had been living on welfare.

Lougheed was virulent that confidential welfare information had been made public and immediately moved to censure Henderson for his "disgraceful effort to discredit a citizen." He demanded that the Committee on Privileges and Elections investigate Henderson's action.

The *Journal* perceived the issue this way: "If the government, keeper of much confidential information, starts digging into its files and uses the information for political purposes against an individual or a company, then 1984 is much closer than the calendar would indicate."

Premier Strom, embarrassed by the situation, tried to clarify the government's policy concerning confidential files, and maintained that "under ordinary circumstances," the confidential nature of welfare files was protected. "But," Strom added, "the case of Noel McKay is rare and exceptional."

During the committee hearings, Henderson presented figures to show that during 1966-67 an average of 600 people in the Athabasca Delta had been on welfare. The year after the dam was built, that figure dropped to less than 500. And Henderson also pointed out that the decline in the welfare rolls occurred while the population of the area increased. The Health Minister also claimed that it was Lougheed and not himself who made public McKay's welfare record explaining that "no one else saw fit to broadcast the information except the leader of the opposition."

On April 22, the standing committee delivered its verdict: Peter Lougheed had, it said, "unintentionally misled the legislature" in the Noel McKay affair, and it attributed his action to "anxieties and inexperience." It also ruled that Lougheed "shared responsibility" with Henderson for publication of confidential welfare information.

Lougheed was not repentant. He would, he said, do exactly the same thing all over again if he had to. Although Lougheed had lost a legislative battle, the public perceived him to be a winner. Had he not exposed the fact that the government could not be trusted to protect the confidentiality of personal files? Everyone expected Strom to dissolve the legislature and call the election, but the house prorogued on April 27 without the government giving any hint of its election plans.

Scrutiny of the budget offered no clues. While it contained no tax increases, there were none of the pre-election give aways. Old age pensioners on public assistance were given a modest increase, and 19,000 civil servants were awarded substantial pay hikes, but that was it. In fact, property owners faced the prospect of higher taxes. Deteriorating relations with municipal governments were strained further as their share of petroleum revenues was fixed at $38 million. Formerly, local governments were entitled to a third of all provincial royalties. But Arctic oil exploration had robbed the treasury of $34 million and a slump in the sale of Crown leases and reservations for development had for the third consecutive year contributed to a growing deficit. Calgary and Edmonton stood to lose millions and warned their residents that because of Social Credit's actions, property taxes would be increased by two or three mills.

"It remains to be seen whether the voters interpret the government's attitude to arrogance or good husbandry, as bigotry or enlightened responsibility," commented the Lethbridge Herald, "a case can be made either way. It promises to be an exciting election, but will the government dare call it?"

Strom's reluctance to call a spring election was well founded. The government had commissioned a California firm to conduct a private poll which confirmed that it was in deep trouble. The independent survey revealed that 46 per cent of the voters were committed to Peter Lougheed; only 24 per cent expressed a preference for Strom.

Several factors combined to work to Lougheed's advantage. Alberta's population was getting younger, it's leadership older. In the decade between 1961-71, the rural population had declined by 12 per cent; at the same time, the urban population has increased by more than 40 per cent.

Redistribution had created ten new constituencies, increasing the number of seats in the legislature from sixty-five to seventy-five; for the first time in Alberta's history, urban MLAs outnumbered rural ones. And for the first time, eighteen year olds would be allowed to vote.

Although the government recognized it was threatened, it lacked the will and the imagination to reform its rural based philosophy. Ageing government ministers and strategists were almost paranoid in their routine rejection of constructive ideas.

In June, Lougheed accelerated his courtship of the petroleum industry, which was clearly pro-Social Credit. He suggested that Alberta offset its reliance on petroleum revenues and encourage secondary industry. "Government policy should recognize the best interest of the people by developing tax measures, financial assistance, and government policies to expand ownership by Canadians and assure greater involvement of our people," he said. And he promised tax policies to "provide incentive and reward enterprise."

The pledge of tax incentives to Canadian independent companies to drill and explore was particularly significant. The multinational oil companies had shifted their operations away from Alberta to the Arctic. To fill the void left by their departure, the small independents, more than 300 of them and their related service industries, had expanded their exploration activity within provincial boundaries. Lougheed's message of encouragement came at a time when the federal government's white paper on tax reform ruled out any tax holiday for the independent companies.

The prospect of an election dimmed in mid-June as Premier Strom flew to Victoria for a federal-provincial conference to approve a new Canadian constitution. Lougheed opposed the Victoria Charter and warned Strom that if the Conservatives were to form the government, they would not be bound by Alberta's acceptance of the draft charter. At the time, the warning was irrelevant. Quebec's Premier Robert Bourassa was demanding complete control over social security and refused the required unanimous consent. The prospect of a Canadian constitution was again deferred.

Meanwhile, the *Lethbridge Herald* leaked the results of the government's confidential opinion poll under a front page banner headline: SOCREDS IN DEEP TROUBLE AS ALBERTA VOTE APPROACHES. The story was not picked up by the major dailies. Instead they dwelt on the prediction of the new NDP leader, Grant Notley, that the government would be lucky to win fifteen seats. "It's obvious," he stated, "the Progressive Conservatives under their new leader will form the next government."

Other polls supported that contention. There were only thirteen so-called "safe seats," which Social Credit could be confident of winning, and only one of those was in Edmonton.

As early as January, Les Young had taken a poll in his own riding of Edmonton-Jasper Place, and discovered to his surprise that he was comfortably ahead of his opponents. There had been a tendency to dismiss the findings as an aberration. But when a second poll in the spring confirmed the earlier soundings, Young was amazed "at the consistency of the anti-government sentiment."

Impatient for the fight Lougheed demonstrated that not all of his advice was sound: he promised permanent election dates at regular intervals; "the election call has no part in a political campaign," he wrote in the *Alberta Conservative*. "I am committed to the principle of having predetermined election dates set at regular intervals." The *Edmonton Journal's* editorial response warned Lougheed "not to let his enthusiasm overwhelm his apparent capacity for sound thinking." It was, as Lougheed later realized, a foolish pledge. In parliamentary democracy the first minister's prerogative to gauge the political climate and to call an election at his discretion is perhaps the most powerful advantage of incumbency.

Premier Harry Strom used that advantage to its maximum on the morning of July 22. As he rode in a motorcade during the annual Klondike Days parade in Edmonton an election writ was issued setting the voting day for August 30, 1971. The election would be held to "seek the affirmation of confidence in good government."

Lougheed was in Banff planning party policy and was

128

caught by surprise but he was aware that during the thirty-nine day campaign the appearance of events would be more important than reality. "We have to make this election an event," he warned," that's the only way we're going to win."

Conservative strategy was to demonstrate that under a Social Credit administration stagnation had set in, and since Albertans had put their faith in rural virtues the Conservatives had to show that the province was being deprived by ignoring urban values. It was not difficult to arouse extravagant hopes even if Alberta was neither stagnating nor deprived. Harry Strom did little to remove the impression. As the campaign began Lougheed's image was that of a bright, new force. He was fresh in a time of shopworn politicians. In contrast it seemed as if "Old Harry" had been recruited to play the role of the tired opposition. The Conservative campaign was designed to demonstrate that "thirty-six years of government by one party is too long" – that change was needed. NOW.

On July 29, the Conservatives opened their campaign in Red Deer with the promise of a provincial bill of rights patterned after the Diefenbaker legislation. There were also promises of more money for the cities, the youth, the aged, and the poor. Included was a $50 million pledge of government loans and grants as incentive to industrial and commercial development. The government platform was a model of financial restraint. At one point Premier Strom advocated that the federal government consider wage and price controls to beat inflation.

For the first couple of weeks the campaign was remarkably low key. The public didn't appear to be interested and the percentage of uncommitted voters was high. Press reports rhythmically referred to Lougheed as "dynamic" – other adjectives frequently associated with his campaign described the Tory efforts as a "blitz" or "bandwagon." Premier Strom was characterized in the press as "a slow moving man" whose style was "casual" and "unhurried." The campaign buses used by the candidates offered a typical point of comparison: Lougheed's $118,000 vehicle was loaned to the Conservatives by Calgary's Proflex Corporation; Strom campaigned in a much more modest $24,000 camper.

The *Edmonton Journal's* John Lindblad recorded that "the Strom campaign arrangements border on the infuriating. ... the press may leave earlier than scheduled, few arrangements have been made for hotels." On the other hand, Lindblad wrote "the PC's run a tour with the precision of those ramrodding a football squad on a road trip. ... no detail was left to chance, and some see it as almost Kennedyesque in how the PC chief is met and led off at a run to blitz the streets and stores." The *Journal's* reporting of the campaign and Lindblad's articles in particular became an issue. Lindblad, a native of Calgary, had served in the Sea Cadets with Peter's older brother Don. He had known the Lougheeds since childhood. His description of Lougheed as "Kennedyesque" raised the ire of one correspondent who wrote to the editor complaining, "Lougheed's tendency to shadowbox with trumped up issues and the prodigious efforts which have gone into creating his smooth public image could, in fact, be more appropriately compared with the campaign style of Richard Nixon." Lougheed was drawing good crowds. An excursion through northern Alberta convinced him that he had challenged and could break Social Credit influence in the area. Government organizers felt reporters were exaggerating the size of the crowds Lougheed was attracting. For example, prominent coverage was given to Strom's visit to Millet where it was noted that "only four people were waiting for the Stromobile, one being the mayor, one being a CBC reporter, and only two possibly there to shake Uncle Harry's hand." Lougheed had his share of disappointments; in one southern Alberta town his reception was chilling. That was conveniently ignored by the news media. Frustrated by what he considered to be biased reporting a Social Credit organizer stormed into the *Journal* newsroom demanding Lindblad be removed from covering the Strom campaign. He wasn't.

Two issues emerged as the contest drew to a close. Social Credit offered a $1,000.00 cash grant to any family earning less than $15,000.00 a year, toward the purchase of a first house. The promise infuriated those who had just bought homes; and it stretched the government's credibility. As someone pointed out, "a year ago Mr. Strom said we couldn't afford all this, now the money's suddenly available." Lougheed's response was to promise subsidies to developers to stimulate greater private investment in housing. The Social Credit proposal, he noted, would merely cause realtors to raise the prices of houses by $1,000.00. The other issue involved the fate of Edmonton Telephones, a utility owned and operated by the city. Social Credit had threatened legislation to restrict Edmonton Telephone's growth by allowing the provincial agency, Alberta Government Telephones, to provide service to new subdivisions in the city. Edmonton argued that it needed the revenues from its own company, but Strom's reply was consistent. "Eventually," the Premier warned, "the only answer is for the province to lease or buy the city telephone service." Lougheed promised that a Conservative government would sell 49 per cent minority shares in AGT and would permit "full boundary growth for Edmonton's telephone system." That position while popular in Edmonton was resented in Calgary and initial sounding indicated that because of it Lougheed's chances in his own Calgary-West riding had diminished, so campaign strategy was altered to allow him to spend more time in his own constituency.

Still the campaign was not getting off the ground. There was a ventriloquial quality to the Social Credit and Conservative platforms. Both supported medicare for the aged; the Conservatives proposed it be free, Social Credit suggested premiums of $1.00 per month. Lougheed promised a universal scheme of kindergartens; Social Credit matched the idea with Project Access, a scheme to produce television series for preschool children. The government's platform also included a promise of $10.00 per capita grants for the construction of community recreation centres.

But as Lougheed explained "we differ from Social Credit in certain important ways. Our emphasis is on the future, our determination is never to be complacent."

The label he chose for himself was "pragmatist." "I am and always will be a free enterprise Conservative on economic matters," he said. "On social matters such as the

131

rights of the individual, mental health reform, privacy, and social isues, we emphasize the progressive and reform character of the Progressive Conservative party. For this reason some people have referred to me on occasion as a 'liberal Conservative.' But frankly I do not believe the terms 'right' or 'left' are meaningful in modern politics. We stand for free enterprise – not socialism. We also stand for social reform and individual rights – not big government control."

The last seven days of August were a watershed for both parties. Lougheed reduced his breakneck travels across the province to concentrate his energies at home and in urban centres. On August 23, he was encouraged by the huge crowds who turned out during a barnstorming visit to two Edmonton shopping centres. The contrast between Lougheed's increasingly solid Conservative front and the fractious Social Credit effort became apparent after both parties staged major rallies in Edmonton and in Calgary.

The Social Credit rally, Wednesday, August 25, coincided with a football game between the Edmonton Eskimos and the Winnipeg Blue Bombers. Half an hour before the meeting was scheduled to begin the Jubilee Auditorium was virtually deserted; organizers spent anxious moments wondering whether they would fill the hall. But, by 8.00 p.m., a capacity audience of 2,700 had assembled, stirred to enthusiasm by a precision marching band. Manning shared the podium with Strom and launched into a personal attack on Lougheed describing him as "the boy with the ultra-brite toothpaste smile, and Avon Lady charm. A Madison Avenue glamour boy image has nothing whatsoever to do with a person's qualifications to govern the province."

The crowd applauded his performance but to many it appeared that his presence conveyed the impression that without Manning's assistance Harry Strom was incapable of conducting his own campaign. Under the circumstances Strom's speech seemed to be filled with alibis: he attacked the Southam Press and the CBC for the failure of his campaign. He charged that Southam's directors in eastern Canada had instructed the *Edmonton Journal* and the *Calgary Herald* to support the Conservatives. "Anyone who has been reading their news stories and their editorials knows they have been following these instructions." It was not the speech of a man in control of a government; it was the speech of a man whose back was against the wall.

Thursday, August 26, was Lougheed's turn and the Conservative replay attracted an overflow crowd of 4,000 to the same auditorium. The orchestra and balconies were a sea of placards, and balloons floated to the ceiling as spotlights swept the stage. As Peter appeared someone from an overhead catwalk spilled a bag of flour narrowly missing him. Undeterred by the incident Lougheed plunged into his speech. Donald Peacock who covered the meeting for the *Albertan* reported that "he went onto the empty stage and performed politically the way Judy Garland used to theatrically in London's Palladium: just the bare stage, the spotlight and him."

Using a radio pocket microphone that frequently gave him trouble he was visibly moved by the reception from the audience.

"We are, in my view, on the threshold of greatness."

The roar from the crowd was delirious.

"Now! Now! NOW!" they chanted. Responding to the buoyant mood Lougheed was cautious in his conclusion: "It's going to be very, very close," he predicted. "I've got that kind of feeling that it's going our way."

The following morning, August 27, the *Edmonton Journal* carried a terse front page:

Premier Harry Strom has been predicting the Journal will oppose the re-election of the Social Credit government.
WE DO.

But even the paper's senior legislature reporter, Bob Bell, was far from convinced that the Conservatives could win. Suggesting that the campaign had "yet to generate anywhere near the enthusiasm some were willing to predict," Bell wrote, "it appears that neither Social Credit nor the Conservatives have been able to make a noticeable impact on the swing voter." Bell was not alone in his view. In the final campaign assessment in Saturday's *Herald*, reporters Don Sellar and Kevin Peterson concluded "the

Conservatives had mounted a strong urban offensive. ...
but Social Credit's traditional strength seems likely to give
the party a tenth term in power."

In the Red Coach Lounge in Lethbridge bookies were offering 7 to 5 take-your-pick odds. The fact that they were
betting on the outcome was in itself remarkable. It was the
first Alberta election in almost forty years in which the outcome was in doubt. But Lougheed's rural lieutenant Dr.
Hugh Horner had no doubts: "fifty-five seats for the Conservatives," Horner boasted. "I'm predicting fifty-five seats
and it could go higher."

Election morning August 30 dawned warm and clear.
Lougheed was reflective and compared the day to a Grey
Cup kick-off: "You become less and less confident once the
playoffs are over." As the day progressed he seemed to have
lost much of the confidence he had exuded during the campaign. "I don't think were going to do it," he told a reporter
and even expressed concern about his own chances for re-
election in Calgary-West.

At 3.00 in the afternoon he returned to his home to await
the election returns. Stepping into the house he flashed a
nervous grin when, perhaps in premonition of the political
forecast, he moved the needle on his barometer from "very
dry" to "change."

Art Smith was upstairs working on three speeches: win,
lose, and draw. Lougheed asked Smith how he thought
things would go. Smith said he felt it would be close but that
the Conservatives would lose. Lougheed agreed and asked
Smith to touch up the "draw" speech.

When the polls closed at 8.00 p.m., a mad scramble of
reporters gathered outside; inside the mood was subdued.
As the suspense began to build, Peter was determined not to
subject his nerves to any unnecessary strain. He retired to
his den upstairs. The television and radio were turned off.
Seymour phoned to say that Lougheed was assured of his
own personal re-election. At around 8.50 the television was
turned on. At that point Peter C. Newman appeared on the
screen and was heard to say "Prime Minister Trudeau has
real cause for concern tonight. A switch in power is certain
as Peter Lougheed heads for an upset victory." Still, the

channel they were watching did not reinforce that assessment. They switched to CBC which was anchored to the southern Alberta desk. The order in which the fragments of the election results were revealed to those gathered in the Lougheed house was deceptive: a disappointing report that Normie Kwong had been defeated by the Speaker of the House, Art Dixon; Lethbridge and Medicine Hat had returned Social Credit MLAs; Roy Farran was in a tight battle; Cardston and Pincher Creek had gone Social Credit; the Conservatives were not winning one seat south of Calgary. Reports from northern Alberta were encouraging but inconclusive. Was it true that Conservatives were sweeping most of Edmonton's sixteen seats?

At 9.13 CBC's co-hosts, Alex Moir and Ron Smith, projected a Conservative win. But it was difficult to appreciate the dimension of what was happening; the television returns continued to be fragmentary and inconsistent. "It was hard to relate realism to fact," explains Harold Millican who was present. "Even though we had been declared the winners, the TV set gave us the distinct impression we were losing." Slowly the numbers, charts and graphics on the screen made the magnitude of victory apparent: Conservatives elected in thirty-eight seats, leading in eleven for a total of forty-nine; Social Credit elected in nineteen, leading in six for a total of twenty-five; only one seat remained in doubt. The new government was clearly urban with a smattering of rural representation.

Peter decided to wait until Premier Strom conceded defeat before leaving the house. Seemingly relaxed he changed to a clean shirt and tie: he had difficulty with his cufflinks and asked Millican to help him with them.

Shortly after 10.00, remote television cameras at Social Credit headquarters in Edmonton's Jubilee Auditorium focused on the ashen figure of Harry Strom as he stepped to the microphone to "accept the fact that the government has been defeated. It appears," Strom conceded, "Mr. Lougheed will be the new Premier."

The excitement in the Lougheed home was restrained. "There was surprisingly little emotion," remembers Harry Hobbs. "Peter had won but it didn't really sink in." It was almost as if Lougheed was quietly resigned to accept what he had felt for so long was his destiny.

A carnival atmosphere prevailed outside the Westgate Hotel as Lougheed arrived to deliver an acceptance speech. There was a stunned feeling in the crowd's euphoria, a feeling of amazement that the win had happened at all. Pausing, as if uncertain of what to say, Lougheed seemed nervous in his flush of victory as he praised the Social Credit League for its "remarkable contribution to the province." There was no tendency to gloat as he made a simple plea to all Albertans to "do a job in the '70's" and "to build the greatest, greatest province."

The results from Edmonton were now conclusive: all sixteen seats in the capital had elected Conservatives giving Lougheed the key to his victory. "We're going to Edmonton," he declared.

Under police escort the Premier-elect headed to the Calgary International Airport where a Lear jet was standing by. He and Jeanne arrived in the capital at midnight. The reception was tumultuous as he repeated his acceptance speech to crowds gathered in the Edmonton Inn.

It was 1.30 in the morning when he boarded the jet for the return trip home. For the first time he had time to ponder the results. The Lougheed team had secured forty-nine seats in the expanded legislature; Social Credit twenty-five. The Conservatives had taken twenty-three seats from the government and had won nine of the ten new ridings. Eight government ministers had gone down to defeat and only seventeen of the thirty-seven Social Credit incumbents were re-elected. In only eight ridings was the Conservative majority less than 200 votes. Their share of the popular vote had increased to 46.5 per cent – 21 points higher than the 1967 results. Social Credit though had declined only 4 per cent from 1967 to 40.4 per cent. The NDP vote had declined 4 per cent as well but the party managed to elect its leader, Grant Notley, in Spirit River-Fairview. The Liberals, who had polled 10 per cent of the vote in centennial year, were obliterated: they scored a humiliating 1 per cent – the Liberal vote had been absorbed by the Tories.

Peter Lougheed almost didn't live to preside over the new

government. The plane carrying him back to Calgary in his moment of electoral triumph came close to crashing in heavy fog that obscured the runway. In its final descent the pilot realized that the Lear jet was going down on the wrong side of the control tower and heading for a crash landing on a parking lot. At the last moment the pilot recovered, climbed into the night, and headed back to Edmonton.

The desk clerk at the Edmonton Inn was not impressed with the exhausted party who had returned after 2.00 in the morning in search of rooms. Premier-elect or not, nothing was available. Lougheed headed across town to his Edmonton apartment and as he left, he turned to an aide and asked: "after thirty-six years do you think there's still anyone around who remembers how in the hell you change a government?"

CHAPTER VIII

Thirty-six years of "God's government" had come to an end. It was an awesome victory for Lougheed but in terms of Alberta's history it was a triumph of style rather than of substance – the secular equivalent of a revival meeting – a new minister had been selected to do a better job than the old one but the faith remained the same. There was no substantive change in political philosophy.

The win immediately established Lougheed on the national forefront. The *Toronto Telegram* recognized "the young political Lochinvar who came out of obscurity to challenge what seemed immovable and now must be recognized as a political figure of national stature." That theme was developed in the *Calgary Herald* which reported that "Mr. Lougheed's victory immediately rouses speculation that the Premier elect may have to resist a draft from the national Conservative party when it chooses a successor to Robert Stanfield."

Only the *Albertan* (which had supported Social Credit during the campaign) remained skeptical: "a substantial number of Albertans expect an appreciably better way of life than they now enjoy . . . they may be disappointed."

In his approach to government organization Lougheed had a clear idea of what he hoped to accomplish, and even before he took the oath of office he began making changes which would give him complete control of both the legislature and the civil service.

In the days following the election he began putting together his cabinet in the backyard of his Calgary home, and at his cottage in Banff away from the distraction of well wishers who kept his telephone ringing at a steady pace. Fred Mannix was one of the first to drop by and offer his congratulations. In choosing his cabinet, he relied on his wife's judgement. "She has an innate ability to judge people. I think perhaps women are naturally better at that than men. Men are more gullible."

There was nothing exceptional about Lougheed's twenty-two member cabinet other than the fact that it was the largest ever sworn in, better educated than Strom's, and with the average age of its members nine years younger than those in the previous executive council.

All of the original Conservative MLAs received appointments. Lougheed's chief lieutenant, Dr. Hugh Horner, became Deputy Premier and Minister of Agriculture. Lou Hyndman was given the Education portfolio and made government house leader. Don Getty, who had his eye on the energy portfolio, was put in charge of the newly created Department of Intergovernmental Affairs. Energy went to Bill Dickie. Bill Yurko was handed the job of heading the Department of the Environment. And, Len Werry was made responsible for Telephones. Lougheed offered Calgary lawyer Ron Ghitter the Municipal Affairs portfolio but Ghitter (for a combination of personal reasons which he won't talk about) turned it down. So, the job went to Dave Russell. Clarence Copithorne was made Minister of Highways and Bob Dowling a Minister Without Portfolio, responsible for tourism.

From among the thirty-eight other MLAs all of them new faces in the legislature, he elevated Merv Leitch to the position of Attorney General. Helen Hunley became Solicitor General. The oldest member in the cabinet was fifty-four year old Fred Peacock, the Industry Minister; the youngest, an exceptionally bright thirty-one year old Red Deer lawyer, Jim Foster, became Minister of Advanced Education. Neil Crawford was made Minister of Health. For his Provincial

Treasurer he selected a cherubic chartered accountant, Gordon Miniely. (Hearing of his father's appointment, Miniely's six year old Jeff boasted "if it weren't for my dad Alberta would go broke." Not to be outdone a schoolmate who happened to be Education Minister Lou Hyndman's six year old son, Bruce, shot back, "Oh yeah! Well, if it weren't for my dad we'd all be dumb" – an assessment that had more than a ring of truth to it. "Long Lou" quickly earned a reputation as one of the most intelligent, accessible, and humane of Lougheed's ministers.) Horst Schmid, an indefatigable, pear-shaped man, was put in charge of Culture, Youth, and Recreation. Dr. Allan Warrack took over responsibility for Lands and Forests. Bert Hohol, a greying man with a starched face, became Minister of Labour and Manpower; Dr. Winston Backus, Minister of Public Works. That left two others without portfolios, Peace River broadcaster Allen "Boomer" Adair and George Topolnisky.

Lougheed took the oath of office and the cabinet was sworn in on September 10, 1971, thirty-six years to the day that Social Credit came to power.

Equally as important as his cabinet choices was the placing of his loyal followers in key positions. During his first term Lougheed took a giant step in reorganizing the civil service, replacing 70 per cent of all senior deputy ministers who held key positions. In doing so he explained "the cabinet need a significant staff of senior people involved as back up resources, much like the privy council in Ottawa." But another source says it was obvious that Lougheed "tailored the government to suit himself. Although he is intensely courteous to his friends and considers their advice as input, the decisions he makes are his and his alone."

He was determined that his government would be as well informed as any in Canada. And, his appointments fall into three identifiable categories.

THE CALGARY CLAQUE: These are the very "close buddies" he grew up with. Across the hall from his office sits Harry Hobbs, a tight lipped, balding man, who moved from a position with the Calgary parking authority to serve as deputy minister of the executive council. Jim Seymour, a tall, dapper man with a knobby nose, ended his career as an oil scout to run the Premier's Calgary office. Harold Millican, a card-carrying Liberal, served as his executive assistant, then became the deputy minister of intergovernmental affairs – a position he held for three years before leaving the government to work with the Canadian Petroleum Association and the Northern Pipeline Authority.

Also included are childhood friends of Peter's older brother Don (who is now vice-president of production at Imperial Oil). John Lindblad, the *Journal* reporter, took a job as one of Lougheed's "red hot guys" in Ottawa. He was director of the Alberta office, sort of a provincial ambassador to the federal capital. Rod McDaniel, a consulting engineer with expertise in the oil business, is relied upon for advice. Lougheed still keeps in constant touch with Mr. Justice Ken Moore[1] and with Clare "Swede" Liden, the lawyer who was instrumental in convincing him to get into politics. Another on the list is Joe Hutton, the news director at CFCN TV, who later worked for Art Smith. Hutton became Lougheed's press officer the day after the election. Lee Richardson, his executive secretary, is not technically part of this group but as a teenager Richardson campaigned for Lougheed in 1967 and served briefly as an assistant to John Diefenbaker.

THE MANNIX CONNECTION: Lougheed remains in communication with his old boss Fred Mannix. But his most important source from his Mannix days is "Chip" Collins, the forth-right, owlish-looking Irishman, who had twenty-two years experience with the Mannix group of companies as both general manager and as president of Manalta Coal, the largest coal mining company in Canada. A former captain in the Canadian Army, Collins started his present career with the Bank of Nova Scotia and is today, as deputy provincial treasurer, the architect of Alberta's economic policy. He sits as a member of the financial and priorities committee, the management policy committee, the deputy ministers' resource committee, and is secretary to both the Treasury Board and the Heritage Savings Trust Fund Investment

Committee. David Wood, who worked with Lougheed in university and at the Mannix corporation, remains involved in election strategy.

THE NEW LOUGHEED LOYALISTS: One of the first people Lougheed called after becoming Premier was Dr. George Govier, a highly respected authority on energy resource conservation and management. Govier, a professor of engineering at the University of Calgary, had served the Social Credit government as a member of Alberta's Energy Resources Conservation Board. He was brought in as deputy minister of energy and natural resources at a time when Alberta was engaged in a dispute with Ottawa over resource policy. Govier, recently retired chairman of the Energy Resources Conservation Board, was later succeeded by Dr. G. Barry Mellon, the former head geologist with the Alberta Research Council.

Wayne Minion, who had worked in British Columbia Hydro's engineering division and had seen service in Brazil as a director of LIGHT, was hired as an energy troubleshooter and later became chairman of the Petroleum Marketing Commission. John Channon, an earthy maverick who had worked in Ottawa for four federal agriculture ministers, was invited to take the position as chairman of the Alberta Grain Commission. Jack Lyndon, now head of the Insurance Bureau of Canada, had been vice-president of the Toronto Stock Exchange and was hired to become Alberta's first deputy consumer affairs minister. Rheal Leblanc, a New Brunswick correctional authority, was brought in as Alberta's first deputy solicitor general. His hiring was considered a coup since the federal government had also been after Leblanc's services. One person to make the transition from the Social Credit to the Conservative governments was Glenn Purnell who became deputy agriculture minister shortly before Lougheed took office. Another, Judy Wish, came from Premier Strom's Calgary office to work as a press officer and in 1978 was appointed Lindblad's successor in Ottawa. Peter Macdonnell is an influential party bagman with a pipeline to the Eastern establishment (he's the nephew of former Governor-General

Vincent Massey). Although not a personal friend, Bob Blair, president of Alberta Gas Truck Line, is an important ally in Lougheed's industrial strategy. The executive director of Lougheed's office, George de Rappard, is a former executive director of the Conservative party and a past national president of Canada JayCees. De Rappard, a former hockey player with the Lethbridge Native Sons, was educated on an athletic scholarship at Colorado Springs College.

Unencumbered by political debts that follow most politicians into office Lougheed was free to do things his own way from the start. Patronage, although it exists, was a minor consideration: porkbarrel politics, familiar in most eastern Canadian provinces, is not practised as much in Alberta. "In fact there were a number of people whose service to the party entitled them to positions, but because Peter was sensitive to that fact, they were denied," says one MLA.

The favourite means of dispensing patronage is for the government to hire "consultants." Lougheed had a code of ethics drafted for the public service prohibiting government employees from "accepting a gift, favor, or service from any individual, organization or corporation." While the code does not govern MLAs, Lougheed himself has attempted to follow it – he once returned a case of expensive wine to a developer who sent it to him as an election victory present. But he had no compunction about accepting free airline passes from both Air Canada and CP Air for personal holiday travel. When the practice was revealed in November, 1978, Lougheed lamely maintained that the travel passes were not gifts but "an opportunity for him to get a break and do a better job for Albertans." The public refused to accept that explanation and Lougheed borrowed $9,000 to reimburse the airlines and he promised never again to accept free travel passes.

Even though government guidelines forbid party fundraising by civil servants, Lougheed condones the unethical practice of directors of public companies serving as members of the Conservative party's finance committee.

His corporate approach to running a government was immediately apparent when he established a slew of cabinet committees, government caucus committees, subcommittees, and task forces. The new government had inherited a potentially serious economic situation and as a source of additional revenue Lougheed's first priority was a review of natural resource royalities. The average price paid for a barrel of Alberta crude oil in 1971 was $2.83; royalties ranged from 8 to 16⅔ per cent on a sliding scale based on a well's production. Natural gas royalties were 16⅔ per cent but the government provided processing subsidies. From the beginning the new government's preoccupation with the symbols and trappings of power was evident and the ambience of the legislature changed radically. The third floor corridor leading to his predecessor's office was blocked off and renovated to accommodate a ring of offices for key advisors. Although he inherited Strom's government limousine, a green Oldsmobile, Lougheed thought it too flashy and turned it over to Don Getty. Instead, he chose a more modest looking but equally expensive Chevrolet (although Lougheed drives he is impatient behind the wheel and tends to be heavy on the gas pedal so he relies on the services of a chauffeur). Government stationery was redesigned, the provincial coat of arms replaced by a bold, graphic Alberta. The legislative chamber itself was redecorated; the green carpet replaced with pile of shades of imperial red. True to his word Lougheed had televison installed in the house, but on his own terms. Sound jacks for television cameras were only put in behind opposition benches, forcing cameras to face the government side of the house. Opposition speakers cannot be filmed head-on and as a result they appear on the screen as disembodied voices.

After a month of sixteen hour days organizing his administration he and Jeanne booked a flight to California and disappeared on a two week vacation. Lougheed surfaced again in Ontario, the star attraction in Premier Bill Davis's October 21, 1971, provincial election campaign. Two days after the election Lougheed was back in Edmonton to host the visit to Alberta of Soviet Premier Alexi Kosygin. Kosygin's tour of the provinces was relaxed and informal. The Soviet Premier, who even donned an Indian head-dress in ceremonies making him an honorary chief, appreciated the break from rigid protocol. In a spontaneous gesture at the moment of his departure he invited Lougheed to visit the USSR. (When Lougheed finally made the trip in June of 1977 Kosygin stretched protocol to receive him and orchestrated a highly successful tour for Peter of the Soviet oil fields in Siberia.)

Early in November Lougheed delivered his first major address to the National Press Club in Ottawa where he stated his intention to expand Alberta's influence on national energy policy. Reminding his audience that under the Canadian constitution Alberta is the sole owner of its resources he promised a "clean, fresh and new slate" in federal-provincial energy matters. He demanded that he be given observer status at any energy discussions between the United States and Canada. "If Alberta poker chips are involved at the poker table," he asserted, "we will be at that table." Two days later his suggestion of a provincial presence at an international bargaining table was routinely dismissed by acting federal Energy Minister Jean-Luc Pepin as "not the proper way" for international negotiations to be conducted.

Lougheed's reputation as a tough negotiator preceded him to the federal-provincial conference which opened in Ottawa on November 15, 1971. There he repeated his demand that Alberta be a fully informed partner in the formation of national energy policy. He warned that he would not stand by and let Ottawa discuss the sale of energy resources without regard to the province's welfare. "Any decision by the federal government which might limit petroleum or natural gas exports or discourage exploration and development by the industry will have a serious, immediate impact on Alberta's economy. Such action could seriously affect Canada's overall position in any discussions of our country's future." The reaction of the Trudeau government was predictable: it dismissed his remarks as so much unpolished sabre rattling.

At the end of November a jarring event occurred which illustrated just how helpless Lougheed was to effect any meaningful change on national energy policy. The Alberta Energy Resources Conservation Board had approved the sale over twenty years of a billion dollars worth of natural gas to the United States. But the National Energy Board ruled that Canada had no surplus gas for export and killed the deal. Lougheed who felt that the decision was motivated by central Canada's natural gas requirements was disturbed. "If eastern utility companies expect Albertans to just simply sit and keep its gas in the ground, surplus to the needs of the people in Alberta until they get around in eastern Canada to use and take advantage of Alberta gas, then obviously that is not a satisfactory situation." Prime Minister Trudeau who had no authority to alter the NEB decision sent Lougheed a perfunctory telegram indicating his willingness to discuss ways of stimulating the Alberta petroleum industry.

During the first week of December the Lougheeds bought a house in Edmonton. They paid $100,000 for a two storey brick and white frame house at 13636 Ravine Drive in the city's posh Capital Hill district. The building is on a secluded street overlooking a wooded ravine and commands a view of the distant legislature.

On December 7, the same day that the Lougheed's bought their new home, Peter learned of the death of one of his MLAs, Jack Robertson, the member for Stettler. Robertson, a forty-three year old bulk oil dealer, had taken the seat from Social Credit with a 300 vote margin. In the subsequent by-election held on February 14, 1972, Wainwright lawyer, Graham Harle retained the seat and increased the Conservative's margin of victory.

As Lougheed was preparing for the opening of his first legislative session, his mother died. Edna Bauld had been ill for some time, but her death came as a shock. "Peter's father never lived to see him graduate from college, and he was particularly saddened that his mother – who had encouraged his political career – never lived to see him as Premier in the legislature," explains a friend. She was buried at the end of February in Calgary's Union Cemetery beneath one of the many identical small white grave markers which identify the resting place of three generations of Lougheeds. Peter himself will eventually be interred in the same family plot.

Lougheed struggled to keep his mourning private during

the traditional pomp and ceremony that marked the opening on March 2, 1972, of the first session of the seventeenth Alberta legislature. Immediately after the reading of the Speech From The Throne, which promised "a more diversified and more balanced economy," Lougheed broke with legislative tradition to introduce his Alberta Bill of Rights. The move was significant in that it represented the first effort by a province to adopt John Diefenbaker's Bill of Rights, which up until that time, operated only within the constitutional authority of the federal parliament. The Alberta bill uses the exact language of the Diefenbaker legislation specifying that in Alberta "there exists without discrimination by reason of race, national origin, colour, religion or sex" six fundamental freedoms: the right of the individual to liberty, security of person, and enjoyment of property; the right of the individual before the law; freedom of religion; freedom of speech; freedom of assembly; and, freedom of the press. In theory the bill differed from the Social Credit government's Human Rights Act in that it took precedence over all other provincial statutes. But in adopting the Canadian Bill of Rights the Lougheed government reserved the right of the legislature to declare and identify certain acts which could operate "not withstanding the Bill of Rights." This clause weakened the Alberta Bill of Rights because the possibility of invading the liberties of citizens at a provincial level is greater than at the federal level. Yet perhaps the most important result of Alberta's adoption of the Canadian Bill of Rights is that all Supreme Court decisions became immediately applicable to the province.

From the start the new government's businesslike approach was obvious. Accounting procedures were tightened. The Provincial Treasurer, Gordon Miniely, discovered that under Social Credit, royalty cheques for "millions and millions of dollars" had been left on the Minister's desk for days and, as a result, the province had lost interest on the money.

The budget introduced on March 18 put a lid on health, education, and welfare spending. For the first time since the depression, Alberta embarked on a $200 million borrowing program which Miniely defended as "more desirable than the alternative of raising additional revenue through increased tax burdens." Lougheed also introduced a program of economic nationalism imposing tough conditions on a consortium of foreign investors committed to building a heavy oil sands extraction plant in the Athabasca tar sands. The Syncrude consortium of Gulf (U.S.), Exxon, Atlantic Richfield, Royalite, and Cities Service had a very modest beginning in 1963 when it proposed to undertake a pilot tar sands plant. But by 1972 Syncrude had reappraised its original proposal and concluded that production would have to be increased if the plant were to be profitable. Before he would give the consortium permission to expand, Lougheed insisted on a new deal which would allow Albertans to buy shares in the company, insisted that there be a Canadian director, and demanded that Alberta technology be used in construction of the plant wherever possible. Finally, and most importantly, Lougheed asked that any products manufactured from the oil be processed in plants established in Alberta.

Suspicion was growing in central Canada that Lougheed was a latent Western separatist, an image he tried to dispel whenever he went east. In a speech to the annual dinner meeting of the Canadian Press in Toronto at the end of April he introduced his theory of decentralized federalism. He soothingly challenged the east to accept Alberta in the mainstream of Confederation, stressing the need for a national industrial strategy to be developed by "the eleven governments of Canada." His remarks – short on detail but long on theory – warned of the danger of forcing any one province into isolationism. It was his first venture into statesmanship and he was nationally applauded. Instead of emphasizing the difference between regions he had dwelt upon the similarities between Quebec and Alberta and pro-. posed greater provincial autonomy to eliminate "deep and strong regional alienation." While his remarks rejected the concept of Western separatism they also rejected Western docility.

As the legislative session progressed in what Lougheed called "new directions" many of the bills before the house took a long range, philosophical view of various problems. It was a cautious approach. Arrayed against the growing confidence of Lougheed's Ministers the Social Credit members appeared to disintegrate as an opposition. More than half of the Social Credit MLAs were as inexperienced as the Lougheed team, and illness kept their leader Harry Strom away from the house for most the session. The sole NDP member, Grant Notley, filled the void and won grudging respect for his abilities. Even Fred Kennedy, the *Albertan's* right-wing columnist, admitted that as a parliamentarian Notley was easily "the number one star." "Here is a chap," he wrote in his newspaper column, "who went from a junior B league right into the majors without benefit of minor professional league experience."

The house had barely settled down to work when Lougheed revealed his determination to get extra provincial revenues by introducing a tax on oil reserves still in the ground. Facing predictable opposition from the oil companies he did not spell out the specifics, but proposed public hearings on the matter. He argued at the hearings that the oil industry in its infancy had been generously treated by the Social Credit government and that such treatment was no longer appropriate or necessary now that the industry had matured.

When his first legislature sessions adjourned for a summer recess in June, Lougheed, as every new Canadian Premier does, made the obligatory pilgrimage to New York for discussion with the captains of North American finance. Specifically he went to Wall Street to explore financing for industrial development which would see construction in north eastern Alberta of "ten or twenty heavy oil extraction plants."

On July 29, after months of public hearings, Lougheed disclosed the details of the first phase of his major oil and gas revenue plan calculated to give the Alberta Treasury an additional $70 million. The plan ensured that the oil industry, although still taxed, would be encouraged to risk exploration capital in the province. It was smart politics, shrewdly devised. The new approach offered the oil companies the option of paying tax on oil still in the ground or accepting a revised royalty system which boosted the province's rate from 16⅔ to 21 per cent. To sweeten the tax pill the industry was offered incentives to step up the search for new conventional supplies and was allowed to claim the new Alberta tax as a deductible item on its federal income tax returns. Lougheed felt that he was exercising reasonable latitude but, in fact, he was laying the groundwork for a feud with the federal government which would see the oil companies caught in a squeeze play.

Having laid the foundation for his game plan Lougheed left in September for an economic mission to Japan, a country which had demonstrated keen interest in developing Alberta's coal and petroleum resources. The size of the mission astonished Canadian diplomatic officials; Lougheed had forty people in tow. As the meetings were about to begin in Tokyo, Lougheed suffered back spasms and had to be hospitalized. Negotiations with the Japanese were conducted by Dr. Hugh Horner who sounded out various officials on active co-operation in the development of oil sands in Alberta while other members of the mission conferred with their Japanese counterparts in business, agriculture, and the oil, coal, and steel industries.

The day Lougheed left for Japan, Prime Minister Trudeau called a federal election for October 30. Upon his return from Tokyo and a three day Hawaiian vacation Lougheed plunged into the campaign for Robert Stanfield although he didn't give him a chance of winning. Discontent had been mounting in the West to Trudeau's economic, regional, and resources policies and Stanfield, at least, held out the promise of giving Alberta "meaningful" consultations on energy matters and of putting a Westerner in charge of a federal Department of Energy, Mines, and Resources. Lougheed campaigned for Joe Clark who was seeking election in Rocky Mountain House, and introduced Stanfield at two major rallies in Calgary and Edmonton. Trudeau remained aloof throughout the campaign, confident that the election was a formality that would result in another four years of Liberal majority rule. "The land is strong" was the Liberal rallying cry but the election results demonstrated in startling fashion that while the land was strong the Liberal party was not. For a few hours on election night as the outcome hung in the balance it appeared that Stanfield had won. Not since 1925 had a political leader come so close, only to have the prize elude his grasp. Trudeau had been repudiated in English Canada. Stanfield made a clean sweep of Alberta's nineteen seats. Had he won three more in the country he might have led a minority Conservative government. While the voters had withdrawn their confidence from Trudeau they did not confer it on anyone else.

When the results were officially tabulated, Trudeau with 109 seats was able to cling to office with the support of 31 New Democrats. The Liberals won only 7 of 68 ridings west of the Ontario border. Conservatives with 107 seats remained in opposition. Commenting on the outcome Lougheed took satisfaction in seeing his machine deliver a unified Alberta block in the Commons. The results he said were a clear indication that the Liberals had failed to recognize freight rate inequities and Alberta's energy potential. "The potentials in this area are being ignored and the Alberta vote, to some degree, reflected that feeling," he warned.

Lougheed wasted no time in using his alliance with the federal Conservatives to launch a major offensive on the crippled Liberal minority government. The second phase of his financial plan for Alberta was revealed to the legislature in mid-November. Lougheed served notice that he would demand higher prices for Alberta natural gas and in doing so pledged a two price system to protect consumers in Alberta from the higher export price. No longer would he provide the rest of the country with 80 per cent of its gas at cut rates. "Past natural gas policies," he explained, "have threatened to thwart the growth of job opportunities in this province by failing to take advantage of this clean, inexpensive, and accessible fuel as a feedstock in such a way as to provide a competitive advantage for Alberta industries to compete with industries in central Canada already enjoying the unfair advantage of inequitable transportation rates."

His innovative two price proposal aimed "to provide a fair and reasonable return to Albertans who own the depleting and non-recurring resources." The Alberta Energy Resources Conservation Board determined that Alberta's natural gas was underpriced by 10 to 20 cents, a situation that was further aggravated by the National Energy Board's refusal to grant export permits to Alberta gas companies on the ground that Canada's future gas requirements would exceed the current available supply. As a result, TransCanada Pipelines Ltd., the sole purchaser of gas for eastern Canada, was put in a monopoly position of no longer facing competition for Alberta gas from U.S. buyers.

Loughed had no authority to establish a well-head price for gas but, exercising his undisputed power to tamper with interprovincial trade, he threatened to cut the supply of gas from the well-head by denying approval of natural gas export permits unless the transmission companies were willing to pay his price. The gas companies were outraged but they were bound to go along with it. But not without a fight. To Ontario, the largest single consumer of Alberta gas, the increase would cost industrial and private users at least $52 million.

The *Toronto Star* questioned whether Lougheed's proposal was constitutional:

> The establishment of a discriminatory two price system for natural gas would have harmful effects not only for Ontario but for Canada as a whole. Over much of the country it would raise the basic cost of production and make Canadian manufactured goods more costly and less able to compete not only in the foreign market but against foreign imports in the domestic market.

The *Ottawa Journal* dismissed Lougheed's contention that Ontario was getting "cheap gas": "industrial consumers in Ontario now pay 56 cents per thousand cubic feet of gas. Alberta industry obtains the same amount for 19 cents. The difference is made up, of course, in transmission and other charges. Alberta producers don't get that revenue, but that doesn't make Ontario gas cheap." The Ontario Assocation of Gas Users demanded that the federal government set the field price for Alberta gas at levels suitable to Ontario consumers. And, at Queen's Park, Ontario Premier Bill Davis appointed Darcy McKeough, his parliamentary aid on energy, to deal with the developing situation. But Lougheed refused to meet with McKeough explaining that as a "first minister" he would only meet with another "first minister." So, on January 17, 1973 Premier William Davis flew to Edmonton to consult with Lougheed on Alberta gas policy. Lougheed took direct pleasure in the Davis visit: symbolically it was an historic occasion. The traditional pattern of Alberta Premiers going east to seek audience in Ottawa, Toronto, and Montreal had been reversed. And, as Lougheed commented, "the east is used to us Westerners coming to them on bended knees. Now we hold the high cards in terms of energy and we plan to use them." For his effort Davis was informed that Alberta would not retreat from its demands and that central Canada would have to accept the fact that the cost of its energy was going to rise.

As the controversy developed over the winter Lougheed prepared to do battle on another front with a new Social Credit opposition leader. A convention to replace Harry Strom had been called for the first week in February and at least two of the leadership candidates presented a potential cause for some concern. Gordon Taylor, one of the most successful politicians in Alberta, was making a second bid for the leadership, and Robert Clark, the former Education and Youth Minister, campaigned on a liberal populist stance offering the party genuine opportunity for reform. Two other candidates had no parliamentary experience. Werner Schmidt, the vice president of Lethbridge Community College, was considered as a Mennonite, too high minded to be a good politician. And, John Ludwig, a Dutch-born educator, was the dark horse. Both Schmidt and Ludwig had sought election in 1971 and both had been rejected by the voters.

There are observers of the Alberta political scene who contend that Ernest Manning influenced the outcome of the convention. Manning, these observers say, had a growing admiration for Lougheed and sent his son, Preston, to campaign for the most ineffectual candidate, Werner Schmidt. (It is interesting to note that Lougheed meets regularly with Manning and even today respects his advice.) On the first ballot Clark led Schmidt 583 to 512; Taylor, who wasn't impressed with either Schmidt or Clark, refused to endorse anyone and the majority of his 406 first ballot votes went to

Schmidt who emerged the winner with a narrow 39 vote majority.

The new opposition leader had no seat in the legislature, so when the house resumed sitting on February 15, Gordon Henderson was named opposition house leader after Schmidt rejected a caucus suggestion that Clark assume the duties.

Ten days after the legislature opened, Telephone Minister Len Werry was killed in an automobile accident on a particularly treacherous stretch of road near Edson.

Werry's death afforded Schmidt the opportunity to seek a seat in the legislature. But Schmidt, who represented the rural elements of Social Credit, made the politically fatal mistake of contesting the by-election in urban Calgary. Urban voters in Alberta do not tend to take seriously rural candidates. He was beaten handily by Conservative oilman Stewart McCrae and his defeat relegated Social Credit to oblivion.

As the house went about its business that spring of 1973 Lougheed set about to make good his Throne Speech pledge that Alberta was entering "a new era of energy." But the Ottawa government threatened to circumvent those ambitions. The federal government slapped controls on crude oil exports considered surplus to Canadian needs. The decision was, in Lougheed's view, an unnecessary step and an overreaction to growing United States demands for Canadian energy. Lougheed insisted that Alberta had enough crude oil production capacity to supply the needs of Canadian refineries and U.S. requests as well.

The fight with Ontario over higher gas prices escalated in April when Premier Davis threatened Supreme Court action on the grounds that Alberta's proposed two price system violated the British North America Act by impeding free interprovincial trade. Davis insisted that Ottawa intervene. "The energy problem is national," he argued, "the policy must be national." Davis returned to Edmonton to plead his case. His welcome was elaborately staged: as Davis's chartered jet approached the airport, a green and gold helicopter carrying Lougheed swung into view. The two craft touched down simultaneously and the two leaders held their discussions in the airport's VIP lounge. Davis insisted that "Ontario is too large a part of the economic community of Canada for the nation to be indifferent to the economic health of the province. It is absurd and mischievous to try and create an image of a deprived West standing up stoutly to a prosperous east." He proposed a three price system for gas in which other Canadian provinces would pay less than United States' customers, a suggestion which Lougheed agreed to consider. As a result of the airport meeting the two Premiers agreed on the need for a federal-provincial conference on national energy policy. But Lougheed ruled out any suggestion that his gas price increase be put on the agenda. That he maintained was not negotiable.

While the federal government remained aloof from the dispute over gas a chastened Prime Minister Trudeau appeared to take a solicitous interest in the West. Trudeau proposed a Conference on Western Economic Opportunities with the object of "shaping a new national policy, a policy to strengthen Canada by achieving a more balanced and diversified regional growth throughout the whole country." For the first time since Confederation a unified block of four Western Canadian Premiers was invited to sit down with Ottawa to tackle the problems of the single region. When the meeting convened in Calgary on July 25, 1973, Lougheed called for fundamental changes to the underlying philosophy of Canadian transportation policy aimed at correcting the Crowsnest freight rates which have for so long angered Westerners. (The Crowsnest rates allow the railways, for example, to charge $2.11 per hundredweight to transport steel from Hamilton to Edmonton. But to keep Canadian steel competitive with Japanese imports on the West coast the rate from Hamilton to Vancouver, a thousand miles farther west, is only $1.35 per hundredweight. Almost all agricultural and mineral resources are shipped from the prairies in their raw form more cheaply than if they are processed in the West. The policy is particularly damaging in Alberta where the railways face no competition from water transport and where competition from trucks is weak.)

The Alberta position paper demanded changes to "clearly

155

place regional economic development as one of the basic objectives of the national transportation policy." Trudeau rejected the idea suggesting that what Alberta really wanted was a transportation system "biased in favour of one region." As the conference proceeded it became apparent that Trudeau had not come to listen to Western grievances but to lecture. After wading through more than three tons of conference documents the only concession the West achieved was a federal commitment to amend the Bank Act so that provincial governments could participate directly in banking.

Lougheed who emerged from the meeting as the unofficial spokesman for Western grievances was disappointed and told Trudeau, "frankly, we would have foresaken any federal dollars, any federal programmes in exchange for understanding."

The dialogue between east and West that had begun in Calgary was undone two months later when the Trudeau government unilaterally introduced its own two price system for oil by imposing an oil export tax of 40 cents per barrel on Alberta crude. Federal Energy Minister Donald Macdonald defended the decision as a way of insuring that Canadians got a "fair price for oil on the export market." "Without the tax," he explained, "US refineries could buy oil from Western Canada at a frozen Canadian price ($4.00 per barrel) below what was paid for their foreign oil ($4.30 per barrel). This would have meant windfall profits for the US oil companies whereas our export tax means that the windfall will go the federal and Alberta treasuries."

But Lougheed didn't see it that way. "The tax upon oil owned by Albertans will siphon off substantial cash proceeds to central and eastern parts of Canada," Lougheed charged, and he arbitrarily estimated Alberta's losses would exceed $300 million. He vowed to strike back against a tax which he considered "detrimental and discriminatory." Lougheed made good his threat by tearing up the existing royalty agreements with the oil companies. He announced that oil leases in Alberta would be reopened for negotiation and that the royalty rates which had just been raised would be raised again to make up the deficit the federal tax would cost the province. "Under the terms of Confederation the provinces formed a union on the basis that the natural resources would be the exclusive jurisdiction of the provinces," he repeated. And, to emphasize the point, he introduced legislation to allow his government to take from the oil companies their authority to set the well-head price of Alberta crude. Oilmen who had considered Lougheed in their pockets were angered and challenged his actions by immediately threatening to cut back exploration and investment in the province. But events half way around the globe abruptly conspired to enhance the authority which so far had eluded Lougheed; events which contributed in a fashion never imagined to the rise of Peter Lougheed and to the economic balkanization of Canada.

Note

1 Lougheed's former law partner, Ken Moore, was appointed to the bench in January, 1972, by federal Justice Minister, John Turner.

CHAPTER IX

On the holiest of Jewish religious days in 1973, Yom Kippur, Egyptian tanks rolled across the windless sands of Suez to invade the Israeli occupied Sinai Peninsula. Simultaneously, Syrian troops surged across the craggy hills of the Golan Heights in an assault on Jerusalem. The Arabs had launched a two-pronged invasion on October 6, to avenge their losses in the 1967 Six Day War. Aided by the United States, Israeli troops stemmed the Arab thrust and delivered a brutal counterattack. Within eighteen days the Yom Kippur War was over; the Arabs had lost the battle but their confidence had not been shattered. They resorted to another initiative that immediately threw the world economy into total confusion.

In Kuwait, Arab oil producers met on October 16, 1973, to determine how best to use their oil reserves as a weapon to pressure Western diplomacy to tone down its support of Israel. At the outset the Organization of Arab Petroleum Exporting Countries (OAPEC) agreed to cut back oil production by an immediate 25 per cent with further 5 per cent reductions each month until a settlement was negotiated in the Middle East dispute. Almost overnight the demand for non-Arab fuel tripled international oil prices as supplies were reduced by the threatened embargo. Oil that had been selling for $3.00 jumped to the following prices: Venezuelan oil rose to $10.00 per barrel; Iran gained bids of up to $17.00 per barrel; Nigeria demanded and got $16.80 a barrel; Tunisia received $22.00 a barrel though on a relatively small scale.

As the energy crisis deepened the Canadian government moved to cash in on the windfall and unilaterally raised the export tax on Canadian oil, from 40 cents to $1.90, then to $2.20 a barrel. In less than three months more than $70 million was siphoned from the Alberta economy to subsidize Quebec and Atlantic Canada which depended on foreign imports for their supply.

	Alberta Oil Exports (barrels)	Return to Alberta	Return to Ottawa
October 73	30,087,025	$114,634,613	$12,035,130
November 73	26,926,662	$102,590,582	$10,770,664
December 73	25,819,962	$ 98,374,055	$49,057,927

Alberta owns its natural resources as designated in the BNA Act and reiterated in the 1929 Resource Transfer Agreement, and in spite of this agreed to export prices to Eastern Canada well below the international level. The extra money obtained by Ottawa on its unilateral price increase was used to buy Venezuelan oil at world prices, instead of giving Alberta the equal international price increase.

Angered by the loss of revenue Alberta took a step equal to severing relations with the Trudeau government when Federal and Intergovernmental Affairs Minister Don Getty announced that Edmonton "can reluctantly no longer participate in energy discussions." In an atmosphere of charged emotion, Lougheed convened a special session of the legislature in early December to strengthen his hand in dealing with the situation. A series of three bills moved to establish a petroleum marketing commission which was designed to usurp the oil companies' authority to post prices. Lougheed also proposed increased royalties which could be paid "in kind, that is, in actual crude in lieu of cash." This move guaranteed the province direct ownership of one-third of Alberta's oil production. (This legislation is viewed by Lougheed as the most crucial he has ever introduced as Premier. Prior to its introduction Imperial Oil and the other major oil companies set the well-head price. Now the government assumed this responsibility. In effect the legislation transformed Albertans from energy tenants in their own province to landlords of their own resources.) "For resource based Alberta, it is not an energy crisis, it is a time of energy opportunity," Lougheed told the legislature.

It was also an opportune time for an election. Advisors urged Lougheed "to jump the gun on Ottawa" and seek a mandate on whether the province's resources belonged to Albertans or to the federal government. When a leading Calgary civic official suggested to Lougheed that such an election might backfire, that Albertans were prepared to put the national interest ahead of their provincial self interest, Lougheed was defensive. "My constituents are Albertans first. They will follow me, they will follow me wherever I lead them." And, in an uncharacteristic gesture, he whipped his handkerchief from his breast pocket waving it like a flag and he added "I will never surrender to Ottawa."

Even though opinion polls indicated that Lougheed could win seventy of seventy-five seats he recognized that an election would prove nothing. It was also an ideal issue for the minority Liberal government to exploit. A federal election fought on the same resource ownership issue could only strengthen Pierre Trudeau's mandate. In fact, Justice Minister, Otto Lang, threatened to use the federal power to disallow the Lougheed legislation. Declared Lang: "No province can impose its own tariffs or export taxes. If the constitution does not make that clear I will fight to make the constitution say it."

Lang's statement is the kind of expression of Liberal arrogance that makes Lougheed wary of Trudeau's continued attempts at constitutional change. The Natural Resources Transfer Agreement of 1929 clearly defined: "It is desirable that the Province of Alberta should be placed in a position of equality with the other Provinces of Confederation with respect to the administration and control of its natural resources." That Act is the touchstone of Lougheed's defence.

In anticipation of a federal election the Trudeau government hastily assembled a new national energy policy which was designed to make Canada autonomous in energy. Trudeau pledged his support to the construction of a Mackenzie River valley pipeline which would carry gas from the Mackenzie valley and Alaska to the Canadian market. And, he introduced a bill to create a national petroleum corporation that would compete with private industry in the exploration for the processing of off-shore oil reserves. He also committed $40 million to study the technology needed to develop Alberta's vast Athabasca oil sands. On January 16, 1974, federal Energy Minister Donald Macdonald further announced that at long last a pipeline to carry Western oil would be built linking Sarnia to Montreal so that Alberta's reserves might be distributed to Quebec and the Atlantic provinces.

Lougheed responded with a $100 million program of his own directed towards an all out effort for Alberta to develop new technology to mine the tar sands. The research program called "Energy Breakthrough" would be devoted to finding ways of recovering 900 billion barrels of crude bitumen from which heavy crude oil could be synthetically manufactured. In his determination to develop the Alberta tar sands, some say Lougheed was inspired by Herman Kahn, consultant to the U.S. Atomic Energy Commission and director of the Hudson Institute in New York. With a reputation as a futuristic thinker, Kahn, at the time, proposed an international consortium to spend $20 billion to build sixteen plants which would employ imported Korean labourers to strip mine the oil bearing sand and would use hot water to separate the oil at the rate of 25,000 barrels a day. Lougheed says that he never for a moment considered Kahn's idea.

His jockeying for resource control earned Lougheed a new nickname – "the blue-eyed Arab of Saudi Alberta" – an appellation that Ottawa's Southam Press news bureau chief Charles Lynch incorporated into a satiric ditty "The Sheik of Cal-gary."

161

I'm the Sheik of Cal-gary
These sands belong to me
Trudeau says they're for all
Into my tent he'll crawl
Like Algeria did it to DeGaulle
The gas we've got today
We just don't fart away
Gas pains don't worry me
Cuz I'm the Sheik of Cal-gary. . . .

Lougheed, who seldom makes jokes himself, is a man who likes to laugh. And when Lynch performed the act in Edmonton, Lougheed appeared to be amused by the performance. The dispute took a less humorous turn as automobile bumper stickers appeared in Alberta bearing the message "Let the eastern bastards freeze in the dark." Although Lougheed personally deplored that sentiment at least two of his cabinet ministers were seen distributing the offending slogans.

Against this highly charged background Lougheed flew to Ottawa for private consultations with Prime Minister Trudeau on the eve of a crucial Federal-Provincial Conference on oil pricing. The seventy-five minute meeting, held at Trudeau's request, was the first of any consequence held between the two leaders since Lougheed's election. When the conference opened in the glare of television lights on January 21, it took the form of widening the fissures and fault lines that divided Canada.

Prime Minister Trudeau adopted a rigid stand in his opening statement, "We would all agree that a provincial government should receive a reasonable price for its resources," but he argued, "wouldn't it be reasonable for a province to receive continuing revenues which would give it the capacity in proportion to its population of say three or four times as much as other provinces?"

It was the semantic play on words that Lougheed enjoys and he argued "reasonable" value was not the same as "fair" value. "For the rest of Canada to ask Albertans to sell below fair value for any extended period of time is simply unreasonable."

While Lougheed may have defined the territory it was the Premier of Saskatchewan, Allan Blakeney, who defended it. As the various premiers staked out their positions, Lougheed was not prepared to be isolated publicly as the "fall guy" and left it to Blakeney to state the case of the oil producing provinces. Blakeney suggested that oil prices be approached in the same fashion as Medicare, under federal subsidy. "I mean the broad concept where Canadians should have access to essential goods and services with the cost shared on the ability to pay." Blakeney proposed a subsidy required to maintain a Canadian price well below the international level be provided through an equalization formula but like Lougheed he was not prepared "to assume the full cost of a subsidized Canadian price by undervaluing the oil itself." None of the premiers had any inkling as to what the federal government would propose and they were aghast when Energy Minister Donald Macdonald unveiled his pricing plan.

What Macdonald proposed in rudimentary fashion was a unilateral $2.00 a barrel increase and of that $2.00, 50 per cent would go to the federal treasury to cushion eastern consumers against the price hike. Of the balance, industry would get 16 per cent, the federal government 6 per cent, and the provinces 28 per cent. Alberta and Saskatchewan immediately rejected this arbitrary proposal as an encroachment on provincial rights. Blakeney called the plan "a rubber $2.00 bill." "You are asking taxpayers of Saskatchewan and Alberta to bear the burden but you are not asking Ontario taxpayers to make any contribution. This is not a policy at all, just a clear proposal for increasing regional disparity."

The distribution of revenue from the federal levy on Canadian oil exports was not resolved. In what Trudeau called a "typically Canadian solution" the conference came to an abrupt denouement. A temporary compromise was hammered out during a private luncheon behind closed doors at Trudeau's residence averting a constitutional showdown. The principals agreed to postpone any price increase for two months, until April 1, 1975. "Nothing," observed Lougheed, "has been agreed except to go along as at present." The conference was a turning point in federal-provincial relations: even if Lougheed had not won, the fact that he had forced a stalemate was evidence that he had not lost. On March 4, 1975, Trudeau and Lougheed met for a three hour luncheon and the Prime Minister appeared sympathetic for the first time to Lougheed's oil pricing proposals.

The first of what was to become a series of new oil pricing agreements was worked out on March 27 during a meeting of First Ministers at 24 Sussex Drive in Ottawa. Domestic crude would go up $2.40 to $6.50 a barrel with the federal government cutting back its oil export tax to keep the foreign price of Canadian oil at the $11.00 a barrel world price level. The new windfall to be generated in Alberta was not to be treated as provincial revenue and therefore would not be calculated in Canada's equalization formula in which the "have" provinces contribute to the support of the "have not" provinces. Instead, Alberta agreed to subsidize lower fuel prices in eastern Canada by agreeing to a domestic price that was $4.00 below the international level.

The increase in domestic prices resulted in new and complicated royalty schedules in Alberta. Lougheed announced the existing average royalty of 22 per cent would apply to the first $3.80 on a barrel of oil. Of the new increase Alberta would take 65 per cent on oil already in production and 35 per cent from new discoveries. The new levies left the industry with an average profit of $1.50 per barrel from the new prices. But the accord did not settle who should derive the ultimate benefit from the sale of natural resources: Ottawa or Edmonton.

Prime Minister Trudeau warned the producing provinces that the federal government intended to take its share of the $2 billion the new oil prices would produce. In letters to Lougheed and Blakeney, Trudeau made it clear that "any action [Alberta] may decide to take in respect of royalties would have to be without prejudice to our freedom of action as regards federal taxation." Lougheed did not appear to appreciate the implication of Trudeau's letter; Saskatchewan's Premier Allan Blakeney did. On March 22, 1974

Blakeney wrote to Trudeau "concerning corporate taxes. ... it would be useful to us if you could indicate what your thoughts are. ... do you have in mind not allowing provincial royalties as deductions from taxable income?"

Blakeney received no reply. The answer to his question came on May 6, 1974 when federal Finance Minister John Turner introduced his budget. The budget toughened the depletion allowance, reduced exploration write-offs and declared that provincial royalties were no longer deductible in the calculation of federal income tax. Under pre-budget conditions oil companies had about $123 million available for exploration, or about $2.00 for a per barrel equivalent. If enacted, the Turner budget combined with Alberta's new royalties and taxes would cut cash flow for exploration to $50 million, or a per barrel equivalent of 90 cents.

The budget did not accommodate the NDP's demands for a two price system on commodities and a cut in the mortgage rate, nor did it accede to Robert Stanfield's demands for the implementation of wage and price controls. Two days after the budget was introduced the Tories moved no confidence in the government. With the support of the NDP who were no longer prepared to sustain the minority Liberals, the life of the twenty-ninth Parliament was ended. For the first time in Canadian history a government was defeated over a budget and an election called for July 8.

That summer, as Richard Nixon's presidency was collapsing in the United States, Pierre Trudeau plunged into a campaign for his government's survival in Canada. Trudeau made it clear that the non-deductibility of royalties would continue to be firm Liberal policy. Oil companies began cancelling exploration plans and drilling rigs began moving out of Alberta in attempts to influence the outcome of the election. During a campaign visit to Calgary Trudeau was jeered by hostile demonstrators. But energy was only an issue in Alberta. In the rest of the country, opinion crystallized over the Conservative campaign pledge to introduce wage and price controls. Trudeau rejected the idea and on election day the voters believed him. The Liberals won a majority of seats, but for the second time in a row

Alberta went solidly Progressive Conservative, remaining the only province without a Liberal representative in the House of Commons.

With the Liberals solidly entrenched and Robert Stanfield's leadership of the Conservative party in ruins, Alberta emerged as Confederation's "newest problem child." Ged Baldwin interpreted the election results as an indication that "there is more potential for dissolution of the bonds of nationalism now in the Western provinces than there ever was in Quebec." And Calgary South MP Peter Bawden agreed. "There will be one helluva lot of Western separatism," he said on election night. "The only salvation we have left is the Premier of Alberta. He's going to have to come through and come through strong."

Within the next six months Lougheed would respond to Bawden's challenge in a way most observers never expected.

On Wednesday, July 24, 1974 Lougheed could be seen on the balcony of his legislative office deep in conversation with three cabinet ministers and his deputy provincial treasurer. The subject under confidential discussion was the financial situation of Pacific Western Airlines, Canada's third largest carrier. Despite a net worth of $40 million, the privately owned, Vancouver based company had issued shares to finance the purchase of two additional 737 jets for its fleet. In order to get the money to buy the two planes, they had to go public, therefore lowering the share values. But a declining market had reduced share values to about $7.75. But once the planes were bought, the shares should have gone back up to the $16.00 that the company's president Donald Watson thought they were worth.

There are those who think that Lougheed was convinced that British Columbia's NDP premier, Dave Barrett, was about to nationalize the airline and that Lougheed decided to pirate it for his own province.

There were two major considerations: one legal, the other philosophical. The Supreme Court had just ruled that the national regulatory agency, the Canadian Transport Commission, had a mandate to see that regional airlines served the public interest. The Aeronautics Act clearly demanded that

166

any organization with transportation interests (such as Alberta) must notify the CTC in advance of taking over other carriers. The second consideration centred around whether a Conservative government, committed to free enterprise, should intervene in the private sector.

The White Pass and Yukon Railway, Bethlehem Copper, John Lab (Labatt's) holdings, and the Canadian Development Corporation were all rumoured to be interested. In short, PWA was a steal for anyone with enough capital to buy all of its 400,000 shares, which PWA said had to be bought outright. This was one of the terms and conditions of sale to which both parties agreed.

Lougheed rejected advising the CTC. "There's no way Alberta will go down on bended knee to the federal government. If we ask we know what the answer will be. It will be 'no.' "

Don Getty reasoned that if British Columbia was indeed about to act, Alberta could not waste time gathering a group of private businessmen, backing them, and allowing them control and ownership of the airline. Not wanting to become involved in a bidding war with private interests, Lougheed decided to act secretly and quickly. No hint of the plan could be whispered in the legislature. The operation to acquire PWA was given a code name: *Patio Project*. Merv Leitch's law partner, Calgary lawyer Ritchie Love, was acquired as an agent. Love telephoned PWA on behalf of "a surprise Western group." His offer: $13.00 a common share or $38 million for the whole company. With the directors' acceptance Love identified his client. PWA's number two man, Rusty Harris, raised his hands in astonishment and mumbled "Jesus Christ." Watson and his board of directors decided to accept the offer.

Within forty-eight hours, 90 per cent of PWA's common shares changed hands in a blitz of market trading. On Friday, August 2, 1974, the identity of the airline's new owner was made public. In announcing the acquisition of PWA for $36.7 million Lougheed explained; "For a land locked province far from population centres, transportation is the key, and air transportation – particularly air freight – is a critical factor. One of Alberta's best known, long term prospects for

167

diversification is to capitalize upon its geography as the gateway province to the north. The acquisition of PWA will strengthen Alberta's ability to do so."

The government's decision to buy the airline, he added, was the result of "concern that recent take-over proposals and schemes threaten the continuation of PWA's capacity to expand and serve Alberta's growth needs. Almost 80% of PWA's revenue originates or terminates in Alberta. We wanted to assure that such a vital part of the transportation system would continue to reflect the needs and interests of the people of Alberta."

He was prepared for criticism of his interventionist policy but did not expect the degree of outrage that followed. The *Albertan* described the purchase as "disturbing. The wisdom of allowing pragmatism (and a bulging bankroll) to override sound political philosophy must remain in doubt." The new leader of Alberta's Liberal party, Calgary oil millionaire Nick Taylor, argued, "the task of a provincial government is to spur competition and treat all fairly." Lougheed was even chastised by members of his own party. One cabinet minister who had not been party to the Patio Project complained that "outsocializing the Socialists is no excuse and we will demand very urgent explanations." The *Toronto Globe and Mail* in a tongue-in-cheek editorial chortled, "they must be sewing the red flags in the basement of the Alberta legislature." In Victoria, Premier Barrett denied his government had been been interested in acquiring PWA and cheerfully dismissed Lougheed as "Peter the Red." Among some Albertans "PWA" had a new meaning: "Peter Wants All."

Saint John's Edmonton Report, however, rationalized the purchase not as an example of socialism but rather as a demonstration of

state capitalism. A kind of hybrid, descended from both Karl Marx and Adam Smith, in which the government neither owns the means of production – which the pure socialists favour – nor leaves them altogether alone – which the free enterprisers favour. What it does is use the power of tax, licence, law, and royalty, to raise its own capital, then intervenes as a participant in the

168

private sector of the economy, making itself partner of one company, competitor of another, owner of yet another. It does all this with a view to forcing changes in the economic structure.

Having acquired the airline, Lougheed professed that the government would not be directly involved in running it. Faced with various injunctions and demands for public hearings, Alberta set about to defend the purchase in the Supreme Court. Transport department officials in Ottawa did not look favourably on the acquisition arguing, "if the Supreme Court should rule Alberta home free, other provincial carriers could be snapped up by other governments."

(In February of 1976 while the matter was still before the courts, Alberta's Minister of Transporation, Dr. Hugh Horner, decided to move the airlines executive head office from Vancouver to Calgary. PWA's president Don Watson opposed the move as an unnecessary $6 million expense that would undermine PWA's profit motive. Watson, who once admitted "he talks too much", argued "the NDP had enough sense to leave the company alone, to make a profit sure, but to leave it alone." Watson, considered by many to be the best airline president in Canada – he was once invited to head Air Canada – was fired and replaced by Rhys Eaton. One year later on February 22, 1977 the Supreme Court supported Alberta's end run on the CTC and upheld the takeover of PWA. The Supreme Court ruling was based on the fact that the Crown is not bound by any law that does not specificially name it; that the airline was purchased by the Queen in the right of the province which parallels the federal government's ownership of Air Canada which is owned by the Queen in the right of Canada.)

Lougheed spent the late summer of 1974 on a Banff holiday. When he arrived back in Edmonton he had to face the grave and continuing uncertainty of federal tax measures. If the federal government was determined to reintroduce its May 6 budget, Lougheed warned it would "damage the confidence and strength of the petroleum industry in Canada." It was not easy to grasp Ottawa's intentions as the House of Commons opened on September 26. Finance Minister John Turner held out the faint hope that he

169

might revise his budget; he toured Western Canada seeking advice on the handling of the economy. But during a stopover in Edmonton he pointedly stated that his forthcoming budget was "not negotiable."

The Alberta legislature resumed its session on October 23, and while the PWA issue dominated the first few sitting days the federal government's budget provisions loomed menacingly.

On October 30, Lougheed had lunch with Prime Minister Trudeau in Ottawa and appealed for a more moderate approach to the deductibility of royalties in a new federal budget. The meeting was spiritless and the following day Lougheed was back in Edmonton to report to the legislature:

> The federal budget proposals of May 6th, 1974, insofar as they were defeated, became an essentially academic document, although they have hung like a cloud over our province since that date. . . . These tax measures would in fact seriously jeopardize the Canadian petroleum industry and the livelihood of many Canadians. To the extent the measures are implemented, we anticipate a decline in exploration, hence a reduction in Canadian reserves of both oil and natural gas. It is our assessment and our judgement that the consequence could well be an energy shortage in about eight years."

(In fact, Lougheed's fears were well founded; in the five months since the May budget was introduced *Oilweek* reported that 32 drilling rigs and 600 industry personnel had left Alberta for the United States.)

On Monday, November 18, 1974, Finance Minister John Turner reintroduced his May 6 budget and went some distance to make room for both provincial taxation and for the industry to retain risk capital. Where, in May, Turner proposed to allow a 30 per cent write-off of exploration expenditures, the November budget upheld the existing 100 per cent write-off. That represented a 26 per cent reduction in the industries $450 million tax bill. But on the contentious issue of royalties being deductible, Turner made no compromise. While acknowledging that "Western Canada is entitled to its place in the sun" and admitting that royalties have "traditionally been deductible as a business expense," he insisted "there are so many kinds of provincial charges and claims that it would be virtually impossible to draft workable legislation which could distinguish between bona fide royalties ... and other taxes and charges."

"We have done our part," Turner said shrewdly. "Now I appeal to the provinces, which have a responsibility to these industries and the Canadian people, to do their part." In bouncing the ball back into Alberta's court, Turner was asking the province to relinquish $200 million of an annual $1 billion windfall so that the oil and gas companies could continue to thrive. The federal position sought a financial compromise to the problem, but in Lougheed's view much more than simple economics was at stake. Under the constitution, resources belong to the provinces and the Turner budget represented an invasion of provincial jurisdiction.

Resonant with anger, Lougheed appeared on national television that night to denounce the budget as "the biggest rip-off of any province in Canada's history." And, as he promptly cancelled the national oil pricing agreement, he explained "the federal government has breached the oil pricing accord of last March, and we are no longer bound by it. The whole concept of taxing the resources of the province is going to destroy Confederation as we know it. It violates the whole spirit of Confederation."

The *Ottawa Journal* suspected that Lougheed had blown his cool, and in an editorial entitled "Alberta Must Compromise" it argued that Lougheed "owes it to Alberta to negotiate for the best possible deal–consistent with a reasonable understanding that there is enough revenue available for everyone to prosper." Even the *Calgary Herald* suggested "Alberta should step back a bit, and allow the industry to receive the extra $1 to $2 million a year that ... it says it needs to do the exploration and development to find reserves." But Lougheed was adamant, he was not about to compromise.

In a letter to Prime Minister Trudeau on November 22 Lougheed wrote,

The point that must be emphasized is that we are concerned about a depleting – a rapidly depleting – resource. We view the proceeds from this resource as a capital asset, the proceeds of which must be reinvested if this province is to maintain its economic stability. Under the [March 27 oil pricing] accord the needs of Canada and Alberta as a producing province were integrated. Your government's actions now require my government to review its entire range of policy alternatives concerning both the future development of this province and the maintenance of a viable oil and gas industry. The provincial leaders unanimously and strongly reaffirmed their responsibility for mining taxes and oil and gas royalties derived from provincial ownership of resources. Until the federal May budget proposals, this principle had always been recognized by federal governments.

Relations between Alberta and Ottawa had not deteriorated so rapidly since the constitutional confrontations of the Aberhart era in the 1930s and with the federal announcement on November 22 that crude oil exports to the United States would be phased out by 1982 they hit rock bottom. Acting on a National Energy Board forecast of insufficient production to meet Canada's domestic needs, Energy Minister Don Macdonald unveiled a new formula to determine export levels in the future. The current rate of 900,000 barrels a day would be reduced to 650,000 within six months and to 200,000 within two years.

Lougheed attacked the cuts as a "marginal contribution" to heading off an energy shortage. "It is difficult to understand, but the recent federal budget measures which worked against a healthy, vigorous industry, were taken by the federal government with the full knowledge of this report. If Canadians read this situation as one which can be solved by reducing exports, they are seriously misreading the NEB report." He argued that a fair price and a reasonable level of taxation were required to encourage the industry to search for major new oil sources, be they in Alberta or in the Arctic.

On November 27, Prime Minister Trudeau raised the prospect of an historic constitutional battle with Alberta. The Lougheed administration, Trudeau concluded, ought to have recognized as early as March that Alberta's oil royalties "would be going too far, because they didn't leave a large enough share for the federal government." During a ninety minute speech ending the budget debate in the Commons, the Prime Minister disputed Lougheed's claim that the provinces were not adequately forewarned about the radical change in the federal government's taxation policy. The Prime Minister argued that total disallowance was the only way Ottawa could maintain its share of oil taxes since any other method would have fallen far short of giving the federal government an equitable share. "I hope this will help to clear up the air that in some way we have broken the oil price agreement," said the Prime Minister as he asked Alberta to compromise so that the stalemate might be settled.

One week later in Edmonton, Alberta's Intergovernmental Affairs Minister, Don Getty, recovering from a gall bladder operation, joined the war of words and in a speech urged Albertans to "fight an outright battle for the future. If Ottawa does not alter its ways, I would not be part of an Alberta government that would not fight with every weapon at its command," Getty told a constituency meeting. "Maybe we will lose. Maybe they can confiscate our dreams and our future, but if they do, let's make sure it is only after we have fought them every inch of the way."

The next night Lougheed was in Calgary for a nominating meeting in his constituency. He invited critics who were calling for the province to offer concessions to the federal government to spell out the concessions in exact terms. "I will never be part of any form of capitulation to Ottawa on the resource question," he told a hushed crowd of 400. "There is no way this government is going to let the futures of present and future Albertans go down the drain." Careful to avoid a public confrontation with oil industry officials present at the meeting, questions from the floor were prohibited, but Lougheed agreed to meet privately with anyone who wanted to question his stand.

The next day Energy Minister Donald Macdonald reacted intemperately to both speeches in the House of Commons and described Lougheed as being "vicious" and Getty as "dripping with venom." After the hysterical exchange Lougheed moved to defuse the situation. On December 12 he loosened the knot around the neck of the petroleum industry by announcing a "revised" and "modified" royalty and corporate tax plan for Alberta. The new Alberta Petroleum Exploration Plan returned $130 million of the province's corporate tax on royalties to the industry. This combined with other modifications increased the oil companies' cash flow from 80 cents to $2.20 per barrel.

"The essential thing," gloated the *Ottawa Journal*, "is that Mr. Lougheed has compromised. He has had the wisdom to back down .... to use the perhaps unfortunate terminology of the cold war, Alberta has blinked." But was it compromise? Those who at the time suggested that Lougheed caved in to Ottawa neglected to appreciate the price Lougheed demanded for "compromise." So that the province might be reimbursed for its concessions, Lougheed also proposed a further $2.00 barrel increase in the price of oil, raising the price from $6.50 to $8.50 per barrel as soon as the winter was over. The long winter of energy discontent was far from over. The international oil cartel involved in the Syncrude consortium entered the struggle for the control of Canadian resources, and Lougheed found himself forced into a morganatic alliance with Ottawa which would contribute to a landmark decision in Canadian energy development.

CHAPTER X

A short fuse leading to highly volatile political charges that would resound through the country for three months was set on December 4, 1974. On that day one of the four partners in the Syncrude oil extraction plant, Atlantic Richfield, announced it was pulling out of its 30 per cent share of the consortium because of ballooning construction costs. Imperial Oil, Cities Service Athabasca Ltd., and Gulf Oil, immediately declared they would have to receive an additional $1 billion in funding or they would close down the project. Syncrude's avuncular president, Frank Spragins, explained that because of inflation, increased labour costs, and unexpected problems related to the geology of the construction site, the original $960 million estimate had more than doubled to $2.2 billion. "The present cost estimate is simply beyond the collective ability of the three partners to carry on without additional firm commitments," said Spragins.

Canadian nationalist, Mel Hurtig, former chairman of the Committee for an Independent Canada, immediately suggested that "either Canadians are once again being snowed by another multi-billion dollar con job or the petroleum industry in this country is so grossly incompetent they should be politely – or otherwise – asked to leave the country."

Lougheed himself expressed doubt as to how costs could have escalated so fast and before leaving for a Californian vacation he contracted five independent economists to assess and evaluate Syncrude's affairs and to re-evaluate the economics of the project. But more than simple economics was at stake. The tar sands represent the future petroleum wealth of Canada; the quantities of heavy oil deposits locked away in northeastern Alberta are enormous, bigger than Saudi Arabia's proven reserves: 26 billion barrels.

In Lougheed's absence Attorney General Merv Leitch and two other ministers, Hugh Horner and Gordon Miniely, moved to entice Ottawa to invest in the project by arguing that since the rest of Canada's need for the oil from the Athabasca tar sands was more urgent than Alberta's, since virtually all the benefits from the project "would accrue to central Canada," the rest of Canada should put up the money to keep Syncrude afloat. But their statements were more plaintive than truculent; collapse of the project would have a tremendous adverse psychological effect on the province.

When Lougheed had originally announced the Syncrude development on September 18, 1973 he emphasized that if it did not proceed it would be detrimental to Alberta and to Canada, not only in the substantial number of lost jobs but also that oil sands development in Canada would be severely damaged if the search was diverted to the Colorado oil shales. In his original announcement Lougheed also revealed the creation of the Alberta Energy Company to help financing: the AEC invited the public to participate in the project as joint equity investors. The Syncrude project, designed to deliver 4.5 billion barrels of oil a year, was an essential development for Canada's self-sufficiency in energy.

During the last week of January, 1975, as the legislature opened for a winter session Albertan and federal cabinet ministers held a series of meetings in Edmonton in an eleventh hour bid to save the project. Their independent studies verified Syncrude's forebodings. Energy Minister Macdonald indicated that Ottawa was prepared to come up with $200 million, that Syncrude's financial problems could be resolved, but that it would take time: that a two or three month extension to the January 31 deadline was required. And Lougheed told the legislature on January 29, "one option is not open, and that option is that the government is in no way prepared to bow to any ultimatum." The unrelenting pressure on Lougheed during the winter of 1974-75 aged him visibly. His rumpled brown hair became almost grey; crows-feet appeared around his twinkling blue eyes. "His soul seems as clenched as his jawline," wrote Christina Newman in the *Globe and Mail* at the time, "and the prime impression he leaves is of a man under great tension handling it with implacable resolution."

A last ditch attempt to reach an agreement was arranged for February 2 at the International Inn near the Winnipeg airport. During twelve hours of tough and often strained negotiations the three governments bankrolled a rescue operation. Westerners, oilmen and politicians alike had long since decided that loans – guaranteed, no interest or low interest – were not to be entertained. No, it was equity – risk equity – or nothing. In this area Lougheed and the oil interests were in accord. Syncrude, after all, was not a manufacturing company. It was a holding operation prepared to supply its products to its consortium members only in relation to their equity. Accounts of the meeting indicate that Ontario originally intended to invest only $50 million; by the end of the day Premier William Davis had doubled the ante. The national government agreed to exempt Syncrude from income tax levies on its profits in Alberta, and agreed to allow the consortium to sell its oil at the international price.

When the bargaining was all over Macdonald concluded that "one of the interesting political consequences – political observations – is that a Federal-Alberta relationship which had been very much at arm's length and very intermittent was conducted with far greater cordiality than for some time."

It is difficult to call winners and losers of such complicated tripartite games, but it is apparent that Alberta emerged the big winner with the oil interests in second place. The basic terms of the final agreement announced in

Ottawa and Edmonton on February 4, 1975, were these:

1. Imperial Oil, Gulf Oil and Cities Service would, with $1.4 billion invested, retain 70 per cent equity in Syncrude;
2. For a $300 million investment for federal government would receive 15 per cent equity;
3. For a $100 million share Ontario would receive 5 per cent equity;
4. For $200 million Alberta would receive a convertible debenture, getting 10 per cent of Syncrude's equity with a long-term potential of owing 40 per cent of the entire venture;
5. Alberta maintained its position as owner of the resource by continuing to receive 50 per cent of Syncrude's net profit by way of royalties.

In the House of Commons the NDP energy critic, Tommy Douglas, called the deal the "greatest sell-out of our national resources in the history of Canada." Alberta's Liberal leader, Nick Taylor, likened the oil companies to having "married the landlord's daughter: you stop paying rent, get the first pork chop and the best bed in the house." Critics aside, in a very real sense Lougheed got what he went after: a large piece of a pie which would have been a long time baking had he not opted for some foreign fingers in the kitchen; a hefty headstart to industrial diversification; and the ability to assure the viability of oil sands exploration to other leaseholders. (In harsh terms, Syncrude was Peter Lougheed's place to fail. But it hasn't and he didn't. The most expensive oil in the world started flowing from the extraction plant at Mildred Lake July 31, 1978.)

In May, 1978, *Fortune* magazine quoting a computer study conducted by Gerry May shows "Alberta doing the best by far with a gain of $468 million; the companies also show a gain of $343 million, the federal government is minus $683 million. The precision of these figures is questionable, but the proportional distribution of rewards among the participants seems reasonably reliable." The C.D. Howe Institute has stressed that the most straightforward conclusion drawn from the Syncrude experience is "the fact that there is a constructive role to be played by governments as risk sharers in cases where there is a sense of national urgency. ... The key policy task is to select the most economic projects and then to ensure that these projects get all the support they need .... whether that support comes from private enterprise or from the political sector."

The story of the Syncrude negotiations became the subject of a critical book *The Tarsands: Syncrude and the Politics of Oil* by Larry Pratt who suggested that "Lougheed was literally acting as Syncrude's political strategist, advising the group on tactics, setting up meetings and trying to smooth the way to Ottawa." Pratt's account, which admittedly makes many cogent points, suggests Lougheed signed a "sweetheart deal" with the oil companies and in the final analysis, Alberta emerged a loser. On the latter point Pratt may be likened to a hunter in search of big game who has been seduced by rabbit tracks. His research was overtaken by events and rendered obsolete before the book reached the bookstores and Pratt later admitted as much.

(The CBC produced a television docu-drama loosely based on Pratt's book but in the winter of 1976 decided to postpone televising the program. The attendant publicity surrounding the network's decision to delay the show gave rise to suspicions in Lougheed's mind that he had somehow been maligned. In a letter to CBC president Al Johnson, Lougheed warned that "if the program depicts the Premier as having improperly, improvidently or incompetently administered his office and trust in connection with the Syncrude negotiations we will promptly recommend the commencement of an action for defamation." The program (advertised as "Tarzan" in one TV guide) was eventually televised nationally on Monday, September 12, 1977. It proved to be neither a drama nor a documentary. Crucial facts were ignored, attention to detail was ignored (the actor portraying Lougheed depicted him as foul-mouthed), in fact, the entire program should have been ignored as a cheap caricature. But Lougheed did not ignore it. Watching the program with his daughter who asked, "Is that what really happened?" Lougheed was reduced to tears of anger. The following day he charged that the TV program unfairly attacked his character and reputation and ridiculed his office. He promptly slapped the CBC with a lawsuit for $2 million in punitive damages and $750,000 in general damages. The case remains before the Alberta courts, and if Lougheed should win, it would set a precedent for Canadian television productions.)

On February 7, 1975, the government broke with protocol and invited guests to crowd the floor of the legislative chamber as Finance Minister Gordon Miniely read what observers considered to be an election budget.

During the speech Government House Leader, Lou Hynd-man, sent a note to the Speaker, Gerry Amerongen; "Since the government changed precedent by having people on the floor as guests, shouldn't government members stand and applaud on the conclusion of the speech?"

Amerongen rejected the idea with characteristic humour: "Some opposition members aren't entirely happy," he scrawled on the note back to Hyndman. "What could I do if some of them claimed the right to stand up and boo?"

There was little to boo in the $2.4 billion budget. It increased spending for health, education, and welfare and gave Albertans the lowest provincial tax rate in Canada. As Miniely pointed out the budget represented a complete reversal of the government's financial position in three and one half years – from a position of dwindling revenues and increasing borrowing requirements to the strongest financial position of any government in Canada. In fact, Alberta's position was so strong that Miniely completely disregarded $600 million in anticipated revenue in compiling his figures.

The budget also announced creation of an Alberta Heritage Trust Fund to "ensure the prosperity of the future generations of Albertans." Tax cuts announced were less than the interest earned on the provincial surplus and the *Edmonton Journal* on February 8, 1975, was less than enthusiastic:

it indicates a self-satisfied administration, devoid of fresh ideas and apparently unwilling to do serious battle with our problems. There is nothing remarkable, after all, about cutting taxes and increasing expenditures . . . . when you have more money around than you know what to do with.

The week-end following the introduction of the budget Peter Lougheed met in Calgary with Prime Minister Trudeau who had come to Alberta to open the Canada Winter Games in Lethbridge. Lougheed later explained that the meeting with Trudeau left him convinced that the Prime Minister would not believe Albertans were solidly behind the provincial government's oil pricing and energy policies. So on St. Valentine's Day, February 14, 1975, sporting a yellow rose in his lapel Lougheed strode into the legislature and launched into possibly the best speech of his political career. In a spirited ninety minute review of his government's accomplishments he attacked the opposition as "constant carping critics," an attack that was loudly refuted by Social Credit member Albert Ludwig. Undeterred by Ludwig's outburst Lougheed said that he needed to be certain that he had the "full confidence of the people" before negotiating higher oil prices in April. He ended his speech by calling a snap election, the third winter election in Alberta's history, for March 26. In holding the vote he defined the issues in terms very few could reject. "You're not just voting Progressive Conservative when you vote for us," he repeated during the campaign. "A vote for Alberta means a vote for Confederation. It's time for Albertans to stand together."

The NDP attempted to fight the election on the Syncrude issue. The Social Credit advocated a conciliatory stance with Ottawa and complained about Lougheed's executive abuse of power. And, the Liberals opposed Lougheed's industrialization policies. The Premier ignored all criticism and reasonably suggested that he needed a fifty seat mandate – one more seat than he had at dissolution – to strengthen his hand in seeking higher oil prices at the impending federal-provincial conference. "I will be there alone," he said, "I need to know that you are behind me." Who would expect Albertans to vote against their own interests? When the polls closed on election day the Conservative juggernaut moved with astounding speed. Within one hour the Tories had accumulated the largest share of the popular vote ever recorded in Alberta (63 per cent) and had elected sixty-nine members. The opposition parties were reduced to six seats: four Social Credit, one NDP and one independent. Both the Social Credit and Liberal party leaders were defeated.

Two weeks after the election Lougheed reshaped his front benches with a wholesale shuffle of his cabinet. Every minister save one was shifted to a new portfolio. Deputy Premier Dr. Hugh Horner was moved out of Agriculture and named to head a new Department of Transportation. Merv Leitch became Minister of Finance; his former job as Attorney General was filled by Jim Foster. Don Getty was shifted from Intergovernmental Affairs to the Energy portfolio replacing Bill Dickie who did not seek re-election. Lou Hyndman went from Education to Intergovernmental Affairs. Neil Crawford became Minister of Labour replacing Bert Hohol who was given responsibility for Advanced Education and Manpower. Crawford's old job of Health and Social Development was split between Gordon Miniely and Helen Hunley. Bill Yurko the former Minister of the Environment and Dave Russell, Minister of Housing and Public Works, swapped portfolios.

Bob Dowling was put in charge of a restructured Department of Business Development and Tourism.

Roy Farran who had been brought into the cabinet as Minister of Telephones in the spring of 1973 – and who was convicted of impaired driving shortly after – was ordered off alcohol by the Premier as a condition to being given the job of Solicitor General. Farran, who describes himself as a relic of Kiplingesque times, was by far the most colourful member in a generally dull group of ministers. A major in the British army he had served with the CID in Palestine before the creation of Israel. His exploits in the Middle East were the subject of a book he wrote called *Winged Victory*. He had run and been defeated as a Conservative candidate under Winston Churchill's leadership in the 1950 British election. He came to work in Canada as a newspaper reporter shortly after.

The fresh slate of new ministers included Julian Koziak, a

boyish looking barrister, who as Minister of Education proposed in his first major address that the best way to help students to learn would be to simplify the English language; specifically, Koziak cited sounds represented by the letters *k* and *f* and complained of the many different ways they can be used.

Also named were Dick Johnston as Minister of Municipal Affairs; Graham Harle, Minister of Consumer and Corporate Affairs; and a genial farmer, Marvin Moore, as Minister of Agriculture. Al Adair was named Minister of Recreation, Parks and Wild Life, and Allan Warrack became Minister of Utilities and Telephones. Dallas Schmidt, Stewart McCrae, and Robert Bogle were all named Ministers Without Portfolio. The one noted exception to the massive shake-up was Horst Schmid who retained his reponsibility for Culture and was given the added responsibility of Government Services.

Lougheed's feud with the federal government over oil pricing did not figure conspicuously or contentiously when he arrived in Ottawa on April 9, 1975, for the federal-provincial conference. He had found an unaccustomed ally: Pierre Elliott Trudeau. In his opening remarks to the conference the Prime Minister signalled an escalation in the price of gas and oil. "We cannot expect Alberta to go on, year after year, selling its oil to Canadians at a price which is far below that which they could get by exporting it. We cannot expect those who search for oil – whether they be Canadians or others to look for it and develop it in Canada – if our prices are far below those in other countries."

Although a specific price increase was not mentioned, Trudeau's remarks went too far for a cautious William Davis who was about to face Ontario voters in a provincial general election. When Lougheed and Trudeau struck a conciliatory attitude, Davis opposed any increase in the domestic price of oil and gas. "If the government of Canada ... permits a rise in the price of crude oil in this time of economic stress, it is directly denying thousands of people in Ontario the right to employment." Davis complained that Alberta and Ottawa were fattening their treasuries at Ontario's expense. And the *Toronto Star* backed Davis's claim by suggesting any price increase would curb industrial production and put 38,000 people out of work. Davis was joined in his opposition by British Columbia, Manitoba, New Brunswick, and Nova Scotia. In an even division of the provinces, Newfoundland, Quebec, Prince Edward Island, and Saskatchewan supported Alberta's notion of an increase. In short, Davis provoked a stalemate. The meeting failed to produce any agreement and Trudeau warned that if there was no compromise by the end of June the federal government itself would work out an agreement with the producing provinces for higher oil and gas prices for the country.

Ontario only managed to postpone higher oil prices. If anything came out of the meeting, it was the recognition that Canadian oil would start a price climb to an international level. And, on June 23, when federal Finance Minister John Turner presented his budget to the House of Commons, the federal government increased the well-head price of oil from $6.50 to $8.00 per barrel – $4.00 below the world price. The price of natural gas was increased to ninety-seven cents per thousand cubic feet – more than four times the January 1974 average of only twenty-two cents. Turner also introduced an immediate ten cent per gallon hike on the excise tax on the price of gasoline to encourage conservation. Facing the prospect of collecting an additional $500 million in annual royalties Lougheed exulted that "the two governments involved are co-operating in the best interests of Canada." "Our assessment," he said amid desk thumping applause in the legislature, "is that there has been very significant progress in the continuing negotiations between Ottawa and Alberta on energy matters. The petroleum industry at last has a sense of stability."

CHAPTER XI

During the spring of 1975
rumours of widespread and reckless spending by the then
Department of Culture, Youth and Recreation drifted
through the legislative press gallery but nothing could be
substantiated. Len Grant, a sanguine, youthful CHQT radio
reporter, had learned from a source within the department
that "money was being pushed out by the bucket to buy
votes." Grant set out to prove it. He invented a fictitious
Gaelic language school and above the name of one C. A.
(Angus) McTaggart applied to the department for an
operating grant for the school's nineteen imaginary
students. Heading the list of those enrolled was the name
Margaret Thatcher, the leader of the British Conservative
party. Grant handed his application to a legislative guide to
be delivered to the office of the Minister, Horst Schmid.

Schmid had once generously donated $4,800 to keep the
Edmonton Press Club from bankruptcy. Ironically, the club's
president was the same Len Grant now bent on proving that
Schmid's department did not know who or what it was funding. Conscious that his application constituted a fraud,
Grant took measures to protect himself from prosecution; he
swore an affidavit stating that his intent was not criminal;
his prank was designed to "point out the deficiencies in
handling government grants."

Within a month Grant received not one but two cheques.
The first, for $285, was for the school's operations. The sec-

185

ond, for $2,000, was unsolicited. A letter from Schmid commended the Gaelic Association for "its efforts in the promotion of Alberta's cultural heritage," and explained the additional funds were for the acquisition of equipment and facilities.

Armed with the evidence he had sought, Grant called on Schmid late one Sunday evening for an explanation. The ebullient Schmid, who was born in Germany in 1933, often comes across as a Bavarian cliché. Schmid emigrated to Canada in 1952, worked in the mines at Yellowknife, studied accounting and got into the export, restaurant, and broadcasting businesses. He was among the earliest of Lougheed's supporters and, with the 1971 election, became the first-post war immigrant to be appointed to a Canadian cabinet. Once described as the "Daddy Warbucks" of the arts in Alberta, Schmid earned a reputation as the most enlightened cultural affairs minister in the country. His most obvious failing – if indeed it is a failing – is that he approaches even the most insignificant problems with the same unbridled energy and attention that he devotes to major ones, which is one of the reasons he spends almost eighteen hours a day at his job.

At first, Schmid did not seem to appreciate the implication of Grant's investigations. But as it became clear, he responded, "Surely there was another way for you to find this out." In his defence Schmid argued that "to deceive someone knowingly is not within the character of most Albertans. If the news media has to stoop to these measures I'm afraid it would reflect on the honesty and sincerity, hard work and truthfulness of every single ethno-cultural group in the province." Keeping his eyes on his desk Schmid added, "I despise a person who would cast that kind of reflection on ethno-cultural groups in Alberta."

On Monday morning, May 5, Grant went public with his story. During his CHQT broadcast he reported that "not one enquiry was made as to the existence of the school. One telephone call to Provincial Companies Branch would have disclosed no such organization as the St. George's Gaelic Language School exists." Grant's revelations led to an investigation by the provincial Auditor General. His *1975*

Report determined that Schmid was responsible "for having created an environment in which there was a complete lack of internal control . . . a situation which resulted in complete mismanagement . . . and enabled . . . assets and services paid for with public funds to be . . . used for personal purposes." Although there were demands for Schmid's resignation Lougheed excused his Minister explaining, "it simply isn't practical for a minister to have full responsibility." While Lougheed acknowledged the principle of ministerial responsibility, he argued that "total accountability" was "impractical."

"There was no evidence that Schmid personally profited from the situation," explained a department official "and Lougheed recognized that Schmid was more of an asset than a liability. He was afraid to fire him, it would have undermined the ethnic support base that Schmid had built for the party." It could also be said this was an example of Lougheed's loyalty to those who support and work for him.

At about the same time two reporters with the CBC in Edmonton, Dave McCrady and Ron Shorvoyce, were investigating irregularities in the Department of Agriculture. The pair had learned that the deputy minister of agriculture, Dr. Glenn Purnell, had profited from the sale of bull semen to Brazil. Purnell, a Cardston rancher, was a major owner of Swiss Brown Bulls, and during an economic mission to South America, he proposed a gift of bull semen to the government of Brazil in hopes of interesting the Brazilians in starting an artificial insemination program. He then sold some semen from his own bulls to the Alberta government which was financing the gift. When the shipment was assembled by the Canadian Stock Breeders Association the CBC learned that two-thirds of it came from animals owned by Purnell. This contravened an Alberta law which prohibits government employees from being paid for "transacting any business connected with official duties." A subsequent inquiry held in the summer of 1975 by the provincial auditor revealed that Purnell received $11,000 for his cut on the semen deal and had been paid twice as much for his stock of bull semen as were other contributing stock breeders. A judicial inquiry later found the deputy minister was "guilty of misconduct," and Purnell was fired. As a result of the CBC investigation the government drew up a code of ethics spelling out restrictions on personal business activities of senior civil servants. (McCrady had earlier turned up information that Purnell's brother, Delbert, had been paid more than $7,000 as a consultant during a Middle East tour of Alberta Export Agency officials. McCrady charged that the department had tried to conceal Delbert Purnell's identity by issuing the cheque to a consulting firm that was not legally established until five months after the trip was completed.)

During the course of their investigation of the Purnell affair, McCrady and Shorvoyce also uncovered evidence to suggest that the Agriculture Minister, Dr. Hugh Horner, had participated through a business partner in a government financed feed mill pelleting operation. Royblu Feeds had built its plant adjacent to property owned by Horner in Barrhead with the assistance of a $200,000 loan from the Alberta Opportunity Company. When Royblu decided to expand Horner transferred the title of 3.37 acres adjacent to the plant to it. The plant later went into receivership. Horner denied any financial involvement with the company and explained that the land transfer was, in actuality, payment of a personal debt to one of Royblu's directors, John Litke.

Horner said that to save legal costs and simplify the transaction the land went directly to Royblu Feeds and he accused the CBC of "mafia-like investigative tactics." At a public meeting in Barrhead, Horner launched a stinging attack on what he called "the CBC - NDP alliance". "If a federally funded organization like the CBC sets itself up as the official opposition to the province of Alberta, where are we, and what kind of banana republic do we live in? I say it very frankly . . . the rest of the media in the rest of the province, including CBC Calgary, have been fair. But I will never appear on a CBC program with Mr. McCrady again because he distorts . . . he deliberately distorts."

Horner, too, could be accused of distortion for he omitted to point out that at the time the CBC did not have a television station in Calgary and even today the city's private television stations do not have legislative bureaus in Edmonton. He may have added that examples of close and searching scrutiny of the government are the exception rather than the rule; a form of captive journalism is practised daily by the Alberta news media; appreciation of Peter Lougheed is constantly promoted. Lougheed learned very early in his career that the press is a business and like any business it could be manipulated.

There are several ways a politician can apply pressure to interfere effectively with the flow of information and news to the public. As outlined in Hillier Kreigbaum's 1972 *Pressures on the Press* they include attempts by the politician to "influence the news itself, influence reporters with all of their individual mores, prejudices and ideals, influence the news gatekeepers – editors and proprietors, and, to influence the ultimate news consumers especially those with indelible stereotypes." Lougheed employs all of these methods in managing information and has invented a few of his own, for in his view, "the basis of politics is communicating with the public and to do that you must depend on the press."

As early as June, 1965 – three months after he became leader of the Conservative party – Lougheed had set up a communications committee "to establish effective publicity channels to the news media and to continually consider and evaluate" his public image. The committee was also authorized to establish a program for "accelerated public exposure" of Lougheed in the provincial media. He began by cultivating the owners and the managers of the major private television stations – the ones with the ratings – and publishers and managing editors of the major newspapers.

A former associate editor of the *Edmonton Journal*, Homer Ramage, recounts one day Lougheed invited himself to sit in on the paper's daily editorial conference, the conference at which editors decide which issues of the day merit editorial treatment. Ramage denied the request but couldn't help wondering where Lougheed "got the nerve to propose something so outrageous." "He was brash and I guess he was feeling his oats at just having won the leadership." Not to be discouraged by Ramage's refusal, Lougheed adopted a

189

"learning posture" as he got to know the "gatekeepers" and media heavies. As a result of his efforts he enjoys the most uncritical press of any politican in Canada.

The tradition of co-operation he established with CFCN's Gordon Love early in 1965 is maintained. Even though the Calgary television station is now owned by Maclean-Hunter, its president Ted Chapman is counted among Lougheed's personal friends. Dr. G. R. A. Rice who owns CFRN television in Edmonton is chairman of Alberta's Government House Foundation and is a conspicuous guest at most government functions. Although revision of Alberta's archaic liquor advertising laws had been under discussion for some time, it may be no coincidence that one of Lougheed's first pieces of legislation permitted beer and liquor advertising on Alberta's TV and radio stations – advertising which contributes an additional quarter of a million dollars to station revenues in the province.

Television ordained Lougheed's election victory and he uses it regularly to "communicate" directly with his constituents. The most obvious manipulation of television is the series "Conversation with the Premier" alternately produced at CFRN and CFCN. The timing of the program is at Lougheed's discretion. Its producer CFCN's Hugh Dunn who also serves as a media advisor to the Premier admits the program was instituted especially for Lougheed after 1971. Dunn describes it as "a prestige vehicle for our stations." "The Premier has a standing invitation to appear on a free-time telecast five times a year where he can explain to a panel of newsmen the policies of his government." A prime time program with a potential viewing audience of 2 million, "Conversation with the Premier" is nothing more than a thinly disguised commercial for the Conservative party. To be fair, it is never identified as a "news and public affairs" production. One television critic, Barry Westgate, assessed Lougheed's performance on one such show and concluded "style is the key – Lougheed never bites back. He debates. Lougheed often doesn't straight-forwardly answer either, but then he spikes everyone's guns by simply admitting it. That his continued neutrality is blithely accepted by the media corps and by the public is a tribute to the painstaking practicality of the man and his unflappable intelligence. He exudes confidence with a reasoning edge. He is one of those 'Here's what I believe, Jim' people who always get the last word simply because they take great pains to seem not to. His persuasiveness will not be shaken by any kind of galling situation."

Marshall McLuhan, the oracle of the electronic media, accounts for Lougheed's success on television this way: "TV will not take a face, it has to have a mask. Lougheed resembles a lot of other people and on television comes across as the echo of a lot of other faces. It's a good corporate face," say McLuhan, "and on TV Lougheed strives for a role rather than a goal."

Before coming to power, Lougheed had the distinct advantage of knowing that most media outlets in Alberta were predisposed to a change of government. Key media executives quickly came to know him on a first name basis. "They know him and like him and that's obvious by the tone they set in their newsrooms. Negative reaction to Lougheed is not appreciated and any reporter who is unnecessarily hostile to his administration has a difficult time of it," says a veteran legislative reporter.

Former CFRN legislative reporter, Doug Shepherd, reveals that he was often instructed to do insignificant stories like "the tenth anniversary of Lougheed's election as an MLA, the first anniversary of Lougheed's election to a second term, on his birthday." Shepherd claims he even received a memo from his boss, Bruce Hogle, stating that Grant Notley, the NDP leader, was not to be given exposure on CFRN's highly rated 6.00 p.m. "Eyewitness" news show. The station's news and public affairs manager, Bruce Hogle, discounts Shepherd's charge as "an outright lie." "I go after Lougheed as hard as any politician," says Hogle who denies that Dr. Rice sets editorial policy. But, Shepherd's predecessor, Geoff Davy, says while he never received any memos "it was an unwritten law at CFRN that Notley would be downplayed. The NDP's bona fide news stories rarely made the 6.00 p.m. news at CFRN. They were always relegated to the night final show which doesn't have half as many viewers. Self-censorship silences as effectively as government decree." Mark Byington, now an executive assistant in Social Credit Opposition Leader Bob Clark's office, says that during his stint as CFRN's legislative reporter it was understood that "political parties received coverage in proportion to their numerical representation which at that time meant for every forty-nine minutes of news devoted to Lougheed, Social Credit would get twenty-five, the NDP one."

The media tends to support so much of the established order because it fundamentally plays on Lougheed's team. For this reason, the disclosure of government failing is somehow equated in the public consciousness as being anti-Albertan. The widespread belief that Lougheed can do no wrong surfaces from time to time even among individual members of the press corps. It is not unusual to see reporters from rural media outlets proudly wearing Lougheed compaign badges in his presence. On one occasion a network reporter assigned from Toronto to cover an Alberta election campaign was required to work with a local Edmonton cameraman. During the kick-off campaign speech in Sedgewick, Lougheed, carried away by his oratory, stepped backwards and tripped off of an elevated podium. When the reporter inquired of the novice cameraman whether he had filmed the incident the cameraman was astonished: "You really don't expect me to film anything like that that could embarrass our Premier, would you?"

By introducing television to the Alberta legislature on his own terms – by making it difficult for cameras to focus on the opposition – he is assured direct exposure to "the news consumer." And Lougheed is not above orchestrating his own coverage in the house. During a speech being delivered by his Finance Minister the Premier noticed that the CBC's cameras were trained on something other than the front benches. He promptly dispatched a note to reporter Frank Dolphin urging him to direct his cameras toward the minister because "this is important to Edmonton."

It's not the only time Lougheed has brought the weight of his office to bear on the publicly owned CBC. A producer for CBC Edmonton's local television news show, Gerry Olson, received a call one evening from the Premier who complained that coverage of the closing of one legislative session did not include a recap of his government's achievements. Olson suggested the Premier stick to running the province and leave editorial decisions regarding the news to the newsroom.

"Any editorial criticism evokes a phone call from Lougheed quite rapidly," admits Cleo Mowers the publisher of the *Lethbridge Daily Herald*. "He takes it upon himself personally to correct what he considers editorial slights." Mowers is philosophical about Lougheed's interference. "In the political game he's entitled to do whatever he can to obtain a good press. He plays the game better than many of the papers. It's up to the media to be on guard against what he's trying to do, and it's sad that some editors have found themselves caught up in his promotion against all rules of professionalism." Mowers diplomatically declines to name such editors but one obvious choice would be Andrew Snaddon, the editor of the *Edmonton Journal*.

Snaddon grew up in the same Calgary neighbourhood as Lougheed and his earliest recollection of Peter is chasing him away from a football game in the mid-1940s because Lougheed was too small to play in the league. While Snaddon is not in Lougheed's social circle he has been an important influence in his public promotion. It was Snaddon who first brought Lougheed to the attention of the national press with a 1967 article in *Saturday Night*: "Are they incubating a future Tory prime minister in Alberta?" (this before Lougheed had even demonstrated his abililty in a legislative session). Although some *Journal* reporters describe Snaddon's relation with the adminstration as "obscene," Snaddon is unapologetic. "I'm an Albertan inside the Canadian context the same way Peter is; we come from the same background and share the same reaction to things. Of course I support him."

One example of the *Journal* being an apologist for Lougheed dealt with the Syncrude negotiations in Winnipeg. When the *Globe and Mail* reported that "Mr. Lougheed apparently walked in with both guns blazing and layed about with a rudeness that startled many at the table. At one point when Ontario was talking about investing $50 million in the oil sands project, Mr. Lougheed remarked sarcastically that Ontario Premier William Davis should have saved himself the plane fare out, then suggested that he take his assistants to another room to help come up with something serious." The *Journal* countered with its own headline "Tough, not Nasty." The *Journal's* article admitted "Davis and Lougheed had quite a scrap all right but it was a good natured one. . . . knowing those two, Lougheed and Davis, they will say quite a few things to each other but it is all joshing. The same happens when they talk about football, one being a Western fan the other being an Eastern fan." The article also quoted Energy Minister Don Getty as denying Lougheed had been rude. "Can you imagine our Premier saying that? Alberta's Premier just doesn't talk or act this way." Alberta's Premier doesn't exactly "josh" either when $50 million is involved. To be fair, the paper has become more critical since the arrival in Edmonton in 1976 of J. Patrick O'Callaghan.

Lougheed enjoys a more distant relationship with the *Calgary Herald*. His calls to publisher Frank Swanson are routinely referred to the paper's editor, Bill Gold, (a former speechwriter for Ontario Premier William Davis) who describes his dealings with the Premier as "extremely formal and correct." While the *Herald* supports Lougheed's central political and economic objectives it has taken a hard line on the government's handling of people issues, opposed the PWA purchase, and demanded Horst Schmid's resignation. Lougheed is not a sacred cow at the Calgary *Albertan* and its editor, Les Buhasz, says "he's never been in direct communication with me." That may be because the paper, which supported Social Credit in 1971, is considered anti-government and beyond conversion.

Even though the editor of the *Edmonton Sun* is a defeated federal Conservative candidate and former CBC reporter Ron Collister, the sensational *Sun* has been aggressively critical of Lougheed in its news pages if not its editorials. Its former legislative columnist, Don Braid, who worked on parliament hill for the *Montreal Star* admits, "I have a more difficult time of it in Edmonton than I did in Ottawa. On the whole government ministers in Alberta are noncommittal. A few ministers won't even talk to me, or if they do talk, they do not communicate."

But it's the rural weeklies that are most venal. They carry government press releases verbatim and almost all dwell at great length on messages from their area MLA. Not surprisingly government advertising in the rural papers has increased dramatically since the Conservatives took office.

Although Lougheed is always amiable with members of the legislative press corps, individual members feel that collectively he regards them with a degree of contempt. Unlike Prime Minister Trudeau and most provincial premiers who schedule regular news conferences each week Lougheed calls them at whim. (However, he does agree to two or three minute "spot interviews" if a reporter is lucky enough to catch him as he arrives for work in the morning or leaves his office for lunch.) CBC's national correspondent Arthur Kent suggests that while he "never feels manipulated by Lougheed, it's a case of 'fine tuning.' Lougheed gauges when it's to his advantage to speak to the media and he has a very acute sense of timing and audience; his approach to reporters is very well thought out and very controlled."

"Getting through to Lougheed," remarks CHQT's Dick Mather, "is not unlike conquering Mount Everest. It's just a matter of trying to wait and get past Joe." "Joe," of course, is Joseph Hutton the Premier's press secretary and alter ego. A stern and leathery man Hutton rides shotgun on reporters' accessibility to the Premier. When *Time* reporter Brian Butters attempted to get a ten minute interview with Lougheed, Hutton refused, saying, "You just can't plug this guy in and out." Butters was justifiably angered when he learned the real reason he couldn't get to see Lougheed was because the Premier was on vacation.

Hutton has been known to "plant questions on reporters" so that the Premier can "spontaneously" respond to an issue that would be inappropriate for him to raise himself. Hutton keeps an elaborate system of television monitoring equipment in his home and can be instantly aware of the quality and content of the news coverage of all three television networks.

Since image is so important to the government, its public affairs bureau has regular seminars for all government department heads and assistants in which administrative personnel and civil servants are taught how to be "at ease with the media."

Curiously, Lougheed shies away from live radio broadcasts, particularly "hotline" interviews. He has explained that there "are just too many of them, and if I did one I'd have to do them all." But Fil Fraser, the former host of CJCA's "Talk Back" suggests the real reason Lougheed avoids open line radio is "because he can't control all the elements the same way he can control televison." A Calgary radio show host explains, "Lougheed is not convincing on radio, his radio voice is not as authoritative as his televison presence. He's the only politician who's declined to appear on my show."

Lougheed has his own way of dealing with photographs that he might consider embarrassing: his aides simply confiscate them. One such picture, a polaroid, was taken of the Premier with his arm draped over the shoulder of an attractive female reporter, Rossi Cameron. Ms. Cameron was telephoned by a member of the Premier's staff who firmly but politely expressed alarm that such a photograph "might be misunderstood if it fell into the wrong hands" and asked her to surrender it. She did.

Conscientious political reporting is rare in Alberta. Many of the reporters who cover Lougheed are timid, anxious, or committed. "The more you like and agree with a man personally, the harder it is to judge him professionally," offers a veteran legislative reporter. The CBC's Colin MacLean is more blunt. MacLean, who covered Lougheed during the 1967 campaign admits, "he sucked us in." What MacLean is saying is that reporters knew they were being manipulated and since the manipulation was clever enough they gave into it. Mark Byington, however, points out that no politician worked harder to obtain a good press than did Lougheed when he was in opposition. "He's today reaping the benefits of his hard work."

There are obvious exceptions to the sycophantic press that Lougheed enjoys but perhaps none so defiant as the

CBC's Dianne Clarke. Clarke, who moved to Alberta from Ontario during the rapid escalation of the energy crisis, listened attentively as Lougheed justified the need for her native province to pay more for Alberta oil. Unconvinced, the brazen Ms. Clarke stared Lougheed in the eye and dismissed his argument with a single word: "Bullshit!"

Any critical reporting of Lougheed in Alberta is seen by the Premier as "Eastern Canadian propaganda – I think there's been a significant degree of news coverage in the Alberta media of Eastern Canadian points of view, which are very antagonistic to the government," he has observed. "There's quite a bit of propaganda of the Ottawa and Toronto viewpoint being circulated in Alberta."

But through the last six months of 1975, the "propaganda" disseminated by the eastern press was decidedly of a subjective nature, designed to persuade Lougheed to seek the national leadership of the Progressive Conservative party.

CHAPTER XII

The Lord Nelson Hotel – that stately incubator of Conservative party politics in Atlantic Canada – was on June 8, 1975, the scene of what many believe was Peter Lougheed's unofficial entry into the national leadership race. Lougheed had accepted an invitation to go to Halifax thinking he would address a provincial fund raising dinner. Upon his arrival he discovered that he would be speaking to the entire Conservative federal caucus – ninety-five MPs intent on assessing his potential.

His presence was the subject of intense speculation, and as he arrived, he delighted the Maritime capital by shaking hands, planting kisses on ladies along the way, and delivering a speech which many thought revealed his interest in Robert Stanfields's job without actually saying so. He mused about his ancestral roots in Nova Scotia and about how he wished his mother could have lived another three years so that she could have been at his side that evening. His remarks were crammed with Canadianisms – about national objectives, national strengths, national opportunities, and he even got in a plug for the family as "the cornerstone of Canadian life."

One month later, Robert Stanfield formally relinquished the national leadership of the Progressive Conservative party, handing Peter Lougheed the chance to master the tides of opportunity and to see how far they would carry

him. Public opinion polls overwhelmingly favoured Lougheed to succeed Stanfield; a *Financial Times* survey in mid-
July indicated he would have 49 per cent of the party with
him if he declared his candidacy. Matched against other
Conservative prospects he ran ahead of the field. Members
of the federal caucus began pledging their support encouraging him to run.

His competitive instincts made him consider the challenge. He was aware that he could become Leader of the Opposition, but observers say he was skeptical about his
chances of defeating Prime Minister Trudeau. He was objective about his liabilities, cautious about Quebec. Further-
more, no provincial premier who made the transition to
federal politics had ever been elected Prime Minister.

He dispatched scouts to evaluate his strength in Ontario,
the key to any electoral victory, and their soundings confirmed his suspicions: he could not win against Trudeau.
(One advisor close to Lougheed insists, "The situation in Ontario wasn't as bad as it was reported. Lougheed made the
mistake of sending bad scouts who returned with bad
news.")

The prospect of becoming Canada's Prime Minister
cramped his thoughts and during a week-end at his Banff
retreat he arrived at a private and binding decision not to
run. He was about to celebrate his forty-seventh birthday
and he had equalled or surpassed his grandfather's accomplishments. He liked being Premier of Alberta, and he
was secure. As Premier, he could influence change; being
Leader of the Opposition did not guarantee him the office of
the Prime Minister and he was not prepared to accept the
inertia that normally attends the role of a federal Opposition Leader. Having made his decision he refused to second
guess it or to indulge in vain regret. But if he was not to be a
candidate he did nothing that summer to discourage the impression that he might be. He accepted the thunderous applause of the crowds who watched him ride as parade mar-
shal in the Calgary Stampede. He announced he would test
the waters of international diplomacy by embarking on an
ambitious trade mission to Europe in September. He

attended the CNE in Toronto, and at the end of July, took his family on a tour of the western Arctic.

Alberta's interest in the Arctic evolved, according to Lougheed, "not in terms of political jurisdiction but simply from practical economics." Edmonton is the chief supply base for mining and exploration activities in the north. The PWA purchase gave the province a monopoly on air freight service into the area. Lougheed viewed the north as "an offsetting factor geographically for Alberta. In other words, a positive factor. As you look at the map of Canada, most of the geography is against Alberta. We don't have the tidewater advantages of B.C. We are the furthest province from the markets of Central Canada. And, the only geographic advantage we have is that we are the natural gateway province to the North and for future jobs for our people. Geography works against us in most cases. The one area it works for us is in the North."

Perhaps it works too well. The late Aklavik missionary, Father Joseph Adam, outlined the possibility of Alberta laying claim to the energy corridor of the Mackenzie River north to Inuvik and Tuktoyaktuk, in order to have seaports on the Arctic Ocean. "No one questions Alberta's right to make an honest profit in the north," said Adam, "but what is happening now is blatant colonialism. Purchases and prices are far in excess of what the distance justifies and it's Albertans who profit."

During the tour Lougheed went as far north as Resolute Bay and as far west as Prudhoe Bay in Alaska and paid a sentimental visit to the Arctic island named after his grandfather. He returned from the trip to find his appointment book filled with a growing list of federal Conservative powerbrokers determined to sound him out on the leadership question or draft him. Throughout August he met with numerous MPs and issued firm denials of federal ambition. At least he convinced Joe Clark; shortly after the two men met, the MP for Rocky Mountain House began his campaign for the leadership. People close to Lougheed, who a few months earlier would hedge when asked about the Premier's intentions, became more confident in saying that Lougheed was not interested in succeeding Stanfield.

Following the failure of the provincial Conservatives to win a majority government in the Ontario general election on September 18, Premier William Davis was abruptly removed from the list of leadership contenders and eastern interests suddenly shifted their allegiance to Lougheed and organized their efforts to persuade Lougheed to throw his hat into the ring. In their arrogance, eastern editorial writers did not believe him when he asked, "Why should I be Prime Minister of Canada when I already run Alberta?" They could be forgiven for believing that Lougheed might, under proper circumstances, be persuaded to change his mind. For, at the end of September, Peter Lougheed embarked on a highly publicized tour of Europe in search of development money, new industry, and new ideas: a mission designed to enhance Alberta's and his own prestige abroad. Included in the delegation were cabinet ministers, oil men, grain experts, businessmen, labour leaders, lawyers, doctors, and professors: eighty in all. The $300,000 trip was divided into six major interest sectors and involved more than 300 appointments in four countries. The *Financial Times* of London introduced Lougheed to its readers as "the most exciting politician to appear in Canada since Mr. Trudeau." The Paris journal, *L' Entreprise*, described him in one edition as looking like Robert Redford; another edition of the same paper suggested he resembled Paul Newman. *Le Figaro* praised Alberta's riches, pointing out that the province was determined "not to be a milk cow for the rest of Canada." (The irony of this is that during the depression in the 1930s Mitch Hepburn, then Premier of Ontario, stated that Ontario would not be a "milch cow" for Western Canada.)

Lougheed addressed the Royal Institute of International Affairs in London where he endorsed Trudeau's push for special recognition of Canada from the European Economic Community, and he formally announced an end to Alberta's dispute with Ottawa over energy policy at home. He spoke in English without a French translator to influential businessmen in Paris at the Chambre du Commerce telling them that Alberta has reached "a stage of maturity" within Canada. He pointed to Alberta's developing ties with Quebec and said the Alberta government had adopted the position that "Quebec cannot be isolated from the rest of Canada for in so doing Confederation itself is weakened."

"The Europeans love us because we're straight shooters," explained Lougheed's press secretary, Joe Hutton. "We've got oil, gas and coal, and right now it doesn't matter what language we speak. Oil is the magic word."

French Premier, Jacques Chirac, invited Lougheed to his residence at the Hotel Matignon. Lougheed addressed the Mid-Atlantic Club in Brussels and hosted a dinner for German industrialists in the Schloss Kronberg near Frankfurt. He met senior representatives of the Rothschild financial empire. He spent almost a day at the "new" Scottish town of Livingston, designed to ease population pressures in major centres. (Lougheed included the town on his itinerary because of his own preference for balanced growth centres in Alberta. Rather than see Edmonton and Calgary reach unmanageable proportions, Lougheed was promoting the idea of twenty towns the size of Red Deer, population 35,000, throughout Alberta.)

He was intrigued with the operation of the European Common Market and spent more than an hour with its head, François Ortolli. Writing of the trip for the *Globe and Mail*, Christina Newman described "Lougheed's performance in every kind of situation" as "remarkable." For a man who prefers a simple meal of meat and potatoes at home, he savoured continental cuisine at places like Maxim's and La Tour d'Argent in Paris; he raised his atrocious monotone singing voice to join in German beer drinking songs while standing on a chair in Frankfurt; and dropped all inhibitions to dance a Scottish reel with two buxom ladies in the Great Hall of Edinburgh Castle. He laid a wreath at the Canadian War Memorial at Vimy Ridge, and everywhere he went he dispensed $5,000 scholarships for post-graduate work by European students at an Alberta university.

All of this, of course, made headlines at home. While the purpose of the mission remained obscure to Canadian readers, Lougheed was taking the limelight away from serious contenders for the Conservative leadership. The *Calgary Herald's* Bill Gold was perturbed that "Lougheed has deliberately or inadvertently arranged things to be in national prominence right up to the eve of the national convention." In a column urging Lougheed to "pipe down," Gold wrote, "if he wants it that's the way to go – but if he doesn't want it, as a good Tory, shouldn't he tone down a bit to let someone else emerge with a little national stature in order to command the party?"

The question of his federal ambition pursued him in Europe and he consistently denied any interest in the overtures of those who suggested he might lead the Tory party in Ottawa. "The answer will always be the same: 'no' " he insisted. At least one reporter on the mission, the *Calgary Herald's* legislative bureau chief, Kevin Peterson, was convinced by the denial. "In six years of covering Mr. Lougheed he has misled, been grammatically opaque, deliberately confused or remained uncommunicative – but he has never lied. To argue that he would run is to argue that he is telling his first lie and is repeating it over and over again . . . That is neither consistent with his character nor an auspicious way to start seeking the job of Prime Minister."

The only wrinkle in the mission came in Germany near the end of the tour when Jeanne, exhausted by a heavy travel schedule, held up Lougheed's arrival at an elaborate and formal wine tasting banquet in a mediaeval monastery hosted by the German provincial Premier, Osswald de Land-Hessen. Lougheed arrived forty minutes late after the assembled guests had already gone through most of the rare vintages.

That same evening, Prime Minister Pierre Elliott Trudeau interrupted Lougheed's mission by summoning the provincial premiers to meet with him during the Thanksgiving holiday week-end. The time of the meeting – designed to introduce the wage and price controls that the Prime Minister had opposed during the election campaign – meant that Lougheed had to cancel an audience with the Queen and an appointment with British Prime Minister, Harold Wilson. Lougheed left Cologne for Ottawa pleased with both the attention that the mission had received and the potential that it had developed. "The fruits of our trip may not be realized immediately," he explained, "but we had to come to Europe to find out who we are." Almost as an afterthought, as he settled into his seat aboard the plane, he expressed regret about not being able to keep his meeting with the Queen and was heard to say in jest, "I hope Her Majesty won't be too disappointed."

Arriving in Ottawa for Thanksgiving dinner at 24 Sussex Drive, Lougheed was upset to discover that the provincial premiers had been summoned, not for consultation, but to hear Trudeau tell them that wage and price controls for the country had been imposed. The Prime Minister had prepared a statement which declared that all ten premiers had agreed to his economic measures – a statement which was hastily revised before television cameras when Lougheed remained the only premier to object to the fact that the wage and price controls were left open-ended at the Prime Minister's discretion.

CHAPTER XIII

The speaker was one of twenty-five hundred delegates summoned to the Ottawa Civic Centre during the last week of February, 1976, to select a national leader for the Progressive Conservative party.

"Peter Lougheed has the biggest political balls in Canada, it's a damn shame he's not in this race. He could be Prime Minister."

The statement reflected the mood of broad dissatisfaction prevalent at the convention. In spite of a multi-candidate field in competition for delegate support, none of the twelve contenders has the mass appeal necessary to spark the imagination of the convention, much less the country.

The national Conservative party was in disarray. The exercise was all the more frustrating because the one man who offered the most tantalizing combination of high purpose and leadership, the choice of the rank and file, had declared himself immune to the virus of Prime Ministerial ambition.

Edgar Peter Lougheed, the Premier of Alberta, whom the *Globe and Mail* praised as "a vigorous and experienced politician with toughness and courage," was not a candidate. He had resisted the pressure to run "as a matter of personal integrity and public credibility," explaining that he was firmly committed to completing his responsibility to the people of Alberta.

Two Alberta MPs, Doug Roche and Harvie Andre, were convinced that Lougheed had a "duty" to run. During the summer of 1975, they spearheaded a so-called "committee of ten" – a group of representatives from each province who agreed to do the necessary leg work to assure Lougheed of a first ballot victory if he chose to enter the race. In their attempts to persuade him, the committee advanced two arguments: The country needed him because of his ability to produce "progressive and unifying policies and to build a consensus around them." And the party needed him because of his ability "to communicate with the public, both personally and electronically."

Lougheed continued to discourage the movement but while he kept insisting publicly that he was not interested, he continued privately to assess the situation. His cardinal political rule has always been "to keep his options open."

To the national press it was inconceivable that a man would place extravagant ambitions for his own province ahead of what it considered the broader interest of the country. Speculation centred on darker motives behind Lougheed's rejection. *Maclean's* suggested that his health was failing; the *Toronto Star* dispatched a reporter West in the belief that the Premier was on the brink of divorce, or that his wife was an alcoholic. But skeletons, real or imagined, were not to be found.

Realizing that a failed Lougheed draft would tarnish whoever did win as a second-best choice, the committee of ten recognized that Lougheed would have to be committed early in the contest or abandoned altogether. Roche argued that Lougheed could best champion Alberta's cause at the national level and, in an interview with the *Ottawa Journal*, Roche was quoted as suggesting that Lougheed was failing the country by not running. Having already made it clear that he was not a candidate Lougheed wrote to the spokesman for the draft committee, Prince Edward Island MP Heath Macquarrie, saying he would not change his mind. "Among other factors," Lougheed explained, "I had to bear in mind the post-Watergate attitude towards political leaders and the cynicism that would have developed – particularly by young Albertans – if I had changed my position and used the Premiership to reach federal office."

The definitive rejection of all efforts on his behalf delivered in Edmonton in November, 1975, three months before the convention opened stated that "in the unlikely event of a so-called 'draft' " he would not "accept such an approach."

Still he was pressed. In mid-January, the *Globe and Mail* urged Lougheed to reconsider. In a major editorial entitled "Where's Peter Lougheed" the newspaper suggested that if he were a candidate "he would be a man of known qualities and attainments against whom the others could be measured. He could give to the whole convention a definition it seems, so far, to be struggling to grasp without success." And at home, the *Edmonton Journal*, which had originally supported his commitment to remain in Alberta, asked him to run because "a federal party without his leadership is disintegrating to a point where its convention could be a disaster." "The party needs him," the *Journal* concluded "to prevent its consignment to the political wilderness for at least another decade." However, even in the scramble to get him as a candidate, he was not without his detractors. The *Medicine Hat News*, for example, bluntly stated that he wasn't seasoned enough to head the government of Canada. The rural daily concluded that he had failed in "major tests in devising the means of investing oil and gas windfall revenues to the benefit of the people of the province." Its position was that "he needs more practice."

"He will still be wanted for the leadership of the national party three years from now when his government's term will be nearing its end. He will probably be wanted even more than he is now."

But he was not to be seduced. Even at the eleventh hour, at the convention, some zealous Lougheed supporters wore blue buttons centred with a white maple leaf which proclaimed "We Need Lougheed."

Without him, there was an atmosphere of strained optimism as delegates turned to consider which of the contenders had the best chance of defeating the Liberal government and Prime Minister Pierre Elliott Trudeau.

Two candidates afforded the party an opportunity to elect a leader who was both bilingual and had enough credibility in Quebec to break the Liberal's traditional stranglehold over French Canada. The forceful personality of Claude Wagner, and the crisp and handsome presence of Brian Mulroney made both of them worthy of serious consideration. Wagner, a former Liberal Minister of Justice from Quebec, had converted to the Tory cause in 1972; Mulroney, a political neophyte with Irish charm, was a labour specialist in one of Montreal's largest law firms. But the aura that shone around the two men was tarnished. There was a suspicion that Wagner's conversion was not entirely ideological but that it was influenced with a "secret" three hundred thousand dollar trust fund. Mulroney, who had never won elected office, seemed to have unlimited campaign funds at his disposal.

All of the other candidates had their own shortcomings and setbacks. On the right, Jack Horner had staked out a categorical conservative position that was rejected as a reactionary ideological base; Paul Hellyer, who had sought Liberal leadership in 1968, was simply a burned out power seeker; and, Sinclair Stevens was branded as a "Bay Street" operator. To the left, Flora MacDonald's greatest liability was that she was a woman, the first ever to contest the party leadership, while Heward Grafftey, a gadfly that pricked the party's conscience, exercised complete tactical independence. The other candidates, Jim Gillies, Pat Nowlan, and John Fraser, with limited regional support were dismissed as "spoilers." The twelfth candidate, Dr. R.C. Quittendon was thought by some to be a nuisance. And then there was Joe Clark, the able backbencher who had represented Alberta's Rocky Mountain constituency for just three years in the House of Commons. In the initial stages of his leadership campaign, the youthful Clark was thought to be a "stalking horse" for Peter Lougheed.

But Clark was not a stalking horse for anyone. He had taken it upon himself to explain why he thought Peter Lougheed was not a candidate. In his rationale he suggested that "the changes in Alberta are called the Lougheed revolution. Provincial matters are what interest him. He knows Alberta very well, but he doesn't know the rest of the country in the same way. He would have to go through the same process nationally as he did provincially."

Clark's explanation was more accurate than most. That Lougheed could win the convention was obvious; winning the country was another matter.

"Peter had come to the conclusion that as an Anglo-Saxon from Alberta, he would be a catastrophe in Quebec," offers a man who had known him intimately for fifteen years. "He recognized the gut bursting effort Robert Stanfield had made to learn French, an effort that paid no dividend in Quebec. Without confidence in French Canada, he felt there was no point in taking on the job." Lougheed counters this statement by saying that if he had become leader he would have had to compromise the Western position to the Ontario establishment.

That conclusion was reinforced by Claude Wagner who paid a courtesy call on Lougheed early in November, 1975, during the Western leg of his leadership campaign tour.

Wagner predicted that a victory of the separatist Parti Québécois was imminent. "Knowing Premier Bourassa and the type of leader he is," he was confident that "separatist popularity had increased alarmingly." He then posed the hypothetical question: "How would Lougheed deal with the problem if the separatists won?" Lougheed did not have an answer, and it disturbed him.

Wagner has made it clear that he did not "presume to have influenced Lougheed's ultimate decision," but a source close to the Premier suggests Wagner did. "Wagner made Peter recognize that if he ran, he might risk becoming a Prime Minister who might have to preside over the dissolution of Canada. His reading of Quebec forced him to accept his limitations at the national level."

So as Peter Lougheed arrived in Ottawa for the convention in the dead of a Wednesday night, he was surrounded by an entourage bent on protecting their star performer. He was determined to remain neutral but there was something self-conscious about his discretion. His car circled the

Skyline Hotel until a spirited demonstration in the main lobby for Jim Gillies had ended. Although it was well after midnight when he checked in, a clutch of at least a dozen reporters, led by the CBC's Larry Zolf, surrounded him as he waited for an elevator; the attitude among the parliamentary press corps was that Lougheed could not resist playing the role of king-maker at the convention. Nevertheless he remained non-committal; he retired to his suite where he taped a brief interview for CTV's "Canada AM" in which he allowed that "it might be a desirable for the party to elect someone who was bilingual." The statement was interpreted to mean that he favoured either Wagner or Mulroney. (Although Clark is practised in the French language, he is not proficient.)

On Friday as Lougheed was motioned to the rostrum to participate in the ritual obeisance to the outgoing leader, the convention delegates rose to their feet in a thunderous standing ovation, the only one given at the convention. On Saturday, the horsetrading began as candidates sought to define their constituency; it would turn out to be one of those conventions where the weak candidates united to destroy the strongest. The press had built Mulroney's image as the personification of brilliance and success. As it turned out, the media had projected his entire campaign beyond the delegates to the nation at large. His political advance was a *trompe l'oeil* that became evident only when he strode into the convention hall. Although Mulroney made a lot of news during the course of the campaign, his lavish spending didn't make much sense to the delegates. His abuse of money hurt him, but on Saturday he damaged himself irretrievably by delivering a weak, self-conscious speech.

Lougheed had taken pains to remain neutral throughout the contest but he was more neutral with some of the candidates than with others. He had been particularly hospitable to Brian Mulroney. Mulroney sat with Lougheed – in full view of television cameras – at half-time during the Grey Cup game in Calgary in November. In December he dined with Mulroney at the home of lawyer Peter Macdonell. "They were on the same wavelength," agrees Macdonell. And Lougheed's final statement of rejection was delivered to the press the same morning that Mulroney arrived in Edmonton to solicit delegate support. Although Lougheed claims the incidents were mere coincidence, no other candidate, with perhaps the exception of Claude Wagner, received such courtesies. In fact, Lougheed refused to be photographed with any of the other aspirants.

It is not hard to see why Lougheed was intrigued with the prospect of Brian Mulroney as national leader of the Conservatives. Robert Stanfield's failure to win a majority in three federal elections combined with the forced removal of former Prime Minister John Diefenbaker as party leader, had crystallized deep ideological divisions within the party. A poll conducted by Carleton University revealed that 49 per cent of the delegates described themselves as being "right wing." Yet a *Toronto Sun* survey suggested that 60 per cent were so-called "Red Tories," on the left stream of the party. As a relatively unknown quantity, Mulroney could be pragmatic in a party facing an ideological split.

He had the flexibility to respond to the national mood. He could draw on his working class background in Baie Comeau, and at the same time could point to his experience in Tory backroom politics. Fluently bilingual, he was as impressive as a Québécois in French Canada as he was handsomely Irish in English Canada. And he had substantial corporate backing. He was a credible political underdog, and Lougheed could identify with that: he himself conquered great odds to win.

On Sunday, the day of the balloting, Lougheed took his seat at the north end of the arena, a position which gave him an unobstructed view of the convention floor, and he remained impassive as the results of the first shakedown ballot were announced one hour behind schedule.

Wagner 531	Stevens 182
Mulroney 357	Fraser 127
Clark 277	Gillies 87
Horner 235	Nowlan 86
Hellyer 231	Grafftey 33
MacDonald 214	

(Quittendon had dropped out of the race and had declared for Wagner)
(Horner, who had won Diefenbaker's endorsement, was a surprising fourth.)

Grafftey and Fraser withdrew, throwing their support to Clark; Paul Hellyer moved to Wagner. Conventional wisdom suggested that Sinc Stevens would declare for Wagner, but Stevens ignored convention and announced his support for Clark. That gave Clark more federal caucus support than he could muster from MPs in his own province. The Alberta caucus was leaning to the right, almost solid in its backing for Wagner or Horner.

After the first ballot, Lougheed's private arithmetic gave the edge to Wagner. The results of the second ballot were announced: Wagner remained in the lead 667; Clark had gained momentum and passed Mulroney 532 to 419; but no one expected him to win. The look on Lougheed's face was enigmatic but he shook his head in apparent disapproval of Clark's strength. Jack Horner increased his firm hold on fourth place with 289.

Lougheed, like many others, was sobered by the results. The hard persuading and arm twisting was in full swing. He had successfully resisted all of the pressures to involve himself, but a situation had developed where he might be obliged to take sides. Because of the incestuous nature of Conservative politics in Alberta, he might be called upon to choose between the Horner family and Joe Clark.

As former director of the Alberta Conservative party during Lougheed's ascendancy, Clark might expect Lougheed's endorsement to add to his momentum. But the Horners, more so than Clark, are a formidable political force in the West with an uncanny ability to tap grassroots sentiment. The Deputy Premier, Dr. Hugh Horner, had resigned his Commons' seat in 1967 to return to Alberta to build a strong rural base for Lougheed and had distinguished himself as Lougheed's Minister of Agriculture. Some of Lougheed's aides were convinced that Dr. Hugh would try to draw the Premier into his brother's camp. The Horners were openly contemptuous of Clark's leadership abilities.

Confusion reigned in Jack Horner's box. Flora MacDonald swung her support to Clark adding to Clark's psychological advantage. Supporters surrounded Horner, their voices a cacophony of advice: some urged him to remain on the ballot; others yelled at him to throw his support to Wagner. The loudest message was to stop "that son-of-a-bitch Clark." It was a bitter moment for a man who, against all odds, had come so far on his own steam. Reporters pressed closer to get a glimpse of what in the trade is known as "the blood on his brow." In his frustration, Horner lunged to grab an offending microphone. A television reporter was spun off balance and tumbled into the stands.

Tempers flared as other members of the Horner family joined the fray. Lougheed, concerned that Dr. Hugh Horner might become involved in an embarrassing row, suggested that two aides restrain his Deputy Premier in a trailer under the stands. Impressed by the political danger posed to his own party by the situation, Lougheed proffered the excuse that the view from his seat was poor, and returned to his suite in the Skyline Hotel to watch the outcome on television.

Jack Horner, with tears in his eyes, made a personal accommodation with Wagner. As right wing support coalesced, the grassroots were crawling with Clark activists. On the third ballot, Clark with 969 votes was only 34 votes behind Wagner. Mulroney's 369 remaining delegates would decide the outcome. Most of his supporters were delegates from Quebec who had joined Mulroney's bandwagon because of their dislike for Wagner. Now they were free to vote according to their conscience.

Lougheed saw the end on television. The suspense of the afternoon reached its climax as the convention waited for an agonizing ninety minutes before it was all over.

Joe Clark, with 1,187 votes, emerged the winner by a narrow margin of 65 votes. It is one of the ironies of Canadian political history that he won, not because of the exceptional nature of his gifts of leadership, but because he was the lowest common denominator acceptable to all the jealous factions of his party. There was nothing Peter Lougheed could do but fall in line and endorse the new leader.

Nevertheless he was wary of the outcome. Clark may

have been a superb political organizer, but was he the man to unite the party into a cohesive force? At the outset of the campaign Clark's support in caucus was negligible. Lougheed thought it would be difficult for him to attempt to run without even modest support from the elected members of the party.

Three days after the convention, as the Premier of Alberta prepared to assess the results for a CFRN television special in Edmonton, a reporter in his dressing room posed a hypothetical question. "If you had been a candidate, do you think you could have won the convention on the first ballot?"

"No," he replied without hesitation, "we would have won it on the second ballot."

If he had any personal regret he concealed it. A pragmatist, Lougheed intuitively recognized what perhaps Mulroney didn't: pragmatism pushed too far is opportunism.

One man in particular was disappointed with the outcome of the convention. When it was all over Bob Stanfield sent a handwritten note to Lougheed. "I fully understand your reasons for not considering the national leadership at this time but I hope you will not rule out the possibility at a future time."

Those anxious to see Lougheed become the eighteenth Prime Minister of Canada base their judgement solely on his impressive record in Alberta. They do so without knowing anything of substance about his position on federal matters. He has never enunciated a policy on capital punishment, bilingualism, abortion, unemployment insurance, or any other of the major issues that plague the country.

Those who suggest that Lougheed did not turn the leadership down but that he took a raincheck on it ignore Lougheed's perception of his own office, the particular kind of identity he has cultivated for himself.

Those who see him in a national role fail to comprehend his assumptions about himself and his commitment to Alberta in a restructured Confederation. But to take liberties with something Alistair Cooke has written: "Once a man is x-rayed for the prime minister's office he is radioactive into

214

his faltering old age."[1] And so, in English Canada at least, it will always be with Peter Lougheed.

Note

1 Alistair Cooke, *Six Men*, (New York: Knopf, 1977).

CHAPTER XIV

O n June 18, 1976 Lougheed set out on a little publicized but highly significant mission to the United States – a mission designed to awaken Ottawa to its economic responsibility in the West. In his quest for economic decentralization Lougheed began his tour in the Pacific northwest, calling on Montana's Governor Thomas Judge, Oregon's Governor Robert Straub, and Washington state Governor Daniel Evans. To all three he held out an attractive if unorthodox proposition: if they would agree to lobby the United States government for lower petrochemical tariffs, he would, in exchange, attempt to persuade the Canadian government to assure their region of a reliable supply of natural gas exports.

Such a bilateral agreement on tariffs would provide Lougheed with a competitive market for Alberta's developing billion dollar petrochemical industry. The average import duty levied by the United States on Canadian products was 20 per cent compared with the 10 per cent Canada levies. Ottawa had insisted that any tariff changes would have to be negotiated in Geneva through the regular international meeting of the General Agreement on Tariffs and Trade (GATT). But Lougheed disagreed pointing out that Alberta was only seeking changes to compete on equal terms in one region of the United States. "If Ontario can negotiate an autopact with the United States surely Alberta can talk agriculture and petrochemicals with the United States."

If Alberta was to diversify its economy a breakthrough in tariffs was essential. A 1973 study of the petrochemical industry in Alberta bluntly stated at that time "there are no chemicals that can be made competitively in Alberta." Laying aside doubts, Lougheed decided to risk encouraging the local industrial processing of Alberta's energy resources as a way of moving "decision making from Central Canada to the West."

(Two world scale petrochemical plants exist in the province: Dow Chemical at Fort Saskatchewan produces ethylene glycol, used for antifreeze and polyester fibre, and the Alberta Ethylene Company in Red Deer pipes a billion pounds of ethylene a year to the domestic market.)

In 1974, building world scale petrochemical plants seemed like a reasonable idea to strengthen secondary manufacturing industries. But since then demand for plastic bottles, antifreeze, and the like dwindled, and without heavy government subsidies the companies were having trouble generating cash flow to cover their capital costs – and that cash flow depended on finding export markets. So it was with some urgency that Lougheed launched his initiative.

Frustrating Lougheed's dream of twenty-one petrochemical plants in Alberta by the end of the century was the federally backed Petrosar Limited. The $600 million Sarnia, Ontario refinery has the capacity of turning 170,000 barrels of oil a day into petrochemicals and in the long run will claim an estimated 16 per cent of Alberta's known reserves of conventional crude oil. Petrosar Limited, close to captive eastern markets, threatens to undermine Alberta's fledgling industry.

Lougheed continued his mission in Texas. In a speech to the prestigious Houston Club he straightened out "misconceptions" the oil industry might have about the investment climate in Canada and explained the intricacies of the division of powers in a confederal nation. (At the time, Saskatchewan had alarmed United States investors by proposing to nationalize the potash industry in that province.) Lougheed's singular exercise in economic diplomacy took him on to New York where he told the Metropolitan Club that the tariff situation existed "clearly to Canada's detriment" and indicated that Canada would have to become "a tough international trader" if it were to survive as a distinct national identity. As an example he pointed out that the Canadian tax on three dollars worth of steak imported from the United States is three cents while the tax on a similar Canadian steak exported to the United States is thirty cents.

He took his own version of a continental energy pact to Washington where he got a sympathetic hearing from Minnesota Senators Hubert Humphrey and Walter Mondale, Pennsylvania Democrat Thomas Morgan (Chairman of the House International Relations Committee) and Washington State Democrat Henry (Scoop) Jackson (Chairman of the Senate Interior Affairs Committee). He also got to see John Hill, Deputy Energy Administrator and explored long-term arrangements for wheat exports with the Agriculture Secretary, Earl Butz. Lougheed was ecstatic at the reception he received at a breakfast with fourteen senators saying he thought they would be "a lot more distant – they were more interested than I expected them to be."

Having committed himself to his goal he pursued it with single-minded determination when the legislature opened on October 13. In a sweeping seventy-five minute State of the Province Address, Lougheed ignited the sparks of the energy war. In a defiant gesture, he moved to block the flow of Alberta oil to the Petrosar complex in Sarnia. Petrosar, Lougheed explained, had applied for the right to be an approved purchaser of energy supplies from the Alberta Petroleum Marketing Commission. The request, he said, had been denied. But he admitted that it was nothing more than a "symbol of our feeling that the Petrosar project is not in the Canadian interest. That Petrosar has a stranglehold on this province." It was an essentially empty gesture for Loughed could not stop Petrosar from acquiring ethylene from Alberta; it just made it more difficult. Petrosar could still purchase its crude oil feedstock from a third party, and Dow Chemical agreed to take Alberta Gas Ethylene's output and ship a third of it to Sarnia.

One week later Lougheed vowed to launch the biggest campaign in his power to recruit American allies to support Alberta's tariff demands against Ottawa. He was blunt. He pledged to "push every pressure point" to "alter the federal bureaucracy's point of view." It was a speech that shocked national sensitivities and, as CTV's Tom Gould noted in his *Backgrounder To The News*, "What [Lougheed] is ignoring, of course, is that national gas exports are a federal matter. In making the proposal to the Americans anyway, and by proposing to go to the United States to seek a change in tariffs, Mr. Lougheed is openly escalating his one province war against the federal government, and indirectly the rest of Canada."

In his eagerness to work out a modified free trade deal with the United States Lougheed ignores that economic partnership of that kind threatens Canadian political independence. For as former United States Undersecretary of State, George Ball, once predicted, "economic integration will require for its full realization a progressively expanding area of common political decision making."

During the first week of November Jimmy Carter defeated Gerald Ford to win the United States presidency, and the Democratic congressmen that Lougheed had met in Washington moved into new areas of influence. Walter Mondale had become the Vice President designate and Henry Jackson was about to take over as Chairman of the influential Energy and Natural Resources Committee. Shortly after the presidential elections Jackson flew to Edmonton to endorse Lougheed's bid for bilateral Canada-United States tariff negotiations. Praising Lougheed for his "leadership role" Jackson noted, "We have built Chinese walls around a number of items on both sides of the border . . . but many of the reasons for them, such as wages, have now been equalized. There is a common market here and I see great opportunities for both countries – the start of a new era. So let's start by lowering tariffs."

California's Governor, Jerry Brown, intrigued by the gas swap idea, flew to Edmonton on October 4, 1977 to discuss the proposal with Lougheed. And, United States Vice President, Walter Mondale, obliquely endorsed the concept during his visit to Alberta on January 18, 1978, citing "trade between Alberta and the northwestern United States – oil and gas, agricultural and industrial products" as examples of "the friendship between the Canadian and the American people."

On November 15, 1976 the entire country was stunned by the extraordinary election in Quebec of the separatist Parti Québécois. In choosing René Lévesque as Premier, the Quebec electorate challenged Canada's future as a nation. In Alberta, the first visible response to the PQ victory was understated. Lougheed observed that unless the events demonstrate otherwise he would view Lévesque's win as "the election of a provincial government in a normal way." Lougheed had never met Lévesque, and when he was told that the new Quebec Premier was "a charming man," Lougheed retorted that he preferred women with charm, but was suspicious of charming men. Lougheed was concerned that the shift in public focus from Alberta to Quebec threatened his own desire to achieve political and economic equality with central Canada. He was suspicious that "central Canada is going to fall into the same trap (as in the mid-1960s) and concentrate so much on the Quebec question that the aspirations of the Western people are going to be further ignored – hence a further alienation developing in Western Canada – then the people (in other parts of Canada) will wake up in surprise sometime . . . and wonder why it is that Western Canada feels so alienated from the centre."

The Quebec election reinforced a critical need for sweeping reform of Canada's federal system; as constituted Canada could not accommodate the autonomous aspirations of French Canadians. Attempts to weave a new fabric in Canadian federalism had been going on periodically since 1927, but it was not until 1969 when Pierre Elliott Trudeau made constitutional reform a personal priority that it compelled an urgent reaction.

The British North America Act of 1867 – Canada's Constitution – is an Act of Westminister and perceived to be a relic of Canadian colonialism. It cannot be brought home to Canada without the unanimous consent of the provinces. But more important, major amendments to the act that would alter federal and provincial powers to conform to contemporary reality requires agreement on an amending formula – a formula which has been as elusive as patriation itself. The BNA Act is virtually a dead document unless the Canadian government can change it.

The earliest clue to Lougheed's position on constitutional reform was revealed in May of 1970 at a national conference in Lethbridge called to study the feasibility of one Western prairie province. Then Leader of the Opposition, Lougheed listed four constitutional alternatives. "The first one is the idea of a separate Western Canadian Nation." That he rejected "unequivocally without any qualification." He could not accept the question of the *status quo* either. "It would do little to overcome the lack of understanding by Central Canada – by the central government towards our problems, towards the aspirations of the area." He was lukewarm toward the emphasis of the Lethbridge conference on the third alternative – the merging of Manitoba, Saskatchewan, Alberta, and British Columbia into one province. However, he gave his support to a fourth alternative, the genesis of which would later become his policy of decentralized federalism, "an alternative providing for a much greater degree of co-operation between provincial administrations than we have had in the past."

A year later, in the summer of 1971, Lougheed was still Opposition Leader when a tentative agreement on patriation and an amending formula was worked out in Victoria. The amending formula under the Victoria charter required that before any constitutional clause could be altered, agreement would have to come from any province with more than one-quarter of Canada's population (Ontario or Quebec), as well as two Atlantic provinces and two Western provinces. At the insistence of British Columbia's Premier, W. A. C. Bennett, that formula was altered to give British Columbia a near veto by providing that approval be obtained from at least two Western provinces representing 50 per cent of the population of Western Canada. If the deal appealed to the then Alberta Premier, Harry Strom, Lougheed was appalled by it. Hypothetically, British Columbia, Manitoba, Ontario, Newfoundland, and New Brunswick together could use the formula to rob Alberta of constitutional control over its resources. Lougheed warned Strom that if the Conservatives won the provincial election that year a Lougheed government would never accept such an amending formula. But the warning was academic; Quebec's Premier Robert Bourassa did not feel that the Victoria charter offered French Canada sufficient authority over social policy and he vetoed it.

Prime Minister Trudeau's abiding objective to give Canada its own constitution was sublimated when the federal Liberals were reduced to a minority government in 1972. But, after being returned to a majority in 1974, he again made it a priority. The provincial premiers seemed disinterested. In the spring of 1976 Trudeau warned that if the provinces could not come to an agreement on an amending formula by September 15, that year he would consider asking parliament to act on its own authority and unilaterally patriate the constitution from Britain. This apparent ultimatum raised Lougheed's fears of Ottawa's intentions about an amending formula, and it was against this background that the country's ten premiers met at the newly refurbished Government House in Edmonton to draft the basis of a new constitution. Newfoundland's Premier, Frank Moores, charged with co-ordinating the various provincial positions on the matter, arrived with high hopes for accord: "We are pretty close to reaching an agreement," he said.

Moores had every reason to sound optimistic; preparations for the conference had been thorough, position papers had been under construction for more than a year, and the provincial attorneys-general had offered their tentative stamp of approval. Following the first day of deliberations the premiers revealed little of their complex discussions as they adjourned to a session the following day at the Banff Springs Hotel. But it seemed that the country was at last on the brink of constitutional agreement. At the eleventh hour, Lougheed in his role as chairman of the meeting, with the support of British Columbia's Premier, William Bennett, announced that Alberta would insist that any amending formula require the unanimous consent of the provinces. It was a sudden and unexpected change in the Alberta position. "None of our people had any insight into the fact that Peter was going to raise this," offered Ontario's Premier William

Davis. What Lougheed's proposal meant was that Prince Edward Island, for example, with a population of 120,000 could veto any proposal agreed to by Ottawa and the other nine provinces. As he adjourned the Banff meeting Lougheed reported that "nothing on the constitutional question is finalized" and that the premiers would resume their discussions on the constitution in six weeks.

Lougheed's veto encountered wrathful opposition in central Canada. The *Toronto Star* took the fallacious stance that "the truth about Alberta's oil and gas is that it is a vital *national* resource too valuable to be entrusted to exclusive provincial authority in any circumstance." Building its case on that false premise the *Star* suggested that "Ottawa and the other provinces should make it clear to Lougheed that he won't be allowed to grab full control no matter what attitude he takes under the constitution." Ontario Premier William Davis followed that transparent argument; "There has to be a recognition that there is a national interest. The federal government has to have some power." But under the existing constitution Lougheed *has* full resource control – barring a national emergency – and that control is inviolate. Lougheed's position resurrects the so-called "Fulton-Favreau Formula" worked out in the early 1960s which suggested unanimous consent for any constitutional change. "The only way to protect the enshrined rights of the provinces is unanimity," Lougheed maintained.

The *Edmonton Journal* derided Lougheed for his sudden shift as "overly rigid and defensive" and pointed out, "if there is to be reasonable scope for constitutional amendment there has to be some potential for majority rule related to the distribution of population and economic activity in Canada." And the *Calgary Herald* proposed a compromise that would see some provincial rights as "inviolate." "These could be natural resources in Alberta's case and language in Quebec's case. A granite bound result shouldn't be necessary if there can be prior guarantees in the case of a limited number of issues considered vital by certain provinces," the *Herald* contended.

The premiers met again in Toronto on October 1, 1976 in an attempt to resolve the deadlock, but at that meeting

Lougheed stood alone and steadfastly refused to back away from his concept of "one province, one vote."

"The country has been treated to the parochial obstinancy of Peter Lougheed," charged *Globe and Mail* columnist, Geoffrey Stevens. "To hell with national concerns. To hell with trying to create a sounder framework for healthy federation. To hell with the needs and aspirations of others. More for Alberta is his slogan and they love him back home for every elbow delivered to the eye of an Easterner." Lougheed ignored the vituperative press comment in central Canada, and his Minister of Federal and Intergovernmental Affairs, Lou Hyndman (who once prepared a list of 116 federal intrusions into provincial jurisdiction), clarified the Alberta position: "We are certainly not saying there should be unanimity on every change proposed for the constitution. All we are saying is that the traditional powers now enjoyed by the provinces, particularly in cases in which a province entered Confederation because of guarantees of those historic rights, those rights will be protected. . . . One thing we can't accept," Hyndman continued, "is that there should be two tiers of provinces in this country, one tier of so-called first class provinces and another of so-called second class provinces. All provinces in Confederation should be regarded as equals."

Following the Toronto meeting Prime Minister Trudeau rebuked Lougheed for attempting to gain extra powers rather than discuss patriation and an amending formula. "The premiers . . . seemed to have turned the process upsidedown and have concentrated on increasing provincial powers," Trudeau wrote Lougheed. "I cannot consider myself to be committed in advance to anything the premiers may seem to have agreed upon when the points of agreement are entirely apart from the central exercise."

Lougheed had turned the ball back into Trudeau's court, and in the spring of 1978 the Prime Minister served it decisively. Making good his pledge to act unilaterally to patriate the constitution he unveiled a discussion paper entitled "A Time for Change." Essentially, Trudeau's plan proposed to change powers under federal jurisdiction by July 1, 1979, and to work out a new division of powers with the provinces by July 1, 1981. Under its own jurisdiction, the federal government proposed to upgrade the role of the Governor-General; abolish the Senate and create a new "House of Federation" to which half of the members would be appointed by the provinces to reflect the composition of the legislatures. Trudeau also proposed to expand the Supreme Court and to entrench a bill of rights in a new constitution. To reinforce his plan he dispatched his Justice Minister, Ron Basford, to London to inform the Queen of his intentions.

Queen Elizabeth arrived in Edmonton in August to open the 1978 Commonwealth Games, and Lougheed's behaviour during the royal tour earned him the enmity of the British press. The *London Daily Telegraph* portrayed Lougheed as an ignorant bore who "upset the royal party by acting during the Queen's tour . . . as if he were campaigning for election." What irked reporters was Lougheed's apparent breach of etiquette by riding in an open car in St. Paul while the royal party followed in an enclosed limousine. Lougheed was also said to have annoyed protocol officials by plunging into the crowds who had come to see the Queen and by animatedly shaking his supporters' hands. "At one point, Prince Philip was unable to conceal his irritation," wrote James Whiteman in the *Telegraph*, "as the Premier followed him at close range through a receiving line shaking hands and talking to local people." Even though the Queen's press secretary Michael Shea could do nothing but deny that Her Majesty was upset by Lougheed's behaviour, Lougheed's actions were in stark contrast to the unobtrusive presence of Saskatchewan's Premier Allan Blakeney and Newfoundland's Frank Moores who had hosted the Queen during other portions of her Canadian tour. And, as the *Medicine Hat News* commented, "Lougheed's conduct . . . was undecorous and unbecoming a man of his stature." Lougheed's defence of his behaviour is that in Alberta things are less formal and that he was merely responding to the well wishes of his constituents who called out to him on a first name basis and "my normal exuberance took over."

At a banquet on August 2 sponsored by the Alberta government, the Queen, reading a speech prepared for her by the Lougheed administration, used the opportunity to talk about Lougheed's constitutional visions, "a society where the individual can find full expression in an atmosphere of tolerance, co-operation and harmony." The following night at a state banquet sponsored by the federal government, Her Majesty indirectly endorsed Prime Minister Trudeau's vision of constitutional change.

On October 20, 1978 the Alberta government released its blueprint for constitutional change: "Harmony and Diversity: A New Federalism for Canada." While Alberta's defence of its natural resources is reasonable, the document, prepared by Dr. J. Peter Meekison, deputy minister of the Department of Federal and Intergovernmental Relations, lists twenty-nine proposals that, if adopted, would virtually eliminate the federal parliament's emergency powers in time of national crisis; dismiss reform of the Senate as irrelevant; advocate a convoluted constitutional court; oppose inclusion of a bill of rights in a new constitution; demand that communications, transportation and culture be shared powers; insist that the provinces be given an expanded role in international relations; and, restrict Ottawa's authority to spend money in a provincial jurisdiction.

Even in Alberta, editorial support for the document was negligible. The *Calgary Albertan* described it as "a master plan for a daring daylight raid on the federal political arsenal; a design for deconfederation that is *provincial* in the worst sense of the word. It is unacceptable." The *Edmonton Journal* recognized that "if fully implanted," Lougheed's proposals "could well leave Ottawa seriously hampered in its ability to control the national economy and to ensure equitable distribution of wealth." And, the *Calgary Herald* noted that the working paper "pushes the advantages of expanding provincial powers without proper regard for some of the adverse consequences of a weakened federal role." But perhaps the best description of the Lougheed policy is coined by the president of the Canada West Foundation, Stan Roberts, who described it as "small c confederation." Or, as Lougheed himself has put it, "the two orders of government, federal and provincial, [would be] equal."

Constitutional shadow chasing resumed again at a federal-provincial conference in Ottawa on October 28, 1978. Lougheed arrived in Ottawa threatening to call a provincial election on constitutional issues. In customary fashion he dispensed with a prepared text and in his opening statement again itemized in his typical point-by-point fashion his consistent arguments. Then, for the the first time anyone could remember, he relied on a quotation from someone else to bolster his arguments. Turning to the Prime Minister he referred to words written by Trudeau's predecessor, Lester B. Pearson, in his book, *Federalism for the Future*: "We are committed to the view that Canada requires both a strong federal government and strong provincial governments. The fields of government are now so wide, the problems of government so many, that it is not a contradiction to speak in these terms." (Lougheed failed to finish the quotation which continues, "The freedom of the individual is more likely to be safeguarded if neither order of government is able to acquire a preponderant power.")

Prime Minister Trudeau adopted a conciliatory nature at the conference and opened seven subjects of federal power to discussion: the control, management, and taxation of natural resources, control and regulation of interprovincial trade, as well as parliament's right to declare public works for the benefit of Canada. He also agreed to "clarify" provincial control over resources, but Lougheed "smelled a rat" in Trudeau's stand and remained the only Premier "who was not encouraged." Even René Lévesque, who opposes constitutional change as irrelevant, was forced to admit "something is finally starting to happen."

The *Edmonton Journal* reacted with a rare front page editorial to Lougheed's intransigence, and argued against his calling a provincial election "that exploits divisions in our country to no meaningful political end." Branding Lougheed "the outcast" the paper cautioned "Alberta's suspicion of Ottawa should know some bounds."

Lougheed tempered his talk of election at the end of the conference but continued to justify his stand: "perhaps some people see my position as too harsh. Look, I want to see progress towards a more united Canada but I want to know what the actual terms of such an arrangement are. There is complete justification – if not for suspicion of the federal proposals – at least for caution. It's simple. If Ontario owned the oil you can be assured that we in Alberta would be buying it at the world price."

CHAPTER XV

At the end of May, 1977, as he began the most ambitious foreign excursion ever undertaken by a Canadian Premier, Peter Lougheed said: "Any Canadian Premier who doesn't have an awareness of what's happening internationally, in my view, isn't doing his job very well." Embarking on a $300,000 tour that would take him half way around the world through the Soviet Union, the Middle East, and Europe, Lougheed appeared determined to strengthen his position not only as Premier but as Canada's senior Conservative statesman.

Although Lougheed was careful to emphasize that the fact finding mission had been arranged in close consultation with the federal Department of External Affairs, a senior Canadian diplomat confessed that arrangements for the tour far exceeded the demands of normal protocol associated with foreign visits of even the Prime Minister. "Lougheed represents a powerful political potential that even External Affairs doesn't quite know how to handle," he confided.

That political potential was not lost on Soviet Premier Alexi Kosygin who, in an extended meeting with the Alberta Premier in the Kremlin, admitted that he attached "great importance" to the visit, and publicly acknowledged Lougheed's growing influence on the Canadian political scene.

The meeting with the Soviet Premier was the climax of a ten day tour of the Soviet Union that exceeded even the most optimistic expectations of the Alberta delegation. The visit was obviously orchestrated by the Soviet Premier himself. Lougheed was quartered at the Sovyetstka Hotel, an unobtrusive building in a residential area of Moscow, in an apartment once used by Winston Churchill. The likelihood of Soviet eavesdropping was raised after a peculiar coincidence: in the privacy of their suite the Lougheeds, weary of the traditional diet of cucumbers, tomatoes, and vodka, expressed a preference for coffee and strawberries. The following morning strawberries and coffee were served. After that, Lougheed seemed withdrawn in discussions with members of his party. The Russians jammed his itinerary with political, social, and cultural events. Lougheed almost fell asleep during a performance of the "Stone Angel" at the Bolshoi, and walked out at intermission during a propaganda folk festival staged at the Kremlin's Palace of Congress.

After initial meetings with Soviet officials, Lougheed quickly tired of the stilted rhetoric that in diplomatic circles is called "an exchange of views." He set out to change the format and before the trip had ended he had, to a modest degree, succeeded. The Premier managed to add his personal touch to the trip, moving easily into discussions of agriculture and energy, and persuading the reluctant Soviets to alter a rigid schedule so that he and his Agriculture Minister, Marvin Moore, could get an on-site inspection of a collective farm near Minsk.

Only about twelve hours were set aside for top level discussions during the ten day visit but Lougheed made the most of them. "What we gleaned from our meeting with Russian Agriculture Minister, Mesyats, was alone worth the cost of the entire trip," concluded the chairman of Alberta's grain commission, John Channon. That session put an end to the myth that the Canadian Wheat Board had any real power to influence grain sales to the Soviet Union.

The Soviet equivalent of the Wheat Board is the Exportkleb, and it is instructed by a Minister of Procurement and a Minister of Foreign Trade to buy grain. The Exportkleb's purchasing power is restricted. What Lougheed learned was that long-term contracts for sales of Alberta grain to the Soviet Union were nearly hopeless; purchase of the first six to eight million metric tonnes that Russia imports annually is guaranteed to the United States. And, it became clear to the Alberta delegation that Russia has no intention of simply purchasing grain. In return, Canada would be required to buy Russian products. Moreover, the balance of trade negotiations had to go on at a ministerial level, not at a provincial level, and not even at the level of the Canadian Wheat Board.

Lougheed laid the responsibility for Canada's poor performance in the sale of Alberta grain at the door of Otto Lang, the federal Minister responsible for the Wheat Board, and he recommended creation of a separate federal cabinet position that would be exclusively responsible for the Wheat Board. "Canada has lost ground in grain marketing and the time has come for a full reassessment of our international marketing strategy." For his part, Lang dismissed Lougheed's suggestion "as a matter of very serious interference and intervention [which] has done more real harm. His criticism of the Canadian Wheat Board is absolute nonsense at a time when Canadian wheat sales have increased and our share of world markets and the prospect for future sales have increased even more."

Lougheed was also honoured by being one of the few Western politicians to visit western Siberia, the Soviet Union's chief oil and gas producing region. It was hoped that the visit to the Samatlar Oil Fields would offer a clue as to whether the Soviets would become a major exporter of oil. If they do, it will have a major bearing on world oil prices, and also on the rate of oil sands production in Alberta. The latest reports indicate the Soviet Union is shipping more oil to the West than to their satellite countries. Soaring Siberian production and high world prices are attracting the Soviets to earn the hard currency they need to buy technology. Although he didn't get all of the answers he sought, Lougheed "saw enough in Siberia to raise questions about the credibility of the CIA report on Soviet energy supplies, which indicates a world energy shortage in the 1980s if the Russians start to buy oil from the OPEC countries.

"Provincial governments have not traditionally become

involved in these areas," Lougheed explained, "and by serving Albertans perhaps I can serve Canada as well."

"If Lougheed got a good deal out of the Soviet trip, the Russians also benefited from his presence," said a consular official in Moscow. "Nothing happens by accident in the Soviet Union, and if the Russians spent money on lavish five course dinners, private planes and motorcades, it's a small price for them to pay for what they can get out of Lougheed's visit if they want to," the official added. Perhaps mindful of that possibility Lougheed seemed reluctant to tour the Khatyn Memorial. Required by protocol to lay a bouquet of flowers at the "mound of glory" – a war monument erected to the victories of the Red Army during the Second World War – he hastily deposited the flowers and quickly moved on, aware of the fact that his visit to the Soviet Union might antagonize the large number of eastern European Canadians living in Alberta. He obviously wanted to avoid any impression that he was cozying up to the Soviets. There was another reason, too: "We are here not as tourists but as traders," he sharply reminded a photographer who tried to manoeuvre him into posing for a picture in Red Square.

His visit to the Soviet Union came at the time when United States President Jimmy Carter had confronted Moscow on the issue of human rights. Before Lougheed's departure, Alberta's Ukrainian community had asked him to follow Carter's lead and to press Soviet leaders on the treatment of dissidents. Throughout the trip Lougheed diplomatically remained silent. That silence earned him the scorn of Leonid Plyushch, a former Ukrainian mathematician imprisoned by the KGB for writing a public letter protesting the arrest of other dissidents. Plyushch, who was tortured in Soviet "mental hospitals" before managing to escape to the West, told a meeting in Edmonton that Lougheed's trade mission to Russia was "opportunism of the Munich type." Plyushch elaborated on the comment saying that the discussion of commerce without reference to the treatment of political prisoners in the Soviet Union was a sellout of those prisoners.

From Moscow Lougheed flew to Vienna, then to Athens

for what was supposed to be a four day relaxation period. But he spent the time in his suite at the Caravel Hotel briefing himself on the Middle East portion of the trip. Expressing an interest in ancient Greek history, Lougheed attempted to visit the acropolis, but when he arrived at its gates he discovered them locked and although he vowed to return the following day, he never did.

He boarded the Canadian Armed Forces Convair Cosmopolitan that would take him to the Arab world, and fifteen minutes after its departure from Athens Lougheed once again narrowly escaped death in a possible plane crash. As the aircraft climbed over the Aegean an exit door sprung one of its hinges, depressurizing the cabin. The plane filled with what appeared to be smoke; oxygen masks were rushed to passengers. Through it all, Lougheed seemed calm but there was one give-away of his true feelings: the copy of *Time* that he intently studied as the plane began its hasty descent remained upsidedown.

The flying seminar continued without further incident to Saudi Arabia and the boom camp atmosphere of its diplomatic, political, and oil capitals: Jeddah, Riyadh, and Dhahran. It was the one portion of the tour where the Lougheed party didn't know what to expect. Lougheed's arrival in Jeddah was overshadowed by the arrival of the governor of Malaysia's Sabah province, Daro Harith Muhammed Saleh. That Lougheed commanded any attention at all was due to the efforts of Canada's new ambassador in Saudi Arabia, Ed Bobinski. "We had to convince the Saudis that Lougheed was of some importance in Canada," admitted one embassy official. "They really don't understand our provincial divisions of power."

Not only did Lougheed get an unusual fifteen minute audience with King Khalid, and the strong man of the Saudi regime, Crown Prince Fahd (who arrived late for the meeting), but he also met the colourful Arabian Oil Minister Sheik Ahmad Zaki Yamani, and the Deputy Minister of the Saudi Monetary Agency, Sheik Khaled Ali Gosetir. Although Gosetir didn't quite know what to make of the visiting Albertans, he was aware that Lougheed was unique in that he was one of the few foreigners "who wasn't coming to borrow money." Perhaps. Lougheed doesn't rule out future Arab financing of projects in Alberta. "If we run into a project of great magnitude, such as another heavy oil sands plant, and we discover a capital shortage in Canada, I don't see any reason why we couldn't consider asking the Saudis for money. However, they must understand they would be asked to supply debt financing, and could not come in on an equity basis," Lougheed explained.

In a prop jet, Lougheed inspected the biggest oil fields in the world. The tour demonstrated just how insignificant Alberta's conventional oil patch is on a global scale. Long after the oil wells in Alberta have gone dry the Saudis will still have oil. "What Saudi Arabia does directly affects Alberta," Lougheed observed. "If we had greater oil reserves in Alberta it wouldn't have such a bearing." The object of his tour to the Middle East was, in his words, "to assess world energy trends and to determine for ourselves whether there will be a world energy shortage in the mid 1980s." Satisfied that there will be a "serious oil shortage in the middle of the next decade" and convinced that the OPEC countries "will become stronger, not weaker" Alberta is accelerating its own energy strategy.

The "blue-eyed Arab" of Alberta seemed content among the Thabus and Kaffeyehs of the real Arab world, although he refused to wear the traditional garb himself. He was particulary proud to tour the Alberta based ATCO construction camp in Jeddah. (ATCO is an Alberta company which pioneered building prefabricated trailers and is now engaged around the world in construction and drilling operations.)

If Lougheed was satisfied with his reception in Saudi Arabia, then he was impressed with how the Iranians seemed eager to please him, down to the smallest detail. A guard of honour was on hand for his arrival in Tehran; Canadian flags, albeit out of proportion and occasionally upsidedown, lined the route of his motorcade in Shiraz. Lougheed himself had to nudge to a close an unprecedented one hour long meeting with the Shah, whom Lougheed admired as "informed and self-assured." The Shah's Prime Minister at the time, Amir Abbas Hoveyda, proved to be an elegant and polished host. A candlelight dinner on the lawn of Hoveyda's residence on the evening of June 21 was held to celebrate the Lougheed's twenty-fifth wedding anniversary.

Lougheed jogged every morning – in London, Moscow, and Athens. Perhaps the most curious scene for his exercise, however, was among the ruins of the ancient Persian capital of Persopolis.

Lougheed's principle reference book throughout the trip was a 300 page report on alternative energy strategies sponsored by the Massachusetts Institute of Technology. Entitled "Global Energy Prospects: 1985-2000," the report offered a critical analysis of the global energy scene with three or four possible future scenarios. Asked if he learned anything on the mission that wasn't covered in the fifteen dollar book, Lougheed offered, "You can't be in the energy business without a feel for what's going on in the nerve centres," and that the trip had given him "a feel – I can't say in a precise way – for the future decision making process in Alberta." Or, as the book suggests as one of its conclusions, Lougheed was learning that "the critical interdependence of nations in the energy field requires an unprecedented degree of international collaboration. In addition it requires the will to mobilize finance, research and ingenuity for the common purpose never before attained. And, it requires it now."

If the purpose of Lougheed's trip was to get on a first name basis with the heads of OPEC countries his visit to Israel was dictated by politics: to balance his visit to Saudi Arabia. Lougheed spent a day inspecting irrigation methods in a kibbutz, where water is allocated by computer – a system that could be applied in southern Alberta. He was unable to meet Menacham Begin, who had just been elected Prime Minister, but he was received by Israel's President, Efriam Katziak, and did get to see Israel's Minister of Agriculture Arik Sharon. There was an impromptu midnight tour of the museum housing the Dead Sea Scrolls arranged by Jerusalem's ebullient mayor, Teddy Kollek, an uncomfortable ride on the back of a camel, and a visit to Bethlehem and other religious sites. Lougheed offered a $5,000 scholarship for an Israeli student to do graduate work in Alberta.

He had offered a similar scholarship for a Saudi student.

As he left Tel Aviv for Geneva, Lougheed dramatically removed the Canadian maple leaf he was wearing in his lapel throughout the mission and replaced it with an Alberta flag pin, a symbolic gesture to indicate that keeping an eye on Alberta's interest was uppermost in his mind as he crashed the General Agreement on Tariffs and Trade negotiating sessions on the final sprint of his tour. Lougheed was not invited to the tariff discussions in Geneva and one member of the Canadian negotiating team suggested "he wasn't particularly welcome." Nevertheless, he continued his quest for bilateral trade negotiations with the United States. He lobbied American, Japanese, and European Common Market negotiators in an effort to make sure that Alberta's developing export market was not handicapped by Canadian protectionism.

There were more than 2,800 tariffs on the negotiating table and Lougheed was not optimistic about his efforts. "All we could do was present our point of view in an effective way," he told a news conference before leaving Switzerland. "The test as to whether we've succeeded in having Western Canadian interests put forward at the GATT negotiations will be determined by the final result of those negotiations, because there's a whole area of requests and a whole area of exceptions."

By October 1978, Lougheed conceded that his efforts to get significant trade and tariff concessions had failed. In his State of the Province address to the Alberta legislature on October 12, 1978 he expressed the fear "that while there were indications that the U.S. General Agreement on Tariffs and Trade (GATT) negotiators were responsive to Alberta's views, Canadian negotiators might yet trade away Western Canada interests for those of Central Canada."

Although Lougheed is still hopeful that the Americans might make concessions, particularly in the area of petrochemical feedstock exports and agricultural quotas, he admitted that that was no longer an absolute condition for increased exports of Alberta gas. As he explained to the legislature, "If we do not start in the next year or two, to move some significant additional volumes to the market place, we're going to find ourselves with a cash flow problem of the producers, and the drive is going to come out of the exploration industry in the province. That means a clearly negative effect upon jobs for Albertans – not the oil industry, as some are so disposed to use the term. Jobs for hundreds of Albertans in many communities. Surely we don't want that to happen. So I think it's a very important question now facing the people of Alberta, whether they support the position of this government that . . . natural gas export clearly can flow on an intermediate term basis to the United States to the benefit of all Canada, because that additional exploration will be to provide new discoveries in the future."

CHAPTER XVI

To understand Peter Lougheed is to understand Alberta, for more than any other Canadian Premier, including René Lévesque, Lougheed *is* his constituency. There is an appealing squareness about the man, a genuine sincerity and aggressive confidence that enhances his credibility. He has come to personify the future – the elusive future that has inspired three generations of Albertans through colonialism, drought, depression, and war. Lougheed's career and personality embody the emergence of Western Canada into the mainstream of Confederation.

Historically, the majority of Western Canadians have felt alienated from the rest of the country and, as Larry Pratt in his book, *The Tar Sands*, published by Hurtig in 1976, has written, "What Peter Lougheed articulates so well are the politics of resentment, the frustrated aspirations of a second tier elite for so long dismissed as boorish cowboys, as yahoos with dung on their boots, by the smug, ruling Anglo-French establishment of Ontario and Quebec."

Although Lougheed could never be accused of moving an audience with his oratory or coining a memorable phrase, the grievances he articulates are not new. Oil has been the conduit between Lougheed's potential and the realization of his aspirations; energy has altered the political and economic relationship between east and West.

Because of this another writer, William Thorsell in an Edmonton *Journal* editorial, has taken the view that, contrary to popular belief, "we are not experiencing the rebirth of the protest politics in the West, but an end of them. A national adolescent stage signified by a century of Western paranoia and Eastern paternalism is giving way to a maturing relationship of equals." Under Lougheed, Alberta has taken a more precise view of its own self interest and its capacity in Confederation. "I believe, I am certain that a very positive Western spirit has developed in the last few years," Lougheed says. "The West has reached a certain stage of maturity. It's no longer struggling for survival but it's just beginning to realize that."

Essentially, the position introduced by Lougheed would redress old grievances, dramatically reduce federal power, and challenge central Canada's market based economy; regional energies would supersede federal paternalism. "Policies that are federal," he says, "will have to work by consensus before they become national." He is determined to see the economic centre of Canada shift from the "golden triangle" of Windsor-Montreal-Ottawa to Western Canada. To this end he advocates more Alberta input into the Canadian Wheat Board, the National Energy Board, and the Canadian Transportation Commission; he believes the provinces should have the right to appoint 40 per cent of all members on federal regulatory boards and agencies that exert strong influence on regional growth and development. The overriding theme that emerges from Lougheed's quest is that his "opponents in Ottawa and Toronto stifle Western Canadian initiative, and as a result the prosperity of all Canadians."

There is a danger in underestimating Lougheed's power and will. For he has given birth to a peculiar brand of Western Canadian nationalism and unless Alberta's grievances, like those of Quebec, are understood and accommodated, confrontation is inevitable.

Lougheed admits that while he is "usually regarded as a pretty strong advocate of Western views," he increasingly finds himself "very much of a moderate compared to some of the intense feelings being expressed in Alberta." With virtually no opposition, democracy in Alberta is just as frail a flower as Trudeau says it is in Quebec. Alberta's political flatness has been exemplified by the province's history of one party systems that stretch through six decades into an all pervading flatness: moral, cultural, social, and topographical. But the province does have economic clout. As the national economy falters there is concern that the federal government has designs on the Alberta treasury, and that through equalization the province may be faced with the burden of subsidizing the Canadian economy.

In August of 1978, the federal government once again challenged Alberta's right to public revenues by seeking "a temporary pause" in its signed agreement with Alberta that oil prices would rise one dollar per barrel every six months until they reached the international level. In order to soften the inflationary impact on the country Ottawa suggested that Alberta forgo the January 1, 1979 increase and lower the price of gas. "The feeling in 1976 of mutual hope and understanding and hope in Canada's future is gone" was Lougheed's response to the suggestion. "There has been a rapid deterioration of good will. We are not talking about power or jurisdiction but in fundamental attitudinal changes." And Lougheed is not prepared to accept these attitudinal changes without greater political influence.

"Canadians do not appreciate the fact that Alberta has contributed $14 billion to the Canadian economy since 1974 by keeping the price of its natural resources below the going price," Provincial Treasurer Merv Leitch pointed out. "That message, that information is totally non-existent in the major population centres of eastern Canada."

Carl Beigie, head of the C.D. Howe Institute Research Centre, has warned, "Alberta cannot be a long purse to finance federalism. The people are getting tired of it." Or, as Lougheed has observed, "The feelings of Albertans are getting very, very intense," and he hints, "a future Premier may be forced to separate the province to protect its own interests." So far, Lougheed is the exclusive arbiter of those "interests." His position of power is unique among Canadian political leaders. He did not inherit the liabilities of a predecessor; he controls a political party which he created in his own image; he controls the cabinet (although individual members may be more intelligent or more familiar with their specific responsibilities, Lougheed has a broad grasp of all portfolios); and, he has contained the opposition.

A man of boyish charm, he is not a diplomat; if politics is the art of compromise he refuses: "I don't have to compromise anything to anyone in terms of Alberta," he has said. His greatest skill is his ability to motivate his subordinates and command their loyalty; his own self-sufficiency and self-testing give him an easy regard for the ambitions of his staff – he works quiet spells on people.

His ambition is no longer exclusively for himself. While he is firmly entrenched in office, it would come as no surprise if he honours a pledge he made early in his political career to step down during his third term. "The way I look at it," he explained in a CBC interview, "is some day I'll walk into my office and I won't be trying to change things. I'll find I'm trying to protect what I've done and I know that's the day I'll start planning to leave." On another occasion he said, "people are more important than party. New blood, new ideas are essential. Once a party forgets that, it is on the road to defeat."

Dramatic evidence of that conviction was the unprecedented departure of nine of his cabinet ministers and fifteen backbenchers just prior to the 1979 election. The ministers who left were Don Getty, Roy Farran, Jim Foster, Bob Dowling, Bill Yurko, Alan Warrack, Bert Hohol, Gordon Miniely, and Helen Hunley. All officially cited demands on their family and financial lives as reason for leaving. In order to exercise complete control over his caucus, Lougheed had made it clear to many of them that in his determination to rejuvenate the party, they may not be reappointed, or if they were, their promotions might be lateral.

His politics cannot be categorized. He is a new breed of Conservative. His background inclines him to be a manager rather than an innovator; behind his smoothness is a tenacious nature. His governing style was forged in the boardrooms of private enterprise and, as one of his backbenchers observes, "When you are part of a successful one-man operation in your formative years you tend to think that is the model for all successful operations." "Peter runs the government like a corporation," complains one urban MLA. "He learned his ways at Mannix and Mannix runs a one-man show. Corporations are, perhaps by necessity, soulless – but it doesn't make for particularly good political participation."

While he supports decentralized federalism, he is the architect of an autocratic provincial bureaucracy larger on a per capita basis than any other province in Canada. (When the Social Credit government left office in 1971 there were 18,518 civil servants; in 1978 there were 48,025 – one government employee for every twenty-eight Albertans.) Although he advocates reconsidered federalism he singularly blocked patriation of the Canadian constitution. His is a mercantile view of Confederation; he does not have the traditional Conservative sense of history and precedent.

Although Lougheed campaigned on a promise to reduce the office of Premier to human scale he is isolated in the prerogative of power. "I believe," he explains matter-of-factly, "the decision making process suffers at the expense of legislative sessions." He counters criticism that he is not accessible to the public by pointing to his many cabinet tours of the province – jaunts that he takes several times each year, to all corners of Alberta. But, visibility is not accessibility. Nowhere is his impatience with the contrivances of politics more obvious than in the legislature itself.

The chamber reveals a lack of parliamentary substance. Although the chamber is inspired by Norman architecture, there are executive boardrooms in Calgary and Edmonton with a greater sense of presence. Redecorated in carpets a shade too red and accented by green marble portals, the room evokes memories of a movie set for a low budget production of Julius Caesar. Even the language of parliamentary debate has been sanitized. The term "backbencher" is discouraged in favour of "non-front bench MLAs." They are not "politicians," but "public servants seeking elected office." The government rarely "spends" money, it "invests" it. Since 1971 only two private member's bills have passed:

an amendment to a municipal act regarding pool halls and a bill governing the use of guide dogs for the blind.

One clue to Lougheed's personality may be found in his office in the southeast wing of the third floor of the legislative building; it is remarkably unpretentious for one of Canada's most influential politicians. Visually strong in panelled walnut, it is dominated by a large desk that reflects uncluttered efficiency. There are two nondescript oil paintings in the room; a mountain scene above an artificial corner fireplace and a view of the Alberta foothills behind his desk. The Premier works facing a canvas by his favourite artist, Rick Grandmaison. The only touches of sentiment in the room are a framed silhouette of the late Len Werry, one of the last photographs taken of the young Minister of Telephones before he was killed, and family portraits placed on a low table. The photograph of his wife Jeanne shows an attractive, cultured women. The ideal political wife, she is tender and easily excitable and conducts her public duties with grace and charm. Although she has been hospitalized several times for lung problems, she refuses to give up smoking. Jeanne describes herself as being a night person; Peter is up at dawn. "The only time we can share intimate moments," she has once said, "is when Peter gets away from the office at noon."

Friends agree that Peter runs the province, but that Jeanne runs the Lougheed household. Peter Macdonnell observes that never has he seen anyone with Peter's ability to "compartmentalize his public life and his private life so well. No matter how difficult his day as Premier may have been, he leaves his office completely behind him once he walks through the door of his house. His transformation from politician to father is remarkable. His dedication to his family is absolute."

Jeanne's influence on their four children is obvious. Stephen, the eldest, received his Bachelor of Commerce degree from Queen's University in Kingston, and is working with ATCO in Calgary. As a teenager he was once caught speeding, and when a police officer was reluctant to give him a ticket because of who his father is, Stephen insisted on receiving one. As a youngster he helped his father campaign, the only one of the Lougheed children to do so. Jeanne was not prepared to see her children merchandised for political gain.

Andrea, nineteen, their eldest daughter, is a shy and willowy girl who is enrolled in the professional program at the Royal Winnipeg Ballet School. Her teachers agree she "is obviously involved in something she wants to do, and while she has a remote prospect of becoming a prima ballerina, she has a facility for dancing." Many of the students at the school do not know who she is. "Andrea's managed to keep a very low profile," says a classmate.

Pamela, seventeen, outgoing and poised beyond her years, is in Edmonton's Ross Sheppard High School. "Pam" is the "free spirit" of the family, and was very vocal in her objections to the security guard assigned to her in Paris when she accompanied her father on a mission to Europe.

The youngest Lougheed, Joseph, at thirteen often described as "a chip off the old block," is in Westminster Junior High School in Edmonton's fashionable Glenora district. Joe's teachers describe him as "kind of a loner. He's not old enough to remember a time when his father wasn't Premier, so he is unassuming about the whole thing." Another family acquaintance believes "Joe really suffers the most from his father's job; he's really lost when Peter is away for extended periods of time."

Lougheed's work is organized; his handwriting firm, bold strokes with a flourish. In spite of his expansive television image, he is not a man given to reveal much about himself in private. As Richard Gwyn has perceived in his syndicated newspaper column, "There are really two Lougheeds. One is the brilliant manager and organizer, the visionary, the Alberta patriot. The other is the little guy who made it to the top and who still can't quite believe it, wary, humourless, crushed by any criticism." He is basically shy, and when he is nervous, he massages the gold university ring on his right hand; the engraving has been worn down from constant rubbing.

The windows of his office command a view of the North Saskatchewan River and of the Kinsmen Fieldhouse, an athletic centre, beyond. (Lougheed keeps a track suit handy, and when time allows, slips over to the fieldhouse to jog at lunchtime.)

It is in his office, and not in the legislature, where the blueprints that will shape Alberta's future are drawn.

Lougheed's administration reflects the hopes, prejudices, and ambitions of the upper-middle class to the exclusion of all others. During his first two terms his cabinet was dominated by ten successful businessmen and nine corporate lawyers. It also included a retired British Army major, a doctor, an architect, a teacher, and a businesswoman. The administration is far more moderate than many of its elected representatives. Consider the views of Mundare farmer, John Batiuk, who voiced concern about money being spent on Alberta's native population (less than $2 million per year). The Vegreville backbencher complained, "for such a small segment of our population such a big amount is being spent." And he continued "Albertans would still be sitting in the teepee chewing at the pemmican" if their white ancestors acted like today's Indians.

Then there is Ira Allison Fluker's attempt at humour at the expense of French Canadians. The auctioneer who represented St. Paul was discussing seating arrangements at the Olypmic Stadium in Montreal when he quipped, "They're removing every other seat and replacing them with lily pads for the frogs." The views are expunged from Hansard but it takes more than a vote of the legislature to eradicate the yahoo image they represent. Fluker will not be a candidate in the 1979 election.

Lougheed does not entertain slights lightly. "If you fall out of his favour it's as if you don't exist in his mind anymore," says one man who has experienced Lougheed's displeasure. "Even though we are in the same room on occasion, he looks past me, ignores me, behaves as if we never knew each other." Another who has encountered Lougheed's wrath agrees. "He has quite a temper and after I publicly opposed one of his policies he wouldn't speak to me for months."

Lougheed's temper is rarely displayed in public. But, in September 1976, when the 300,000 member Alberta Chamber of Commerce charged the Premier with "creating a climate of confusion and uncertainty" through his "increasing involvement in the private sector" and asked him to "seriously reconsider where he wants to take this province," Lougheed angrily stormed out of the meeting.

Lougheed perceives his role as not only that of Premier but also as "something of a national opposition leader" to keep pressure on the federal government to move decision making to the West. "The West has to represent itself," he has said, "because of the nature of Confederation the provincial governments have to do it."

Lougheed's greatest strength in this regard is the Alberta Heritage Trust Fund. When the fund was created on May 19, 1976, it set aside one-third of Alberta's resource revenue for "future generations of Albertans." Capital contributions from petroleum income and income on investment multiplies at the rate of $2,000 a minute. As oil prices continue to rise so do the revenues of the fund: by the end of 1979 it will have accumulated $5 billion, the largest public savings account in the Western world. Few understand the nature of the fund, which represents a sound if unimaginative arbitrary economic self-denial based on the insecurity of the thirties. The Provincal Treasurer, Merv Leitch, has explained, "$5 billion is one year's budget in Alberta, five months' in Ontario and one month's in Ottawa. The trust fund is the equivalent to a person having one year's salary saved when he retires." And Lougheed has rationalized, "For those who propose that we spend these monies today on current needs, they should realize that the province is already spending more for services to people than any other provincial government in Canada. We are already utilizing 70 per cent of our resource revenue for today's needs."

The money in the Alberta Heritage Trust Fund is administered by three separate divisions: the Capital Projects Division which allocates 20 per cent of the fund to provide special long-term services to the people of Alberta – education and medical facilities, parks, and irrigation projects. The Alberta Investment Division represents about two-thirds of the fund and is invested in relatively low yield, short-term investments and provides money for such projects as Alberta's share in Syncrude, the Alberta Housing

Corporation, Alberta Telephones, and the Alberta Energy Corporation. The return on these investments is modest, less than 9 per cent and opposition critics point out that the fund is losing to inflation. The third division, the Canada Investment Division, is authorized to invest outside Alberta within the country and although the division has accumulated about $600 million, only $275 million of that has been used so far to provide low interest loans to Manitoba, New Brunswick, Newfoundland, and Nova Scotia.

This pool of wealth, expected to swell to $10 billion by 1980, gives Lougheed the leverage he needs to dictate economic change in Canada. For, if Quebec seeks cultural sovereignty within Confederation, Alberta seeks economic sovereignty in a cultural union. Lougheed has joined the ranks of the world's leading "petrocrats." World leaders such as United States Vice President Walter Mondale, British Prime Minister James Callaghan, and Saudi Arabia Sheik Ahmed Zaki Yamani now include visits to Lougheed when they come to Canada.

Lougheed and his ministers have created an intermesh between board rooms and the provincial cabinet which the leader of the NDP, Grant Notley, says threatens the legislature. Notley views "the government-corporate complex as a lesser but equally dangerous version of the military-industrial complex in the United States. Just as the arms merchants and generals seized control of U.S. foreign policy," Notley charges, "the Conservatives and their corporate allies have grabbed Alberta's economic policy and run it in secret." Both Notley and the Social Credit Opposition Leader, Bob Clark, bitterly complain that 80 per cent of the Alberta Heritage Trust Fund is used by the cabinet without advance legislative approval. Clark doesn't believe the fund should be there for generations in the future. "The bulk of the funding should be put to use today," he argues.

Just prior to the 1979 election Social Credit implemented as policy a resolution promising legislative approval over the use of the fund. "There is no reason for secrecy," says Clark, "because the legislature is supposed to be supreme over the financial management of the province. Major investments should be submitted to the legislature for prior approval." The Provincial Treasurer, Merv Leitch, is "astonished by that allegation. . . . I don't know any place where there is anything like the amount of information given the public about the Alberta Heritage Trust Fund. First of all, we put out both annual and quarterly reports. That's only the beginning," says Leitch. "We start appearing before a legislative committee and answer any questions that are asked. In addition to that, we have the Heritage Trust Fund Review Committee which answers questions about expenditures – and that doesn't happen with the regular budget. In addition to that," he continues, "any question about the fund can be asked during the regular question period in the house."

But Leitch's defence ignores the opposition's basic objection that the Heritage Trust Fund is nothing more than a "slush fund adjunct to the provincial budget" and that all of the information available comes after the fact.

One of the most effective critics on the accountability issue is one of Lougheed's own backbenchers, Ron Ghitter. "Historically, governments that have endeavoured to circumvent the legislature in any way . . . have often been washed upon the rocky shores of electoral defeat," Ghitter warned during debate on the bill to establish the Alberta Heritage Trust Fund. Quoting the 1839 Durham Report which led to the establishment of responsible government in Canada, Ghitter noted, "It is encumbent upon the elected body to have the right and the responsibility to deal with the allocation of funds in public so that there will be public scrutiny to avoid misapplication and misuse." And he warned that the concept of investing surplus oil and gas revenue is "fraught with difficulty, dangers and political hazards of immense consequences."

In creating a fund the Lougheed government has raised expectations which in spite of massive government spending programs do not appear to have been delivered; every special interest group has proposed its own way of utilizing the enormous cash reservoir.

Municipalities and school boards decry inadequate revenue sharing. Opposition Leader Bob Clark proposes that 10 per cent of the revenues collected from oil, natural gas, and other resources – almost $400 million a year – be given directly to the municipalities. Teachers want to the see the quality of education improved, and for the first time since the 1920s went on strike in Edmonton in September, 1978, to back their demands. Hospital service workers, held to a 6 per cent wage increase, have gone on strike; labour relations in Alberta have reached a new low. The president of the Alberta Federation of Labour, Harry Kostiuk, charges the government continually intervenes on behalf of employer interests.

Small business complains that it has been neglected, and renters complain that they have no protection against exorbitant and arbitrary rent increases. Lougheed counters all criticism by appealing for consensus. "I do not accept that this Conservative party is anti-anything, anti-union, anti-any group. We are a government that represents all of the people, in every corner of Alberta. Let us therefore continue to be an open party of *all* of the people of Alberta."

Lougheed's most visible response to indicate to Albertans that they are benefiting from their resource revenue was to eliminate the provincial gasoline tax making the price of a gallon of gas in Alberta the lowest in the country – a move that cost the provincial treasury a mere $100 million per year. In his exercise of economic power, in his quest for dollar dynamism Lougheed appears to lack a human and social reach. Still, Albertans have much less to complain about than other Canadians; their personal income tax is the lowest in Canada (38.5 per cent) and there is no provincial sales tax.

What the Lougheed government possesses to an extraordinary degree is determination and an exceptional vitality. And, if vitality is the mark of an emerging society, then Alberta today is the Canadian present and future. Under the leadership of Edgar Peter Lougheed it is an exciting and an occasionally disturbing place.

About the Author

Allan Hustak, a born and bred Westerner, has been a reporter with the Canadian Broadcasting Corporation for five years. His assignments have taken him to Europe, the Soviet Union, the Middle East, and Iran, and he has spent the last four years hot on Premier Lougheed's trail as a reporter in Edmonton.